The Servant-Ethic in the New Testament

American University Studies

Series VII
Theology and Religion

Vol. 196

PETER LANG
New York • Washington, D.C./Baltimore
Bern • Frankfurt am Main • Berlin • Vienna • Paris

Philippa Carter

The Servant-Ethic in the
New Testament

PETER LANG
New York • Washington, D.C./Baltimore
Bern • Frankfurt am Main • Berlin • Vienna • Paris

Library of Congress Cataloging-in-Publication Data

Carter, Philippa.
The servant-ethic in the New Testament/ Philippa Carter.
p. cm. — (American university studies. VII, Theology and religion; v. 196)
Includes bibliographical references and index.
1. Service (Theology). 2. Love—Religious aspects—Christianity. 3. Bible.
N.T.—Criticism, interpretation, etc. I. Title. II. Series: American university
studies. Series VII, Theology and religion; vol. 196.
BT738.4.C38   241.5—dc20   96-31808
ISBN 0-8204-3393-4
ISSN 0740-0446

Die Deutsche Bibliothek-CIP-Einheitsaufnahme

Carter, Philippa:
The servant-ethic in the New Testament/ Philippa Carter.
– New York; Washington, D.C./Baltimore; Bern; Frankfurt am Main;
Berlin; Vienna; Paris: Lang.
(American university studies: Ser. 7, Theology and religion; Vol. 196)
ISBN 0-8204-3393-4
NE: American university studies/07

The paper in this book meets the guidelines for permanence and durability
of the Committee on Production Guidelines for Book Longevity
of the Council of Library Resources.

Printed in the United States of America.

For
Kristina Bedford
and
my grandparents
Iris and Harry White

Preface

The following pages undertake a modest task: to identify and describe a characteristic aspect of the earliest Christians' ethical self-understanding. At no point do the writers of the New Testament use the phrase "servant-ethic." This phrase is handy, however, to describe an ethical stance that was fundamental for these writers, and, one assumes, their intended readers. It is, of course, impossible to know how well the early Christians lived up to this standard: Paul's correspondence to the Corinthians, not to mention the history of Christianity since its inception, suggests that the ideal is one that has rarely been achieved. In addition, Christianity is the not the only religion, nor is it the first, to insist on the ethical priority of the interests of others. This book is not a work of Comparative Ethics; nor is it an attempt to trace the history of a moral paradigm. It's mandate is simply to demonstrate that a degree of ethical uniformity pervades the earliest Christian literature extant (i.e. the canonical writings of the New Testament) thereby constituting a fundamental part of the earliest Christian kerygma.

I am indebted to five members of the Department of Religious Studies at McMaster University for their encouragement and support: Travis Kroeker, Adele Reinhartz, Eileen Schuller, Stephen Westerholm and Peter Widdicombe. My family's generosity and patience helped enormously: many thanks are due to Ann and Eric Carter and to Joe, Daniel, Chiara and Benjamin Padovani. The following people also played significant roles in the writing of this book: Sheryl Dick, Mavis Fenn, Tinamarie Jones, Rex Kay, Jack Laughlin, Maggie Martineau, Alison Miculan, Richard Ratzlaff and Wendy Robinson. Jennifer Nettleton took time from a very busy schedule to proof-read the manuscript and I am grateful for her assistance. Finally, I acknowledge, with much gratitude, all I have been fortunate to learn from the scores of students in the courses I have taught over the past few years.

CONTENTS

ABBREVIATIONS

BAGD	W. Bauer, W. F. Arndt, F. W. Gingrich and F. W. Danker, Greek-English Lexicon of the New Testament
BDF	F. Blass, A. Debrunner, and R.W. Funk, *A Greek Grammar of the New Testament*
BZ	*Biblische Zeitschrift*
CBQ	*Catholic Biblical Quarterly*
ExpTim	*The Expository Times*
HBT	*Horizons in Biblical Theology*
HTR	*The Harvard Theolgical Review*
Int	*Interpretation*
NTS	*New Testament Studies*
NovT	*Novum Testamentum*
JAAR	*Journal of the American Academy of Religion*
JBL	*Journal of Biblical Literature*
JFSR	*Journal of Feminist Studies in Religion*
JSNT	*Journal for the Study of the New Testament*
JTS	*The Journal of Theological Studies*
RAC	*Reallexikon für Antike und Christentum*
RB	*Revue Biblique*
SE	*Studia Evangelica*
SEÅ	*Svensk exegetisk årsbok*
SJT	*Scottish Journal of Theology*
SR	*Studies in Religion*
TDNT	*The Theological Dictionary of the New Testament*
TynBul	*Tyndale Bulletin*
WTJ	*Westminster Theological Journal*
ZNW	*Zeitschrift für die neutestamentliche Wissenschaft*

Chapter I

INTRODUCTION

Scholars have long noted that the ethics of the New Testament is not systematic and that it is impossible to derive a coherent moral system from these early Christian writings. We are assured that the early Christian communities were diverse in matters of ethics.[1] That no systematic ethic can be found or extracted from the New Testament is hardly surprising, scholars tell us, considering the number of authors and genres found therein. Despite this anomaly in the Christian scripture, there are many professional Christian ethicists at work today, who endeavor to describe what he or she sees as the foundation for Christian conduct given the Christian kerygma or proclamation. Ethicists depend on the New Testament to a greater or lesser extent to formulate answers to the moral questions Christians face, because it is there that they locate the founding story of the Christian community. For Christian ethicists, the problem of scripture, of how it should be understood and used, is often the first issue that has to be tackled. For the early Christians, lacking as they did an undisputed canon, such questions were secondary. The moral dilemmas they faced had to be addressed based on their faith and experience. The role of reason was often subordinated to the primacy of religious conviction.

The writings of the New Testament spoke to the early Christians in ways that illuminated their self-understanding as part of the people of God. The person of Jesus, crucified and resurrected, represented a momentous work of God in history. Their response to this act, to the extent that it involved human conduct, was ethical in nature. It follows that despite the diversity of these communities, ethical principles must have existed that permeated their self-awareness as Christians. These diverse groups of people, each of which was moved to believe that God had performed a unique and decisive act in human history, did express this common conviction in comparable ways in their reflections on human conduct. Throughout the New Testament there is fundamental agreement about how the human response to this divine act should be characterized in concrete action, and which betrays, in terms of ethics, the self-understanding of the early Christians.

Love is often identified as *the* Christian virtue. Love is a prominent motif in many of the early Christian writings and believers are exhorted over and over again to love their fellow Christians, their neighbors and even their enemies. But love of neighbor is essentially an abstract principle in the sense that it needs to be defined in terms of the actions to which it gives rise.[2] Nevertheless, related to love, indeed having their source in love, other ethical themes can be found which point to a degree of moral coherence throughout the New Testament.

One of these themes is the "servant-ethic." This ethic entails the consistent denial of one's own interests in favor of those of others, and the willingness to stand unfailingly ready to serve others. The servant-ethic represents the "other-directedness" and self-sacrifice which is a recurring note throughout the New Testament and which characterizes the self-understanding of the early Christians. It is advocated for many reasons and is carried out in many different ways, but its paradigm is the Son of Man who came to serve and to give his life as a ransom for many (Mark 10:45).

The New Testament motif of ἀγάπη often coincides with the servant-ethic. Garth Hallett examines six rival versions or descriptions of love advanced in Christian thought, to see which comes closest to the New Testament concept of 'αγάπη. The six versions he identifies are: (1)self-preference, (2)parity, (3)other-preference, (4)self-subordination, (5)self-forgetfulness and (6)self-denial. This is a continuum of sorts in which the interests of the self are pitted against the interests of others to a greater or lesser degree. Hallett believes that the New Testament comes down in favor of self-subordination.[3] He says:

> In this understanding of neighbor-love, *one may and should give independent consideration to one's own benefit, but only on the condition that maximum benefit to others is first assured (whether directly or indirectly), through benefit to oneself.*[4]

Hallett allows, however, that some parts of the New Testament are more extreme, implying that self-forgetfulness (in which the benefit to the self is not given any independent weight), and even self-denial (in which benefits to the self are never sought save to maximize benefits to others), are required. Hallett concludes that while the διάκονος and δοῦλος vocabulary of texts such as Mark 10:42–45; John 13:14; Phil 2:5–7 and Gal 5:13 might suggest otherwise, his category of self-subordination is echoed most consistently in the New Testament:

> From texts like these, no strictly logical inference can be drawn to the norm of Self-Subordination (countenancing good to self only when it does not conflict with others' good). However, the texts do, on the one hand, clearly suggest a more purely altruistic norm than Other-Preference (which permits the agent's good to compete, if only minimally, with others'), but do not, on the other hand, suggest a more total self-denial, disconnected from service.[5]

While Hallett's evaluation may be overly schematic, his estimation of the New Testament approach to neighbor-love is correct. In addition, the fact that Hallet can engage in the task of plotting definitions of love on a continuum suggests that love means different things to different people. We are less concerned with how to define ἀγάπη than with the attempt to delineate the ethical implications of love as manifested in the New Testament, which calls for believers to become servants of others. This does not mean that the servant-ethic and love always coincide completely, although they do overlap often. The servant-ethic has to do primarily with the self-understanding of the believer in relation to others and less to do with any positive response. It is this dimension of the believer's self-understanding that is most critical in terms of distinguishing the ethic from more general affirmations of love, and, as we shall see, the emphasis that many scholars place on the expectation of love to be responded to and reciprocated. Exhortations to love others are relevant, therefore, insofar as they require a self-conscious stance of servanthood before others. Consequently, this study will employ terms such as "self" and "other" in ways largely foreign to the New Testament, but consistent with describing individuals as moral actors in relation to other individuals.

Respect for the interests of others and self-denial can be found in all religions, so the earliest Christian believers do not have a monopoly on self-sacrifice and empathy. The servant-ethic, however, is fundamental in the New Testament. Its requirements are extreme and are affirmed again and again throughout the earliest Christian documents. The servant-ethic is a connecting link which points to a degree of coherence in New Testament ethics. It offers a normative standard for Christian conduct involving relations with others. While the writings of many traditions encourage their adherents to consider the wishes and needs of others, few, including much of modern Christian thought, consistently couch this requirement in such extreme terms of self-denial and servanthood as do the early Christian documents. While the Christian is undoubtedly to look to the interests of others, however, the New Testament's view does not favor the absolute denigration of the self. Nevertheless, the call to serve others is consistently invoked in the New Testament. The earliest Christians had a view of ethics that was fundamentally coherent and consistent and was described in similar terms by disparate groups.

The New Testament summons those who understand themselves to be people of God to relinquish their own interests in order to serve others. The true disciple, the authentic believer, is one who renounces the self and becomes "other-directed." Such "other-directedness" is not, however, "self-forgetfulness" in the sense of attaining an altered consciousness akin to that advocated in esoteric Hindu and Buddhist schools. It also is not the kind of self-denial which involves deliberate "mortification of the flesh" and the pursuit of bodily affliction for its own sake. The servant-ethic, in its New Testament form, does not recommend that one endeavor to overcome the limits of human consciousness, or deliberately seek after suffering. Rather, it promotes humility, the acceptance of one's weakness before God, and empathy in the face of another's suffering.

The servant-ethic flouts convention by inhibiting and rejecting ambition and social prestige, while accepting the lesser position and acquiescing in the face of conflict. For the New Testament writers it was the mark of those who had become part of the people of God.

The Extreme Nature of the Servant-Ethic

The biblical tradition is unequivocal in its avowal of the just nature of God. He is portrayed as fair and impartial while at the same time acting as the defender of his people. Stephen Mott points out that in the Bible justice often is found to be closely linked with grace.[6] Mott understands God's justice, which his people are to emulate, to entail especially the protection of the poor, the weak and the oppressed. He points out that biblical justice is not simply punitive, but "also vindication, deliverance, and creation of community."[7] God has bestowed grace on his people because of his love toward them and they, in turn, are to act justly towards others. Citing Deut 10:18–19, Mott asserts that for God's people performance of justice is not based on considerations of personal worth or merit but upon need and the awareness of God's grace. Justice bears both grace and love and "it is this assumption which allows justice to be expressed by the principle of equality" between persons.[8]

We need to ask, however, if and when the well-being and freedom of the other become *more* valuable than those of the self. The New Testament seems consistently to invoke the principle that one's own interests should be subordinated to those of others even when one's own may be asserted justifiably. In other words, God now calls his people to become the weak and oppressed in the sense that rights and privileges that may be claimed often are to be surrendered.

The call to love one's neighbor as oneself is a good starting point to determine the limitations, if any, of the servant-ethic. Does the New Testament ever suggest, or even hint, that in certain circumstances the love of oneself supersedes the love of one's neighbor? The short answer to such an inquiry is no: the situation in which the interests of self take precedence is the situation in which the neighbor is loved less than oneself. Nevertheless, as modern Christian theologians and ethicists often point out, the love of self sometimes comes into a real and painful conflict with the love of neighbor. Joseph L. Allen attempts to resolve this dilemma by arguing that love of self can be distinguished from "serving the interests of the self." His argument illustrates how extreme the New Testament requirement to serve actually is.

For Allen it is possible for the inner disposition of the self in relation to itself to be one of love even when external actions lead to self-sacrifice on behalf of others.[9] He also distinguishes between selfishness and self-love by defining self-love as self-acceptance and self-affirmation. This acceptance and affirmation is derived from God's act of accepting and affirming the self independent of any merit.[10] In Allen's view, the solution of impartiality in which the self attempts to treat others and itself in exactly the same way is more often than not impossible. Indeed, for Christian thinkers this is usually held to be non-Christian. The interest of the other outweighs the interest of the self, according to Allen, for two reasons based on the Christian's faith in God. First, this faith leads to reliance upon God to provide for one's needs. Pointing to Matt 6:25 Allen says that "faith...frees a person from the kind of self-concern that would lead to defensiveness...about getting an equal share, at least where justice to others does not depend upon justice for the self."[11] Allen then notes the positive side to this negative elimination of self-concern. This is the liberating aspect of faith, "freeing one for concern for the other":

> Faith is that by which the self not only has a *right* to sacrifice its own interests for those of others, but also is *inclined* not to be anxious for the self but to give of its resources to serve others.[12]

Allen, however, wishes to pursue his course still further to discover whether such self-sacrifice on the part of Christians is, in fact, a duty or obligation. He suggests that one *"has a strong but not an absolute duty to give priority to the interests of others."*[13] While acknowledging that in the New Testament "concern for the interest of others clearly takes priority over concern for the interests of self,"[14] he also insists that the self also remains obligated to itself. His reservations are based on the observation that self-sacrifice for its own sake can lead to self-destruction which benefits no one. "The point is that self-sacrifice is not an end in itself, but a means to the service of others."[15] Using such arguments Allen defends the position that on many occasions one should advance one's own interests in order to advance the interests of others, or to illuminate the injustice of others' acts. Finally, Allen argues, the occasion often arises where the interest of the self should be protected so that it may serve others at a future time.[16]

The problem with Allen's argument in the context of our study, a problem that he himself acknowledges, is that it would seem alien to the earliest Christians. In the New Testament, the consistent call to serve the interests of others first leaves little room for considering future benefits for others by asserting one's rights, or assuming that one will make a useful contribution to the well-being of others later on. Each instance of encountering another person—that is, the neighbor—becomes the point at which a believer must decide whom to serve. The future is in God's hands: the future of the self and the future of the other. The decision is to be made, according to the New Testament, based on faith and the understanding of God's will for that moment.

In the New Testament it seems clear that such occasions demand the denial of self as the Christian responds by faith in freedom and love to the call of God's grace as represented by the earliest kerygma. The New Testament takes a more rigid stance than Allen on the question of serving the interests of others. Questions of justice, of rational self-interest, become subordinated to the insistence of putting others first in the immediacy of the moment.[17] In short, prudence, even if defined as practical wisdom, becomes less important. Some scholars suggest that this apparent ethical urgency is the product of the eschatological outlook of the early church. The need for prudence, they argue, is diminished if one believes the eschaton is at hand. An example of such an evaluation is found in Jack T. Sanders' consideration of the ethics of Jesus. He insists that Jesus' ethics are so closely interwoven with his eschatology that it is impossible to separate the two.[18] As we shall see, however, the servant-ethic does not in fact seem to be closely tied to eschatological expectations. Indeed, for Paul the effect upon the community's future cohesiveness on earth is often a strong motive for calling his readers to fulfil the servant-ethic even to the point of suffering injustice (e.g. I Cor 6:1–11).[19]

While Allen's discussion may be persuasive, it contradicts the New Testament position. Allen is just as interested in love, for example, as the primitive Christian writers, but his conclusions are at odds with the New Testament at times. His work serves, therefore, to highlight the strange and radical nature of the language of the New Testament servant-ethic.

The Social Context of the Servant-Ethic

The primitive Christians understood themselves to be called by God to be servants to others, to thwart egotistical ambition, and to surrender their own rights and privileges. The language used to describe such behavior is often extreme in its connotations. Words such as δοῦλος (slave) and διάκονος (servant) and their cognates are by no means flattering in their implications. The former especially smacks of debasement and humiliation. We need to consider the ramifications of such language and its possible sources. Δοῦλος and διάκονος and their cognates often occur in passages that delineate the ideal moral stance of Christians; in many passages they are called to become slaves or servants *of others*. What can such language mean in an environment that recognized a slave as the occupant of the lowest level of the social pyramid, or, metaphorically, as a description of the pious individual before God?

Although the δοῦλος was situated at the bottom of the social hierarchy some slaves managed to turn the situation to their own advantage. At the turn of the era many slaves managed to wield a certain amount of power and influence by virtue of their role as aides to powerful and influential men. The first part of S.

Scott Bartchy's study *First Century Slavery and I Corinthians 7:21*, and the first chapter of Dale B. Martin's *Slavery and Salvation* both emphasize the amazing complexity of institutionalized slavery in the Greco-Roman world. Bartchy notes that legal limitations began to be placed upon the rights of masters under Roman law, and that the status and disposition of the slave-owner markedly influenced the quality of life enjoyed by his slaves.[20] This resulted in the paradox that it was often better to be a rich man's slave than a poor man's employee, for the former was at least guaranteed shelter, food and clothing.

Both Bartchy and Martin note that slaves performed many jobs also undertaken by free and freedmen and that it was not simply the menial or unhygienic tasks that were reserved for slaves. Slaves often occupied positions of trust as financial managers, and of influence as educators in the households of more wealthy individuals.[21] Nevertheless, under Greek and Roman law the slave had virtually no legal status whatsoever. The idea of voluntarily becoming like a slave to another, even if only in a figurative sense, would have been alien to Jew and Gentile alike. Aristotle likens a slave-mentality not only to the status of those who are slaves but also with those who are bereft of virtue.[22] Later Greek thinkers equated slavery with enslavement to passions and taught that even a slave could experience true "inner freedom." The Stoics, for example, held that a slave could be virtuous but saw no benefit in free and freed men thinking of themselves as servants of others in any concrete sense. The writings of the Stoic Epictetus are especially intriguing because they come from the pen of a former slave who experienced first-hand the oppression and harshness of a life deprived of autonomy.

The Stoics were primarily concerned with achieving an inner harmony and disposition that bred indifference to external hardship. This harmony extended to an individual's relations with others and was dictated by one's duty and social position. For Epictetus the most dangerous form of bondage was enslavement to vice which upset the serenity born of reason and seeking the highest good. Thus, even when maltreated, Epictetus seeks to respond with equanimity:

> If...we define the good as consisting in a right moral purpose, then the mere preservation of the relationships of life becomes a good; and furthermore, he who gives up some of the externals achieves the good. "My father is taking away my money." But he is doing you no harm. "My brother is going to get the larger part of the farm." Let him have all he wants. That does not help him at all to get a part of your modesty, does it, or of your fidelity, or of your brotherly love? Why, from a possession of this kind who can eject you? Not even Zeus. (Epictetus, *Diss.*, III.iii.4–12).

This principle of striving after the highest moral good and cultivating a tranquil disposition leads, for Epictetus, to true freedom. It is not social but rather moral freedom (ἐλευθηρία) that is most important for Epictetus and his fellow Stoics:

No man who is in fear, or sorrow, or turmoil, is free, but whoever is rid of sorrows and
fears and turmoils, this man is by the self-same course rid also of slavery (Epictetus,
Diss. II.i.24).

The clearest exposition on this question of moral freedom is found in *Diss.* I.i.
Here Epictetus explains how even free men are enslaved if they do not
understand that striving to satisfy a desire is a sinister form of slavery. Freedom
is achieved when desire is destroyed (*Diss.*IV.i. 175). Thus, even a slave who
manages to buy his emancipation is not truly autonomous unless he can destroy
his desire for money and finery (*Diss.* IV.i.33–40). Despite this, Epictetus does
not use the language of servanthood or slavery to describe one's ideal relations
to others. His disciple, Marcus Aurelius, says, moreover:

Pass through the remainder of thy days as one that with his whole soul has given all that
is in his trust to the gods, and has made of himself neither a tyrant *nor a slave to any
man* (IV:3, emphasis mine).

Such relations are marked by indifference if one is treated unjustly, which may
appear similar to the principle of turning the other cheek; but the goal is personal
equanimity and moral integrity, not to become "perfect" (Matt 5:48).

Likewise, in Jewish thought, an individual could be a servant of God but there
are clear biblical prohibitions upon Hebrews enslaving other Hebrews (e.g. Lev
25:35–55), and the servant-vocabulary is not characteristic of Jewish writings
when one's ethical relationship to others is considered.[23] It is also difficult to
determine to what extent Rabbinic literature can be used to investigate slavery
in the first century C.E. E. E. Urbach is adamant that there are no grounds for
assuming that Jews did not practice slavery in the period of the Second Temple,
and indeed afterwards. He insists that Mishnaic references to slavery are not
necessarily hypothetical.[24] Paul V. Flescher demurs, however, and says that
"Urbach's attempt to use laws as evidence of actual historical practice
is...misguided."[25] According to Flescher, Urbach interprets the laws in the
Mishnah as descriptive rather than as prescriptive.[26] Whatever the relation of the
Mishnah to actual historical circumstances it has much to say about slavery.
Flescher describes the Mishnaic view of the slave as different from that of
Aristotle:

In brief, the Mishnah's framers recognize the bondman as a complete human being, but
as one whose status as property prevents him from achieving his full potential. Sages
do not portray him as a sub-human "monster," that is, as something lacking the full
rudiments of humanity.[27]

Like the Greek and Roman situation the circumstances of slavery as portrayed
in the Mishnah are complicated and ambivalent. According to Urbach, rabbinic

Judaism understood slaves to be under the complete control of their masters. Even the former's property and money belonged to their masters so that manumission could only be paid for by a third party. Urbach shows that "the *Halakhah* sensed an incompatibility between being the beneficiary of an assignment of property and servile status, and pronounced that such a transaction carried as its consequence complete emancipation."[28]

Although scholars have shown that many slaves enjoyed a certain degree of power and wielded some influence over their own fate,[29] it is clear that the word "slave" as such denoted a person with no rights, who was indebted to and under the authority of another. When speaking of the use of the δοῦλος word-group in the LXX, K. H. Rengstorf notes that "it always stands in opposition to the thought of freedom. It thus expresses with singular force both the extreme of power demanded and exercised on the one side and the extreme of objective subjection and subjective bondage present and experienced on the other."[30]

The social milieu and the extent of influence of Greek and Jewish literary traditions cannot be surveyed extensively here. Despite evidence of powerful and influential slaves, scholarship has shown that to become a slave to others in any sense was not especially desired. Slaves were essentially bereft of rights, although masters were encouraged to treat their slaves humanely and manumission was an option under certain conditions. It is this lack of rights in relation to others that is particularly important for the servant-ethic. In the New Testament the requirement to place the interests of oneself last often is couched in terms of servanthood. This requirement does not simply describe the believer's relationship to God and those in authority, but to all people. Believers, moreover, are to understand themselves voluntarily as servants of others.

This use of servant vocabulary and of the model of the slave as an ethical ideal can also have sinister aspects which must be faced. It is no secret that some New Testament texts have been used in the past to justify and perpetuate oppression, including institutionalized slavery.[31] Many Christians are embarrassed by the lack of an outright condemnation of slavery by any New Testament writer. This aspect of the text has to be accepted. It also has to be placed in its historical perspective. The early Christians lived in a world of slaves and masters. This dimension of the social structure provided a model for Christian ethical conduct.

The New Testament, in fact, neither condemns nor encourages slavery. Where slavery exists it is accepted but there is no text that encourages individuals to acquire slaves. The emphasis is upon promoting behavior appropriate to the Christian life in the social context within which one finds oneself. The subjugation of an individual by another is prohibited, not only in the sense of perpetuating slavery but in other matters as well. Christians are not actively to seek to dominate others, even in the sense of imposing their own views upon their fellow believers. In his discussion of eating sacrificial foods Paul encourages his readers to halt such practices if they offend others, even though such behavior may not in itself be idolatrous (I Cor 8-10; Rom 14:13–23). It becomes morally wrong to assert one's own rights and privileges as a Christian at the expense of another's conscience. How can a Christian, who has accepted as truth the paradox of the crucifixion, insist on advancing her or his own rights as a Christian "free in Christ"? The servant language imparts to the New Testament writers' ethical discussions a ready model for the Christian's relations to God and to others.

The use of such language raises potential moral problems because it can be abused, but it also sharply depicts the radical nature of truly Christian conduct. Claims about God's action in history in the death of Jesus are elucidated by the early Christians' self-understanding regarding their status as slaves to others. Luther's paradox of being lord of all yet slave of all follows as the ethical consequence of early Christian beliefs about the moral significance of the paradox of the crucifixion and resurrection. As Paul tells his readers in Gal 5:13, freedom in Christ means the freedom to become a slave to others in love. The believer becomes free to serve: in responding to God's grace the Christian has chosen to eschew ambition in order to advance the interests of others. This is no longer merely a duty, it is the result of a conscious decision and is the hallmark of a true believer.[32]

The communities that gave rise to the New Testament writings were not only constituted of masters and slaves but of men and women. The implications of the servant language has not been ignored by feminist biblical interpreters over the last fifteen years or so, given the claim that not only the social context in which these texts originated, but the texts themselves and their interpretations are patriarchal and androcentric.[33] This assertion is relevant to this study insofar as the ethical ideals of service and self-denial promulgated throughout the New Testament are immediately deradicalized if the bulk of their original audience is comprised of people whose lived experience is one of subordination and subjugation whether by sex, social status or both. At the same time, however, the persistent calls to service on behalf of others and self denial, given the text's androcentrism are "hyper-radicalized" when the hearer(s) of the text participate in the privileges enjoyed by elite males. Then the servant-ethic is nothing less than a challenge to voluntary disempowerment on the part of this audience. Nevertheless, the servant-ethic, as an ethical ideal, calls for self-denial in circumstances that seem largely oblivious to the social circumstances or lived experience of the audience.[34]

The New Testament consistently indicates that an individual, upon becoming a Christian, surrenders personal rights before others. While the human inclination is to seek higher status in society, the New Testament seems firm in its insistence that such ambitions are inappropriate (e.g. Mark 10:42–45; I Cor 7:21). All Christians are called to understand that as Christians they become slaves to one another (Gal 5:13): that by seeking to obey God they are required to serve other people. They become servants, not only of God, but of others as well. The example of Jesus as slave or servant (Phil 2:7; Mark 10:45; I Pet 5:5) gives shape to this conviction and reinforces the attitude that leads to submission to others. The New Testament writers do not transform the meaning of δοῦλος or διάκονος; rather they embrace it as a way of identifying those who, by following Christ, are willing to make sacrifices, even of life itself (Mark 8:35). Based on these considerations the δοῦλος vocabulary in the New Testament goes beyond symbolism by influencing the conduct of Christians towards others.

In his discussion of Paul's attitude to slavery Peter Richardson understands the symbolic import of the concept to explain Paul's ambivalence and conservatism on the question of institutionalized slavery. For Richardson, "service not slavery was the point."[35] Yet in some sense Christians were enslaved: they were called to a radical subservience to the interests and claims of others. For the early Christians, institutionalized slavery was part of the social fabric and organization. The christological hymn of Phil 2:6–11, which describes Jesus as taking the μορφὴν δούλου, would have had a far greater impact for the early Christians than it does for moderns because of the implications of the word δοῦλος at that time. A δοῦλος could be coerced in ways that undermine many ideals that we who live in liberal democracies believe are important for human dignity.[36] To *become* a slave means a voluntary surrender of personal autonomy. This is an extreme, perhaps even pathological, manifestation of self-understanding. It seems to be what the New Testament consistently requires, however.

The Parameters of the Servant-Ethic in the New Testament

Much has been written by scholars on Jesus' role as a servant, Paul's self-styling as a slave of Christ, and the implications of texts such as the *Haustafeln* which give instructions to slaves in the form of general paranesis. These passages will not figure prominently in this discussion since we are concerned with the early Christian self-understanding regarding the believer's role as a servant/slave of others in the realm of ethics.

The requirement to place the interests of others first, or rather, one's own last, sounds a consistent note throughout the ethical considerations of the New Testament writers. We need, therefore, to look beyond the occurrences of διάκονος or δοῦλος, and to consider those passages which require the servant-ethic whether or not they explicitly use this vocabulary. Jesus' call to go the second mile is an example of the servant-ethic even though the words δοῦλος and διάκονος are not mentioned. The requirement to look to the wishes and interests of others and to eschew one's own rights even when they may be asserted justifiably, bespeak an attitude of servanthood, even slavery, which is thematic in New Testament ethics.

Our primary objective is to delineate how fundamental the servant-ethic was to the self-understanding of the early Christians by demonstrating that it occurs throughout the earliest Christian documents. We shall examine the Synoptic gospels in order to demonstrate that the evangelists' sketch of Jesus portray his conduct as paradigmatic, and his teaching as exacting a self-conscious stance of servanthood amongst his disciples. Texts that are especially important here will include Mark 10:42–45 and its parallels, parts of the Sermon on the Mount and the calls to discipleship. The Johannine literature presents a special challenge. Here special attention will be paid to the footwashing episode of John 13 in order to show that, while in many respects the fourth gospel differs from the Synoptics, the underlying sentiment regarding the self-awareness of Christians as servants of others is similar. The undisputed writings of Paul elaborate the servant-ethic most explicitly, but are full of paradox and ambiguity on the matter of ethics in general. In examining Paul's approach we do well to keep in mind that the "apostle to the Gentiles" sought to fulfil God's will, not practice ethics. Finally, an examination of the remaining books illustrates how consistent and persistent the servant-ethic is in the New Testament as a whole.

This study does not seek to demonstrate that the ethics and the self-understanding of the early Christians were homogeneous or universally consistent. What it does attempt to show is that there was an element of consistency in what the New Testament writers understood about the self-awareness of Christians in their relations with others. This self-awareness tempered Christian conduct, in theory at least, so that ambition, prestige and social status—in short, the interests of the self—were placed last out of obedience to the will of God. "For Christianity, ethics are not self-contained or self-justifying; they arise out of a response to the Gospel."[37]

Chapter II

THE SERVANT-ETHIC IN THE SYNOPTIC GOSPELS

C.G. Montefiore says of Mark 9:35: "True greatness is service: service is true greatness . . . . A grand paradox."[1] This requirement of humble service and sacrifice is most succinctly stated in Mark 9:35 and in similar texts (Mark 10:43–45; Matt 20:26–28; 23:11–12; Luke 22:24–27), but other passages also invoke the same moral pattern. The Synoptic gospels reveal a consistent call to renounce "self-interest" even in situations where it may be asserted justifiably. The communities that perpetuated the traditions about Jesus clearly found something compelling and vital in such calls to serve others.

The Content of the Synoptic Servant-Ethic

The call to serve others is fulfilled in two separate steps according to the Synoptic gospels. First it can only be obeyed if an inner transformation through repentance has taken place in the hearer of Jesus' teachings. As Günther Bornkamm has pointed out, repentance does not mean the performance of pious exercises before God in order to atone for sins committed. Repentance is the acceptance of God's invitation to salvation. "If Jesus' call to salvation is at the same time a call to repentance, the call to repentance is at the same time a call to rejoice."[2] The wholehearted response to God's offer of salvation and Jesus' call to repentance instills a willingness to put aside self-interest as the individual turns from self to God. The second step involves putting into practice the concrete ethical action that is appropriate for those entering the kingdom. One of the cornerstones of such action is service to others. The call to take up one's cross functions as a warning that the decision to follow him will lead inevitably to self-sacrifice (Mark 8:34–35; Matt 10:38–39; Luke 14:27).[3] The various strands of the servant-ethic that can be drawn out of the Synoptic gospels are all marked by the paradoxes and hyperbole that, as scholars have noted, are so characteristic of Jesus' speech as recorded in these accounts.[4] We may identify four aspects of the content of the servant-ethic as it is depicted in these gospels.

1. Love of Neighbor

The Synoptic gospels are unanimous in their call to love of neighbor (Mark 12:28–31; Matt 22:34–40; Luke 10:25–28)[5], but only Luke gives a concrete example of what this means in the parable of the Good Samaritan (10:29–37).[6] The lawyer's correct analysis that the one "who showed mercy" was the true neighbor to the robbers' victim offers a clue as to what this command to love entails.[7] True love of neighbor is revealed, although not exhausted, by those who show mercy, who look upon the downtrodden, the beaten and the oppressed, and are moved into action to alleviate their suffering.[8] While neither Mark nor Matthew include a parallel parable, Matthew, like Luke, includes the "Golden Rule" with a note that "this is the law and the prophets" (Matt 7:12). The Synoptic tradition understands love of neighbor to include not only the capacity to empathize with the hapless circumstances of another, but also the willingness to alleviate them, even if those circumstances have befallen one outside of one's usual social and/or religious group. It involves assuaging the suffering of the hungry, homeless, naked, sick and imprisoned (Matt 25:35–40). Fundamentally, the calls to love others involve identification of the believer with the one who suffers.

Most important in this regard is the Christian understanding, grounded in the gospel teaching, that the neighbor is any other person and that person is to be loved, as Kierkegaard insists, unreservedly.[9] The command to love neighbors becomes a call to indiscriminate compassion towards others (Matt 5:46–47) which, by the very nature of love itself, often involves degrees of self-subordination and abandonment of self-interest.

2. Love of Enemies

The injunction to love one's enemies is, perhaps, the most radical directive that involves placing one's own interests last. In Matthew's Sermon on the Mount there is a gradual build-up to the injunction that begins with 5:25–26 (the command to make friends with one's accuser), intensifies in 5:38–42 (the call to supersede the *lex talionis*), and culminates with 5:43–48 and the bald demand to love one's enemies, and to pray for one's persecutors. This passage concludes with the call to "be perfect (τέλειος), as your heavenly Father is perfect."

Matt 5:38–42 is an arresting illustration of what it means to subordinate one's own rights and interests. The command not to resist evil is illustrated by the example of offering the left cheek if the right is struck.[10] The blow is unjustified, and the disciple, rather than seeking to extract a fine mandated by such abuse (400 denarii, according to the Mishnah), is to offer the other cheek to the attacker. Justice, in the sense of defending one's rights, and the *lex talionis*, are thereby set aside. Similar concerns are expressed by the example of Matt 5:40. The call to surrender one's cloak as well to the one who merely sues for one's coat, illustrates a deliberate effort to forego justice for oneself.[11] The third example given in Matt 5:41 of going the extra mile probably reflects enforced conscription by Roman soldiers who compelled civilians to carry their supplies and paraphernalia a certain distance.[12] Jesus' followers are not simply to obey the soldiers of the occupation but are to exceed their demands. Luke includes the command to love one's enemies in his Sermon on the Plain with several variations (Luke 6:27–36). The command is repeated twice (6:27, 35) bracketing specific examples of how the command is to be put into practice: doing good, blessing those who curse, praying for abusers, turning the other cheek, surrendering the inner as well as the outer garment, giving to all, lending with no expectations. Furnish notes the special focus the command to love has in the Sermon on the Plain and that it has pragmatic connotations for the believer's life. It means the compassionate serving of whoever stands in need, active "doing good" even to one's enemies.[13]

Both Matthew and Luke, then, point to the requirement to exceed the usual practices of the day and both conclude by insisting on a degree of perfection (in Matthew) or mercy (in Luke) that is similar to the Father's.[14] Loving one's enemies in these texts entails the waiving of justice for oneself. This echoes Kierkegaard's insistence that love and justice must be understood to be in opposition. For Kierkegaard, there can be no reconciliation between love and justice. He calls love a "revolution" which necessarily disrupts justice.[15] To love one's enemies means that one refrains from returning violence with violence (e.g. Matt 5:39; Luke 6:29), and from insisting on fair treatment at the hands of another (e.g. Matt 5:40–42; Luke 6:29–30).[16] Jesus does not supersede the *lex talionis*, but rather stops short of it. Vengeance will occur but in an eschatological rather than immediate context. To be sure the wicked do prosper, often at the expense of the godly, but as the writer of Ps 73 makes clear, true refuge is found in God whose mercy and justice will eventually restore the balance. Jesus encourages his followers to trust that this is the case. As Davies and Allison say, "the law of reciprocity is not utterly repudiated but only taken out of human hands to be placed in divine hands".[17]

This injunction to surrender one's rights sometimes proves problematic for modern theologies. The focus of liberation theologians is the pursuit of justice. This immediately recalls Kierkegaard's claim that love and justice are irreconcilable. One senses however that Gustavo Gutierrez, for example, is thinking along lines very different from Kierkegaard when he promotes the view that theology has to serve the declaration of "the reign of love and justice." Love and justice are in the process of transforming history. Gutierrez says that "liberation theology made this perspective its starting point as it attempted to show the meaning of the proclamation of the gospel for the history of Latin America."[18] According to the Sermon on the Mount, however, God "makes his sun rise on the evil and the good, and sends rain on the just and on the unjust" (Matt 5:45). The call to love is seen as prior to any pursuit of justice. God's love extends to all, and is thereby paradigmatic for his people. Such impartiality on the part of God is thematic in the Biblical and Rabbinic traditions.[19] The problem hinges on how justice is applied to the ethic of loving one's enemies. Common sense dictates that it is better to struggle against an oppressor than to submit and allow injustice to affect others. Jesus, however, appears to leave not only retaliation but also the struggle itself to God.[20]

3. Service to the Poor

While Luke has a special interest in the poor and the Christian's responsibility towards them, the Synoptic tradition as a whole reflects this concern. Concerns about earthly possessions are to be disregarded in favor of alleviating the suffering of the poor. As Birger Gerhardsson says of Matt 5:17–48 "'overflowing' obedience toward God comes to expression in a sacrificial, generous attitude toward one's fellows . . . . When one loves God with one's whole heart . . . people are beneficiaries."[21] There are three passages that we shall consider to illustrate this: Matt 25:31–46; Luke 14:12–14 and Luke 16:19–31.

In the first of these Jesus describes the eschatological judgment that awaits those who fail to offer concrete acts of service to the poor, or more specifically the hungry, the thirsty, the stranger, the naked, the sick and the imprisoned. Many scholars believe that the "poor" are Christians and that the audience of Matthew's gospel is being reminded to live up to their responsibilities towards their fellow-believers. The primary grounds for this view are founded upon the references to prison visitation (unusual in a list of "works of love"), which are thought to refer to Christians incarcerated for their faith.[22] It is also possible, in view of other statements of the Matthean Jesus, to see here a reference to the impoverished in general (Matt 5:43–48).[23] Nevertheless, the fact that the possibility is envisioned that some members of the Christian community will fail to carry out such service to the poor suggests that not all members of the community are living up to their calling as servants of others.[24] In this passage, to serve the poor, whomever they might be, is to serve the Son of Man himself.

In Luke 14:12–14 Jesus tells the Pharisee who has invited him for a meal that he should invite to his banquets the poor, destitute and maimed rather than his friends, family and rich neighbors since he can expect no reciprocity from the former. In this way the host can expect to be blessed at the resurrection. Jesus reveals that generosity is of no value, in eschatological terms, if it is displayed with expectation of imminent benefits for oneself. The prominent Pharisee should not seek what Fitzmyer terms "selfish recompense" but should display real love "which never reckons with recompense; and because this is so, generosity will find its reward at the resurrection."[25] The reward for such generous hospitality is not to be sought in subsequent invitations to elegant and grandiose parties but rather in the hope of the approval and blessing of God.[26]

In Luke 16:19–31 the eschatological implications of failure to provide even the slightest service to the suffering poor are highlighted with the striking parable of the rich man and the beggar Lazarus. As Fitzmyer points out, the rich man's lack of concern for the beggar is only implied,[27] but the reader infers from the judgment upon the former that he deliberately withheld even his crumbs from Lazarus. 16:13 anticipates the parable as Jesus insists that one cannot serve God and be a lover of riches.[28] Luke does not say that the rich necessarily stand condemned, but the story insists that the honorable use of wealth includes generous provision for the poor. The conclusion of the story, with its unmistakable reference to the resurrection of Jesus, reveals that for those whose hearts are hardened against God, and therefore against the suffering of others, even the testimony of one who has been resurrected will not change them.

The disciple's empathy with the impoverished should arise naturally from the change of heart that taking up one's cross entails.[29] That service to the poor is not in and of itself adequate, however, is starkly reflected in the Synoptic writers' accounts of the anointing of Jesus by a woman (Matt 26:6–13; Mark 14:3–9). In Matthew the disciples object to the extravagance, claiming that the profit from selling the ointment could have been given to the poor. In Mark the reaction is much the same, although the word μαθηεται is not used. In both these accounts Jesus responds by suggesting that the anointing is a "beautiful thing" and that it involves preparation for his burial. He then reminds his listeners, "you always have the poor with you, and whenever you will, you can do good to them; but you will not always have me" (Mark 14:7).[30] There are always opportunities to give and to help others, service which in the Synoptic tradition also constitutes giving to and helping Jesus, but the occasions for extraordinary displays of service to Jesus himself are rare indeed.[31]

Finally, in the passage about the rich young man (Mark 10:17–22; Matt 19:16–30; Luke 18:18–30), both Matthew and Mark, as well as Luke, illustrate that service to others is demonstrated in concern for the poor. Jesus' love to the man (Mark 10:21), at least in Mark, is demonstrated by the observation that the man lacks one thing: "Go, sell what you have and give to the poor and you will have treasure in heaven."[32] Self-denial by giving to the poor is the prerequisite, in this case at least, to acquire heavenly treasure.[33] In all of these examples, service exceeds alms-giving and becomes a deliberate and voluntary choice to become "one" with them. Jeremias sums up the attitude towards material possessions as a "revision of values" in which material possessions are no longer a means of security in light of salvation. Rather they are to be sacrificed in love.[34] This deliberate forsaking of material wealth illustrates the self-understanding of the servant-ethic.

4. Rejection of Social Hierarchies

This "revision of values" of which Jeremias writes[35] is also reflected in the attitude that disciples should have toward social hierarchies and political power structures. In endeavoring to fulfill one's obligations as Jesus' disciple, an individual must not look for recognition and honor, but rather seek the least prestigious position and become a servant. It is at this point in the Synoptic tradition that the servant ethic can be most clearly distinguished from the ideal of ἀγάπη love, since it reflects a voluntary relinquishing of authority. Authority is not, in and of itself, necessarily at odds with love. Those seeking positions of power may bestow love on others without necessarily surrendering their own privileges and status. This is not to be amongst Jesus' followers, however. Believers are required to renounce the lust for power and the temptation to pursue it within the community. This is a persistent theme in the Synoptic gospels and is indicated by the calls to become as a child or a servant (Matt 18:2–4; 19:4; 20:25–28; Mark 9:35; 10:15; 10:42–45; Luke 9:48; 18:17; 22:25–27), and to become last of all. These sayings represent a corrective of human ambition that is to be adopted by those who would follow Jesus. Jesus is himself paradigmatic of this: he represents the true servant (Mark 10:42–45) and is symbolized even by a little child (Mark 9:37). As Allen Verhey observes, by responding to Jesus' message individuals also respond to the coming kingdom in which the order of first and last is to be reversed. "To welcome the coming of such a kingdom is to welcome Jesus, and. . . joyfully to surrender the rights and privileges of social status and convention and to serve." For Verhey, humble service "is a part of the concrete shape of repentance in view of the coming kingdom and its present effectiveness in Jesus."[36] We find this ethic specifically invoked in the calls to reject prestige (e.g. Matt 23:8–10; Luke 14:7–11), whereby Jesus' followers are to be indifferent to the honors that social reputation brings. In this way human ambition, which by definition is at odds with God's kingdom and rule, is corrected.[37]

Social conventions and customs that arbitrarily lend more prestige to some than to others based on wealth, learning or ancestry are rejected in favor of the dominion of God. In a sense, this teaching is subversive in that it makes counter-claims to the requirements of social protocol.[38] Those with the least rights in society—slaves, women and children—provide the model for Jesus' disciples. The disciples are to become ones who serve, who no longer seek their own advantage but rather endeavor to minister to others.[39] The inclination to serve comprises a major theme in the Synoptic record of Jesus' teaching, and also reflects the concrete response to the various commands to love. To cite Furnish's words, "'Service' not 'security' is the watchword of this ethic."[40]

The Synoptic Motives for Serving Others

Each of the Synoptic gospels provides a rationale or motive as it advocates the servant-ethic as a fundamental aspect of the moral vision. Disputes about greatness amongst the disciples sometimes form the context for Jesus' call to serve others (Mark 9:33–35; 10:35–45; Matt 20:20–28; Luke 22:24–27). In each of these passages squabbling amongst the disciples precedes Jesus' insistence that service to others rather than personal ambition is required of his disciples. Because different emphases develop in each text we will consider each gospel in turn rather than using a topical arrangement.

1. Mark

In Mark 9:35 the disciples of Jesus have made a decision to follow him and, according to Mark, have already been told that their choice requires self-denial (Mark 8:34–38). Jesus now tells them, in Mark 9:35, that this self-denial, as we saw above, is, in part, to take the form of concrete service towards others.[41] The phrase "If anyone would be first" (Εἰ τις θέλει πρῶτος εἶναι), can be interpreted two ways. Either the desire to be first is affirmed as good, but Jesus insists that the goal be achieved through service; or the desire to be first, and personal ambition as a whole, is seen as evil and must be set aside in following Jesus. Vv 36–37 offer the strongest clue that the call to serve is a corrective to such ambition, at least in this gospel. In these verses Jesus insists that the disciples welcome or receive a little child as if they were receiving Jesus himself.

In Mark 10:42–45 the impetus for such an ethical stance becomes even more explicit. Here a self-conscious posture against emulating the methods of those who rule over the Gentiles is part of the motive. Those who are considered "great" by the Gentiles exercise authority. This, however, is not to be part of the disciples' self-understanding. Rather they are to thwart personal ambition and the desire for dominance over others by becoming servants of all and last of all. Jesus challenges the disciples' ambitions and seeks to correct the attitude that lies behind the request of James and John in v.37. It is too cynical to assert that servanthood is portrayed as the means to attain greatness; i.e., that for those who become servants Jesus promises them the personal glory they are vying for. Dan Via Jr, however, comes close to stating this when he says that "well-being (being great or first) is present as the object of will and, by implication, as the intentional reason for human action." He continues that one attains this well-being by becoming a slave of all and that 10:43–44 "expresses the ethical actualization of the faith stance (8:35)."[42] More caution is required here. Human conventions concerning greatness no longer apply, yet the language of greatness is still employed to illustrate the consequences of faith. This is the paradox of the servant-ethic as articulated by Mark: the transformation of the human heart impelled by responding to Jesus' call makes such categories as greatness irrelevant, yet they are used metaphorically to illustrate the outcome of faith and discipleship. Gnilka overcomes the paradox in part by pointing to greatness in service here that arises not from ambition but from a willingness to serve.[43] More fundamentally, the example of Jesus himself also figures as part of the motive in this passage.[44] The pursuit of social prestige is to be set aside, deliberately and self-consciously, after the manner of the Son of Man.

While other passages in Mark express similar ethical concerns, variations in motive can also be detected. In Mark 8:34–35, for example, self-denial and taking up one's cross is encouraged on the grounds that it is by losing one's life for the sake of Jesus and the gospel that one ultimately saves it. In the context of this passage Jesus lays out the conditions of discipleship, conditions that always involve self-sacrifice. The motive for such sacrifice is simple: it is the means by which one's "life" is "saved."[45] The sacrifice spoken of here does not refer only to the crisis of martyrdom, although some see this as the correct interpretation of the passage,[46] but also to a consistent denial of one's own interests. Ernest Best prefers to interpret the passage metaphorically. He points out that persecution, rather than martyrdom, is a more prominent motif in the New Testament, and that the idea of self-denial in the Markan text points away from a literal understanding of the verse. "Self-denial is the inner attitude; cross-bearing is the outward activity which should accompany the inner attitude."[47]

Best concludes that because taking up a cross corresponds to a particular event in Jesus' own life there is clearly a call to imitation in this passage. "That the disciple's cross-bearing need not be literal as Jesus' was does not affect this since Jesus' cross-bearing is symbolic of all his loving activity."[48] The call to *follow* Jesus requires different obligations according to Martin Hengel, than those obligations incumbent upon those who simply answer the call to repentance. The followers of Jesus took on special roles, but the act of repentance was required of everyone. Everyone needed to repent and acknowledge their guilt before God and subsequently fulfill his will. Those who did had to "renounce all self-glory . . . and to will unconditionally to practice forgiveness of their neighbor, in response to the uninvited forgiveness, through God's goodness, of their own immeasurable guilt."[49]

Although historical considerations compel us to see the circle of disciples as a group distinct from the numbers who responded to the message of salvation, in terms of the early Christian ethical understanding the distinction becomes less important. Bornkamm acknowledges "that the disciples must be distinguished as a more intimate group from Jesus' followers in the wider sense" but insists that "what [Jesus] demands from them does not in fact differ from what he asks of everybody: to repent in light of the coming kingdom of God."[50] In the post-

Easter communities the passages about the call to follow were surely interpreted as a summons to faith in Christ, as Hengel contends.[51] Another important text that might help illuminate the motives of the Markan requirement to serve is Mark 12:30–31, the love commandment. A scribe asks Jesus to name the greatest commandment. Jesus replies by iterating the oneness of God and that one should love him completely. He then says, "You shall love your neighbor as yourself" and that there is no commandment greater than those requiring love of God and neighbor. In praising Jesus' response, the scribe also provides part of the motive for loving one's neighbor as oneself: it "is much more than all whole burnt offerings and sacrifices." Such rituals are pleasing to God, and imperative according to Torah, yet to love God, and others as oneself, is even greater. This judgment is confirmed because the scribe's insight and wisdom prompt Jesus to tell him that he is not far from the kingdom of God. Here, then, the motive boils down to the confirmation that a better way than ritual worship to honor God, is not only to love God, but to love one's neighbor also. This is not to suggest that the author of Mark, or any of the New Testament writers for that matter, would suggest that love for neighbor can substitute for love for God. As Birger Gerhardsson makes so clear, service to God (λατρεία, Matt 4:10) is inextricably tied to service to others: "In the final judgement 'deeds of mercy' are asked after (25:31–46). Διακονία is counted as λατρεία."[52] Although the ones counted as sheep rather than goats are unaware that they have served God by serving others (Matt 25:37), the implication of the passage suggests that it is their desire to fulfill God's will that led to their self-understanding as servants of others. Jesus is the exemplar of how διακονία counts as service to God. Matt 20:28 (Mark 10:45 par.) reveals that Jesus' crucifixion is not simply sacrifice in the sense of atonement, but is sacrificial service to others.[53] Those who desire to serve God must also be willing to love their neighbor as themselves.[54]

A final motive is the calculated strategy to repudiate, at least amongst Jesus' followers, the order of things as they currently stand. Thus, Jesus' disciples are not simply to avoid behaving like the rulers and authorities of the Gentiles—they are to take deliberate steps to become the exact opposite, to become διακόνοι and δοῦλοι.[55] While some have accused the Markan community of attempting to "retreat from the world and its problems,"[56] Verhey suggests that Jesus' call to serve points rather to the creation of a "counterculture" which exists in contrast to both the religious and civil establishment by reinterpreting the meaning of power.[57]

The theme of discipleship is central to the Markan record.[58] Jesus' followers are not to seek power over others, nor are they to aspire to personal greatness on their own behalf. The call to serve in Mark is motivated by a desire to emulate Jesus, to honor God and thereby reject norms and mores that lead to arrogant self-seeking. In other words it is motivated by a desire to realize full discipleship in the Jesus movement. Susan Lochrie Graham points out, however, that the verb διακονέω is never used of male disciples in the gospel.[59] Women engage in service (e.g. Mark 1:30–31), but the verb is never used by Mark to describe the actions of male followers.[60] The self-sacrifice required by the text leads to "salvation" (Mark 8:34–35). This theme of reward, however, is not developed as fully as in Matthew.

2. Matthew

In Matthew, although many of the pertinent passages are parallels to those we have considered in Mark, the increase in material and varying contexts also mean that perhaps a different motive is envisioned in the calls to serve others. For those passages which have parallels in Mark many of the motives are similar in Matthew. Matt 20:25–28 (which parallels Mark 10:42–45) is almost identical to its Markan parallel in wording. The primary difference here is that the mother of the sons of Zebedee makes the request for their prestigious position in the kingdom and thereby gives the impetus for Jesus' saying. Minor differences aside, Matthew's account of this incident seems to provide similar motives to those we have suggested can be found in Mark 10:35–45. Jesus seeks to thwart personal ambition in favor of an attitude of willingness to serve others even unto death. His disciples must not assume that the kingdom of God emulates worldly hierarchies or political regimes.

This rejection by Jesus of the order of the day is also reflected in Matt 23:1–12. Much of this passage is bound up with a ringing condemnation of the "scribes and Pharisees" for which little direct parallel material is found in Mark.[61] This critique of the Pharisees serves, however, as a contrast to the correct attitude that must be found amongst Jesus' disciples. Unlike the scribes and Pharisees, who "love the place of honor at feasts and the best seats in the synagogues," Jesus' disciples are not to covet places of honor or prestigious titles. The reference to the "place of honor at feasts," as well as having a direct parallel in Mark 12:39 and Luke 20:46, represents the Synoptic injunction to serve rather than to seek a prestigious position, especially at the eschatological banquet prepared by God (e.g., Luke 14:7–11; 22:26–27). The one who is greatest among believers shall be their servant and only those who humble themselves will be exalted. As well as seeking to correct personal ambition, this passage also makes explicit the promise of exaltation for the humble. While we need not suggest that this is the primary motive for serving others in this passage, we must not shrink from the fact that the Matthean Jesus offers such a reward as a consideration in promoting appropriate behavior. While Schrage's insistence that "it would be wrong to interpret Matthew simply as an exponent of a spirituality based on merit,"[62] these and other verses imply reward constitutes part of the motive to serve. In this passage, then, Jesus' followers are called to humility and service so as to avoid the ambition and arrogance of some of the religious authorities, and thereby gain exaltation by God.

The exaltation of the humble is a prominent theme throughout the biblical tradition. The people of God are repeatedly reminded that despite their lowly status they can look forward to ultimate exaltation and vindication (e.g., Prov 3:34; II Sam 22:28; Ps 18:27; Job 5:11), although in many of these examples the lowliness or humility of God's people is a pre-existing condition and not one that is deliberately sought. The issue is whether one seeks reward from other people or from God—whether one chooses to be esteemed by others or to seek the exaltation that only God can give. In this Matthean passage Jesus' followers are called to eschew any impressive appellations that may be bestowed upon them, secure in the assurance that they will be duly exalted. The context of the call is the grace that God has seen fit to bestow upon them and their gratitude for it. No one, according to Matthew, has a strict claim on God.

Reward as a motive for responding to Jesus' call to serve is also apparent in the Sermon on the Mount, although it does not seem to be the primary impetus for making the interests of others paramount here.[63] The Matthean Jesus calls his followers to exhibit much behavior that goes beyond religious norms and expectations. As far as Jesus is concerned divorce and oaths are prohibited (5:31–37), every outburst and look of lust is condemned (5:21–22, 27–28) and those at odds with their "brother" must be reconciled before they approach the altar (5:23–24). This recalls the scribe's response to Jesus in Mark 12:33 in which the love of God and neighbor is deemed "much more than all whole burnt offerings and sacrifices." There is, however, no parallel for this latter saying in Matthew, perhaps because he is more reluctant than Mark to portray Jesus as supplanting Torah (e.g. Matt 5:17–20), but probably because he finds the sympathetic portrayal of the scribe in Mark at odds with his own portrayal of them. Matthew, too, insists on the priority of the love commandment over ritual demands (9:13; 12:7). More significantly, as we have seen, Jesus insists that his followers "not resist one who is evil" (5:39–42). The reward that constitutes the motive for the injunctions of Matt 5:43–47 is the fulfilment of the desire to become sons of God (Matt 5:48). This reward is not found in earthly acclaim, it is the approval of the Father.

The command to love one's enemies is central to the Sermon on the Mount and to the Synoptic tradition as a whole.[64] In Matthew it is especially highlighted and Schrage goes so far as to say that "the real standard for correctly interpreting the law is the law of love."[65] It is in these verses that we find a central motive for the ethical teachings presented in the Sermon on the Mount. The religious desire to be like God is, therefore, the motivating force behind the fulfillment of the ethics presented in Matt 5:21–48. These verses do not suggest that by loving one's enemies the enmity will cease, although some have detected such a "strategic" motive in this passage and its parallel in Luke. For example, in his article, "The Inadequacy of Selflessness God's Suffering and the Theory of Love," Stephen Post insists that these passages are addressed to believers whose love for outsiders is evangelical. Love seeks to expand "the circle of reciprocity to include new participants. . . . An attitude of forgiveness is recommended without which the sphere of mutuality cannot enlarge."[66] Luise Schottroff comes to a similar understanding of these passages.[67] For these two scholars love of enemies is a missionary or evangelistic tool that promotes the Kingdom. Jesus' followers love the enemy in the hope of making an ally. While such an interpretation may be valid in light of New Testament ethical injunctions as a whole, the texts in question do not explicitly make such a claim. Furnish interprets the text more accurately when he says that "it is a. . . distinction of Jesus' love command that such love does not await, anticipate, or require a response in kind."[68] For Furnish enemy-love is not to be conditional upon the response of the enemy. The believer's love is not explicitly motivated by the desire to overcome the enmity of the other person. Piper disagrees with Furnish's analysis by relating the Lord's prayer (Matt 6:9–13) to the antitheses in Matt 5. For Piper it is inconceivable that prayer for enemies does not include the wish that they come to do God's will and thereby eradicate the enmity. "That a man should pray for his enemy and not request that the enmity between them be removed would be a questionable manifestation of love, to say the least."[69] Despite the proposals of Post, Schottroff and Piper, I find no indication in the text at hand to suggest that love of enemies is commanded in order to bring more people into the Kingdom. The emphasis is on the disciple's actions and how the disciple should behave. The aim of the text is to bring the disciple into harmony with God's will, rather than the enemy, although the latter may ultimately come to the Kingdom also. Reinhold Niebuhr notes that the text does not claim that enemy-love will transform enmity into friendship and suggests "that social and prudential possibility has been read into the admonition of Jesus by liberal Christianity."[70] The behavior required by the command to love one's enemies involves deliberately rejecting the pursuit of justice for oneself, while allowing the enemy the opportunity to willfully trample one's rights. Lohfink notes that according to the calls for enemy-love fighting for one's legitimate rights is now forbidden God's people. Rights cannot be imposed through violence. Followers of Jesus "should give to anyone who asks. They should be willing to let themselves be forced."[71] That the command to love one's enemy is motivated by something other than enlightened self-interest or evangelistic concerns is especially apparent in Luke where 6:31 the Golden Rule concludes the first section on love of enemies. Harvey says in his comparison of Jesus' positive version with Hillel's negative that "you can never be sure that if you treat people kindly they will show equal kindness in return. . . . Stated quite generally as Jesus states it, the maxim (unlike its negative counterpart) goes beyond the most enlightened common sense."[72]

Ulrich Luz captures the essence of the passage by noting that enemy-love is not advocated "because it is reasonable or natural or promises success but because the one who makes it is as the risen Lord with his community all the days to the close of the age." Questions of whether enemy-love can ever succeed are subordinated, therefore, to the awareness on the part of the believer that it is Jesus who gives the command. Luz further notes that "the question is not directly whether it is tactically or psychically realistic but whether the experience of grace which is presupposed in it is so strong that the human being can become free for such a love."[73]

The failure to take up the challenge to love one's enemies is perhaps the clearest instance of how the Church from early in its history up to the present has been especially selective in its response to the teachings in the gospels. Luz, for example, believes that by mistaking the love of enemies with some ultimate goal the Church has compromised the intention of Jesus [and of Matthew].[74] We need to recognize, therefore, that for some of the earliest Christian communities, this injunction formed an important part of their self-understanding and played a role in the development of their ethic. Harvey, explains why this command is so captivating while rightly acknowledging that most attempts to rationalize it somehow fail. It is

> one of those maxims that gain their power over us, not because of their enlightened good sense or religious motivation, but because of their appeal to a potential that lies deep in the human spirit, and can occasionally be activated by the challenge of a totally unconditional demand.[75]

The perfection called for in Matt 5:48 is moral perfection—the imitation of God's perfect love.[76] This love, which manifests itself in humble service, is the fitting response to God's grace and invitation to salvation. The desire to be like the Father, because one seeks to become his child, is, in and of itself, the primary motivation. The believer does not seek to be perfect in love because he or she wishes to transform the world, but rather because there now exists the desire to conform to God: "love is not being required because it will set the world right. Instead one's motivation to love arises out of a desire to be like God."[77]

The believer is motivated to attempt to fulfill this ethic not only to fulfill the role as a son of the Father but also because it is Jesus who prescribes it. Those who would obey God hearken to Jesus' words.[78] On Matt 5:21–48 Davies and Allison note that while imitation of God (5:45, 48), escaping eschatological retribution (5:22–26, 28–30) and even reason (5:34–36) are given as motives, obedience to Jesus as sovereign Lord is the primary impetus for fulfilling the ethic presented here. One should "faithfully follow the way of the Sermon on the Mount because the voice in it speaks with divine authority."[79]

Matt 25:31–46 and its account of the coming of the Son of Man illustrates how the motive for service in Matthew can extend beyond imitating God and Jesus, and even beyond radical submission to the authoritative word of Jesus and thereby the will of God. Here righteousness is equated with acts of service toward others which are in fact acts of service toward the King.[80] Thus while the passage can be interpreted as simply a promise of the kingdom to those who feed the hungry, clothe the naked, and visit the sick and incarcerated, and eternal punishment to those who do not, it also provides another motive. The "least" represent the Son of Man and must be served.

In Matthew we find similar motivations to serve others as we noted in Mark. We also find, however, more references to reward as a motive. Nevertheless, like Mark, Matthew portrays Jesus' ethic as running counter to what the gospel itself presents as the conventional morality of his day. Those who are "sons of their Father in Heaven," who seek to inherit the kingdom and eternal life, are those who are willing to serve others.[81]

3. Luke

In Luke different emphases can be detected in the discussion of motive concerning the servant-ethic. Like Matthew and Mark, Luke seeks to present the consequences of, and motives for, discipleship and service in his gospel. Luke, however, is especially concerned with wealth and social prestige.

In the first chapter of Luke we find what Schrage terms "his encouragement of humility and warning against lust for power" in Mary's Magnificat (Luke 1:51–52).[82] These verses reveal his belief that God has a special concern for the lowly and the humble. Believers are not to seek prestige or power. God does not exalt the arrogant, and the example of Jesus is one of service. This is especially apparent in Luke 22:24–27, in which Jesus tells his disciples that although the one who sits at the table is usually considered the greater, he (Jesus) is among them "as one who serves."

The Lukan account of this episode (a parallel of Mark 10:42–45 and Matt 20:25–28) is important because in the third gospel we find the dispute occurring at the Last Supper, following the institution of the Eucharist, rather than at an earlier point in Jesus' ministry.[83] This points to a certain similarity to the footwashing episode in the gospel of John, in which Jesus washes the disciples' feet and insists that they imitate him during the Last Supper. Both Luke and John portray Jesus as one who explicitly serves during the Last Supper.

The comparison with the Gentile authorities (Luke 22:25–26) also varies from the Markan and Matthean accounts. One difference is that the word "benefactors" (εὐεργέται) is substituted for "great men" (μεγάλοι) in the two other accounts.[84] Assuming Luke knew Mark, his use of the word "benefactors" may well reflect that he recognizes that Gentile leaders are capable of "good works" but that within the community of Jesus the measure of what is right involves more: a transformation of self-understanding and the relinquishing of social status and power. Also important is the Lukan omission of Jesus' saying in Mark 10:45 about the Son of Man serving and giving his life as a ransom for many.[85] Instead Luke has a verse in which the verb διακονέω is used in its more literal sense of serving at table, although there is no doubt that such service performed by Jesus is to be exemplary for the disciples.[86] As in Matthew and Mark, one of the motives for the servant-ethic is the example of Jesus himself.

Another of Luke's primary motives for serving others and putting their interests first is reflected in texts dealing with money and possessions.[87] For Luke it is necessary to adopt a certain perspective on wealth if one is to exhibit true discipleship. Indeed, one could say that one thread running through Luke-Acts is the idea of service by surrendering personal possessions and wealth (e.g., Luke 6:27–36; 12:13–21; 19:1–10; Acts 2:44–45). Luke 6:27–36 is parallelled in Matt 5:39–48. In Luke, however, loving one's enemies is also exemplified by lending, "expecting nothing in return." The ostensible motive, to receive a great reward and become "sons of the most High," is similar to Matthew's. Like Matthew, however, Luke seems to assume that true disciples will incline towards such behavior. Zacchaeus, for example, upon receiving Jesus, immediately sets about making restitution for his past failings. Zacchaeus is a stark example of the transforming power of true discipleship (Luke 19:1–10). As Verhey says, how one uses one's money is "a sign and symptom of the arrival of the kingdom." Zacchaeus' actions to give recompense for his fraudulent past illustrates that Zacchaeus has indeed responded to the message of Jesus. "Generosity and alms are not *merely* illustrative; they participate in the reality to which they point—the reign of God."[88] No motive for Zacchaeus' action is explicit here—it seems to be the natural outcome of his reception of Jesus and his consequent salvation. His willingness to place his possessions at the disposal of the poor (who apparently have no explicit claim upon him), and those he had deliberately defrauded in the past, reflects how his life has been transformed by his encounter with Jesus. Zacchaeus has been integrated into the new community—those who respond to Jesus and his mission. His attempts at restoration exemplify his μετάνοια. Right use of material possessions occurs when one seeks to serve God by serving others.[89]

The passage concerning the unfair inheritance (Luke 12:13–21) is also important to establish Lukan motives for the command that one put one's possessions at the disposal of others. In this passage Jesus warns against covetousness by reminding his listeners that "life does not consist in the abundance of possessions." The motive here, then, for eschewing one's right to part of an inheritance should one's co-inheritor wish to deny it, is a desire to repudiate selfishness. This will naturally occur, the passage implies, amongst those who place their trust in God to provide. The parable of the foolish rich man, which follows this saying (Luke 12:16–21), concludes with the remark that the one who "lays up treasure for himself" is like this foolish example rather than one who is "rich towards God" (Luke 12:21).

This attitude of indifference to material wealth is reflected in Luke's account of how the early community at Jerusalem distributed their possessions to those in need (Acts 2:44–45). Again there is no clear motive for this sacrifice, other than to illustrate the new life in the Christian community which seeks to alleviate the suffering of others (2:45) by surrendering personal wealth, and the implicit transformation of self-understanding that accompanies it. Luke 16:9 probably reflects this sentiment. Schrage, while acknowledging the difficulty of interpreting this verse, concludes: "The crucial point is to use earthly possessions in the service of love . . . . This love . . . controls and restricts the use of possessions lest they become a source of idolatrous dependence."[90]

Finally in Luke 17:7–10 we have the clearest instance of the evangelist's belief that service to others is the natural outcome of following Jesus' way. Leaving aside the exegetical and source-critical questions that are inherent in the interpretation of these verses,[91] it is evident that these verses show first that service is the "natural" outcome of discipleship and second that such service can never be completed—the servant can never anticipate reward or recognition. The believer can make no claim on God and any reward for service is a bestowal of grace. At the same time the passage is an affirmation of the condition of servanthood, especially since it implicitly repudiates the ungrateful master. The reader is surely meant to recall this passage upon reading Luke 22:27.

In Luke's account we have found it more difficult to discern specific motives for serving and placing oneself (and one's possessions) at the disposal of others. While reward is mentioned, and there does seem to be an attempt to present a stance that deliberately repudiates ambition and the lust for power, Luke, more than either Matthew or Mark, appears to see serving others as the natural outcome of discipleship. Verhey notes that repentance in Luke is integrally bound up with sympathy to the poor and practicing fairness and generosity towards the outcast.[92]

4. Connecting Threads

The Synoptic tradition, as a whole, presents an ethical challenge which, if taken up and discharged, declares the kingdom and identifies its subjects. There are at least four threads that unite in the motive for the servant-ethic in the Synoptic gospels.

i)*The Desire to Imitate God and Christ*

In resolving the squabble of the disciples about who is the greatest Jesus reminds his listeners that the Son of Man came not to be served but to serve and that he is paradigmatic (Mark 10:45 and par.). Self-denial and the abandonment of one's own interests are enjoined using the example of God who acts towards the evil and the just impartially (Matt 5:45). Believers are to be merciful, even as God is, to the ungrateful and the selfish (Luke 6:35–36). The call to serve others and abandon the pursuit of personal justice is fulfilled in part, but not completely, by a conscious attempt to emulate some aspect of God or Jesus. There is here a dimension of self-awareness that provokes the believer to consider how his or her actions correspond to the divine example. This self-awareness arises from the other factors that are part of the Synoptic motives to serve.

ii)*The Recognition of Jesus as Sovereign Lord*

Such imitation of Jesus and God arises from the recognition that God's authority resides in Jesus. Jesus' pronouncements are authoritative because they are his and thereby God's. When he enjoins his followers to serve others and to relinquish their rights, even to be prepared to surrender life itself, his admonishments are sanctioned because he speaks prophetically, as God's representative. Those who respond to Jesus' authority by undergoing μετάνοια recognize in Jesus' words *God's* call to repentance and his requirement for subsequent service to others. Serving others is the fulfillment of God's will and arises from the desire to carry it out.

iii)*The "Natural" Result of μετάνοια*

True discipleship brings about a change in disposition that makes the interests of others paramount, and that naturally leads to serving others, or at least to the inclination to do so.[93] Thus, although the promise of reward is often included in exhortations to such behavior, the Synoptic tradition tends to imply that true disciples will be inclined to serve others as a result of their decision to follow Jesus. Such a decision also involves a readjustment of priorities. Those who follow Jesus, who seek to become a part of the βασιλεία of God, must no longer pursue selfish ambition according to established norms. Their experience of μετάνοια brings about the realization that true wealth is treasure in Heaven rather than on earth, and that true greatness lies in service rather than social prestige. To serve even a little child as one would serve Jesus, is to honor God and obey his will. It is, as Jeremias says, an expression of gratitude for God's grace that is part of repentance.[94] It is at this point that the response to the call to serve surpasses calculated strategies to ultimately advance one's own advantage or diminish others', and becomes joyful participation in the kingdom. Μετάνοια involves a total transformation that not only includes a turning to God, but also a turning away from conventional human norms and standards.

Success and failure, wealth and poverty, honor and rejection, are all measured on a far different scale by the one who has experienced repentance in recognition of God's grace. Μετάνοια gives rise to a "transvaluation of values" that encourages, to use Bultmann's phrase, "the overcoming of self" rather than the pursuit of self-interest.[95]

iv)*The Hope of Eschatological Reward*

The response to God's grace as it is manifested in the servant-ethic arises primarily from gratitude and not hope of reward. The promise of reward is never the primary motive for placing one's interests last. Despite this apparent idealism, it must be faced that the Synoptic record speaks of reward often and it constitutes part of the motive to serve. Jeremias is mistaken in suggesting that Matt 25:37–40 "is an abolition of the idea of reward."[96] Perhaps one could suggest that the promise of heavenly reward may motivate an individual to take up his or her cross, but that once that decision is made, the disciple spontaneously places the interests of others first.[97] Jeremias is then correct in his insistence that "in the sphere of [God's] reign another *motive for action* takes the place of the idea of merit and the claim to reward: gratitude for God's grace."[98] Jeremias, as well as many other scholars, goes too far in asserting that Judaism emphasized the idea of merit while Jesus' teaching did not. There are many passages in Jewish writings which refute the notion that one fulfills the law to gain "brownie points" in the eyes of God. Likewise, as we have seen, many Synoptic passages promise reward to those who are obedient. The crucial point in both traditions is to honor God's will (e.g. Luke 17:10).

v)*Summary*

The response to the Synoptic call to serve is motivated, then, by a complex of incentives that depend upon each other and are integrally related. They are grounded in the experience of grace that the early Christians believed was manifested in Jesus, and arise from the self-understanding of believers as participants in the βασιλεία. As we have said at the outset, we are not claiming that the earliest audiences of these injunctions to serve actually succeeded in living out their daily lives as servants of others. They probably did not set aside their own interests consistently and rigorously. The Synoptic record reveals, however, that the ethical reflection of the writers included a characteristic note of self-denial that was fixed in their convictions about the nature of Jesus and his ministry, and the appropriate response to him. This had to have had some resonance in the earliest audience and therefore must have been manifested, if only sporadically, in their daily conduct. All human behavior is based on some kind of motivation and the Synoptic gospels are clear that for believers self-denial is the ideal to be pursued based on their experience of God's grace.

Limitations upon the Synoptic Call to Serve

We now need to consider whether there are any limitations upon serving others in these texts; that is, situations in which prudence or justice, for example, might restrict the call to self-denial and the surrender of one's own rights.

The first limitation or contradiction that we have to face is the vast gulf that Joseph Klausner and others discern between Jesus' preaching and practice of his own ethics. Klausner points to Jesus' habit of addressing the Pharisees with such epithets as "hypocrites" and "serpents" and his violence against the money-changers in the Temple.[99] Davies and Allison confront this critique with five possibilities:

i)Jesus is exempt from the commandment to love: he is rather the judge.

ii)By their rejection of Jesus, the scribes and Pharisees have become enemies of *God* and the command of enemy-love applies only to personal enemies.

iii)The contradiction cannot be overcome.

iv)The rebukes are required in order to correct error but are motivated by love.

v)Ideas and abuses rather than individuals are attacked, so the reprimands are general and are not directed at specific persons.

Like the evangelist, Davies and Allison draw no definitive conclusions on this matter.[100] The least satisfactory options seem to be (i) and (ii). In the case of (iii) it is only to be accepted if one insists that there is indeed a contradiction between Jesus' preaching and practice. In the context of the dawn of the βασιλεία, or more generally, of experiencing the grace of God, (iv) appears to be most acceptable. Love of others often involves attempts to correct error in the hope of averting future harm to the beloved. The prophetic tradition is replete with hyperbole as God's people are called to righteousness. Jesus' table-fellowship with Pharisees and his approving words to individual members of the religious establishment reveal that (v) is also to be given consideration. The key to the servant-ethic in the Synoptic gospels is the response to God's invitation to the Kingdom. Once an individual has repented he or she becomes open to the will of God. Selflessness and a complete willingness to serve others becomes the moral guide-post. Any act in which the interests of the self are placed before the interests of others constitutes a violation of God's will. As L. H. Marshall has said, "the rule of self is abandoned for the voluntary acceptance of the rule of God."[101] Thus it is possible to envisage situations in which an individual serves others by resisting evil, though Jesus nowhere makes this explicit. For the resistance to be Christian, according to the Synoptic teaching, it must not be done out of revenge or for personal benefit. Christians have long wrestled with this very question, and today many struggle to find the appropriate response to such endemic problems as totalitarianism and racism.[102]

Reinhold Niebuhr points out that the prosecution of justice can often be undertaken selectively for personal benefit:

> From the first restraints upon blood vengeance to the last refinements of corrective justice, the egoistic element of vindictiveness remains both an inevitable and a dangerous alloy in the passion for justice. It is inevitable because men never judge injustice so severely as it ought to be judged until their life, or life in their intimate circle, is destroyed by it.[103]

Jesus' teaching, as reflected by the Synoptic writers, does not call for institutional morality or "official" ethical positions—it reflects the values of the βασιλεία. The gospel teaching tends to concentrate on the everyday, on the personal. The Synoptic Jesus does not tell his listeners how they, as a group, should react to the oppression of living in an occupied land; he tells them how to respond to personal rebuff, to particular but often extreme situations, with the implication that the broader questions of political and social injustice depend upon the believer's self-conscious awareness of her or his role as a child of God and servant of others. Consequently, Jesus' teachings may well have relevance to the situations noted above, and it is certainly appropriate for modern Christians to seek the resolution of such dilemmas in the gospel texts. The sum of the Synoptic gospel-message must be taken into account, however, and not simply such texts as Matt 5:43 or conversely 10:34.[104]

A useful illustration of the dilemma is the fact that some Christians believe that there are cases when war is justified to thwart tyranny and to serve the interests of innocent victims. Others believe that participation in armed conflict is always forbidden. Reinhold Niebuhr warns against attempts to translate too directly Jesus' ethics into social or political policy because it "usually has the effect of blunting the very penetration of his moral insights." Niebuhr insists that the call for non-resistance cannot simply be translated into an injunction against violence because "it ceases to provide a perspective from which the sinful element in all resistance, conflict, and coercion may be discovered." Niebuhr suggests that those who are most vocal in advocating non-retaliation are often those with the "economic power to be able to dispense with the more violent forms of coercion and therefore condemn them as un-Christian"[105] Contemporary Christian pacifism that is based on an interpretation of Synoptic and biblical principles, however, has manifested itself in social and political activism that has had profound consequences. The civil-rights movement in the United States during the 1960's (subsequent to the publication of Niebuhr's book) is a startling example of how a group with limited economic power managed, on the whole, to "dispense with the more violent forms of coercion." Of course, the principles of individual rights inherent in classical liberalism were already in place in America, but only the most cynical would deny that during those years of struggle the West witnessed a profound social and political transformation that was inspired by the belief that oppression should not be overcome with violence. That this movement gained its initial momentum in the African-American churches of the American south testifies, in this instance at least, that the inspiration to seek social transformation can be found in the gospel.

It is not unreasonable to suppose that such dilemmas also confronted the earliest communities of believers, especially since we have the historical records of divisions within Judaism over such questions. It is always useful to remind oneself that in its genesis Christianity was a Jewish sectarian movement amongst many, and that most of the social and political questions that confronted Jews in first-century occupied Palestine and in the communities of the Diaspora must also have challenged their Christian contemporaries.

Despite the fact that the focus here is not on whether the servant-ethic was ever realized in the day to day conduct of any of the earliest believers we need to consider whether or not the gospel texts, especially Mark 10:42–45 (and par.) and the related texts examined above, require adult free(d) male believers to serve those below them in the social hierarchy. Would such a believer, upon hearing these words, understand himself to be required to serve a woman? Or his male (or female) slave? Luise Schottroff answers such questions affirmatively although she qualifies her optimism by observing that these texts may be read "with the suspicion that, by some trick or other, free men regain their privileges."[106]

For both the earliest and modern readers of the Synoptic record there is the sense that no one can claim to be promoting God's will if her or his actions spring from selfish interests. Selflessness, not selfishness, is to guide the moral decision-making of a Christian. To do the will of God is to be the primary incentive of all Christian action and, as we have seen, this is the over-riding motive for the Synoptic call to serve. Obedience is required not only to Jesus' words but also to his example.

The general impression that there are no limitations upon the Synoptic call to serve, which becomes most overt upon reading the extreme examples in Matt 5:34–42, has led many scholars to identify the ethic itself as a limitation or liability: in their view it is impossible to fulfill.[107] When the Synoptic tradition is read as a whole, there is no limit to the injustice a follower of Jesus must be prepared to suffer at the hands of another, or to the lengths that a believer must go to serve. According to the Synoptic texts, however, even Jesus, despite his crucifixion, does not *deliberately* seek opportunities to suffer injustice. In Matt 12:15–16 Jesus' command that he not be made known is not part of the "messianic secret" as it is in Mark, but is rather an attempt to avoid the persecution of the Pharisees who seek to destroy him (12:14). Immediately following this Matthew inserts the quotation from Is 42:1–4 that speaks of the servant who proclaims justice to the Gentiles. William Klassen speaks of how this passage in Matthew illustrates that "by the way Jesus receives injustice, he becomes a king who brings justice to others" and that "by retreating from the conflict and refusing to assert his own rights or engaging in public demonstrations or affirming his essential benevolence, Jesus leads justice on to victory."[108] It is *God's* justice that Jesus proclaims, which always involves divine grace, and not human approximations that involve rights and claims and privileges. In this case, in Matthew, Jesus avoids his opponents' attacks but the evangelist is careful to note that in doing so he fulfills his role as God's servant. It would be perverse to equate the Synoptic call for self-denial with deliberate attempts to seek after mistreatment and persecution. The language used in the Synoptic record speaks of giving one's life or of losing it, and of surrendering one's material possessions. Questions of justice in the sense of protecting one's own rights are set aside.[109] Prudence, in the sense of protecting one's future interests, is waived in favor of fulfilling God's will in the present.[110]

We should, however, infer from the gospel texts that one's fulfillment of the call to serve others must not impede the honor due to God. The first part of the love commandment requires love of God and many texts which describe the conditions of discipleship insist that the demands of human relationships be subordinated to those of God (e.g. Matt 10:34–39; Luke 14:26). God and his kingdom have unrivaled claim upon each disciple and the believer's obedience to him must not be compromised in serving others. Love is to be mirrored in every action and in all human relations. Thus, although the community of Jesus stands counter to society, it does not take up an adversarial stance towards social norms and requirements. Rather, its members voluntarily surrender their rights in order to reflect the authenticity of the new order God is establishing.

Questions of conventional prudence, propriety and common sense become secondary in light of the kingdom. Compromise, as the rich young man discovered, is out of the question. God demands full allegiance, which is achieved, in part at least, by relinquishing human ambitions in favor of serving others.

Nevertheless, the ethic of service as presented in the Synoptic tradition does seem to permit resistance to evil on behalf of others. This can only be inferred since there is no definitive text. The idea that a follower of Jesus would stand by and witness the abuse of an individual and thereby claim that this was to fulfill Jesus' admonishment not to resist evil seems ludicrous. On a personal level, the Synoptic Jesus encourages his followers to forego retaliation for injustice suffered, but he is always quick to champion the cause of the oppressed, in the sense that he deliberately seeks out the poor and the marginalized as recipients of a special invitation to the Kingdom. The neighbor is not loved if the believer does not prevent him or her from being harmed whenever possible. The aim of the servant-ethic in the Synoptic gospels is not simply self-denial but also other-directedness.

Conclusions concerning the Ethic in the Synoptic Gospels

As we noted at the beginning of this chapter, Montefiore understands the call to serve as part of a "grand paradox": it is the path, according to the Synoptic writers, to true greatness. The paradox is even greater, however, than the biblical promise of exaltation for the humble and the lowly, when the motif becomes incorporated into the early Christian theological complex. Jesus is not only Son of Man and Son of God, according to the Synoptic writers, but the servant who gave his life as a ransom for many (Mark 10:45, par.). For many interpreters it is the latter part of this saying that is most interesting because of the problems of historicity. As P.H. Boulton notes, however, greater attention needs to be paid to the first part of the verse and the motif of service.[111]

For the Synoptic tradition, at least, the call to serve is an intrinsic part of new life in the kingdom, and protects against the dangers of human ambition and hubris. Following Jesus leaves no room for arrogance or condescension toward others. It is the way of sacrifice and self-denial that is epitomized in the crucifixion of Jesus himself. As Jesus came "not to be served but to serve," so his disciples are called to a similar self-understanding.

In the Synoptic tradition we find the call to serve others, and to place one's own interests last, reflected primarily in an attitude of indifference toward seeking justice for oneself, toward material possessions and toward social prestige. The appropriate response to this call is manifested rather by fulfilling the double commandment of love of God and love of neighbor. "One's response to God—setting aside self-will, renouncing one's own claims—is to be paradigmatic for one's relation to his neighbor."[112] The Synoptic writers present us with a Jesus who called his listeners into a new relationship not only with God but with other people; a relationship that eschewed social convention as meaningless and which inverted usual ways of thinking about personal worth. Mark 10:45 presents Jesus himself as the model for meeting this challenge. A positive response to Jesus' call and his invitation to take up one's cross—in other words, a willingness to surrender life itself—is the impetus that leads to an existence of service and self-denial. True service can only be carried out, according to the Synoptic tradition, if some inner transformation (μετάνοια) has occurred. This manifests itself as a willingness to sacrifice everything and to place one's own interests last in obedience to the will of God and out of gratitude for the experience of his grace.[113]

Chapter III

THE SERVANT-ETHIC IN THE JOHANNINE WRITINGS

James Gustafson suggests that the obligation to seek the good of one's neighbor is characteristic of Christian ethics.[1] Traces of this requirement are to be found in passages such as I John 3:16–18, and perhaps Rev 2:19. These texts suggest that the members of the Johannine community also knew the requirements to serve others and to put the interests of others first. The most important indication of this tradition amongst Johannine Christians is the footwashing episode of John 13:1–20. By examining this passage and its relationship to the rest of the Johannine literature, we discover that John confirms the Synoptic tradition in terms of the principle of self-denial and the role of believers as servants of others.

The gospel of John presents a picture of Jesus that is quite distinct from that found in the Synoptic gospels. There are, however, points of contact.[2] In terms of Jesus' teaching the footwashing seems to reflect the same kinds of ethical concerns about serving others that we find in the first three gospels. In John this one striking episode serves to highlight an insistence upon loving, mutual service amongst Jesus' followers. At the same time there is a disturbing element in the self-abnegating actions of Jesus. His act of stooping to wash his disciples' feet makes him seem no better than a slave. Peter's horrified response to Jesus' behavior emphasizes this aspect of the passage. It is in this passage that we find the clearest articulation of the servant-ethic in the Johannine literature independent of any reference to love.

The problems of interpreting John 13 are extensive, especially if one seeks to uncover the traditions that lie behind the passage. Scholars have reached a consensus on few aspects of the text, although most seem to agree that the footwashing episode as it now stands is the result of a combination of two different traditions. Because we will focus upon how this passage reflects the self-understanding of the early Christians, such concerns are not so relevant.

The Motives for Footwashing and Service to Others

In a sense there are two motivations for submissive action on behalf of others. The first is the impetus for Jesus' act and the second is the motivation for his followers. Because we are primarily concerned with the self-understanding of the early Christians it is most important for us to examine the motivation for Jesus' disciples. Nevertheless, we shall first tackle the more complicated question of the motive for Jesus' action because this too will reflect the concerns of the writer.

M–E. Boismard understands 13:3 as the key. He believes that the object of Jesus' knowledge is that he has received from God the power to give eternal life. In addition, according to Boismard, this is bound up with an awareness of his mission: "he had come from God and was going to God." Boismard says that Jesus washes his disciples' feet because of his own self-understanding of having been sent by God to give life. He insists that there is a close connection between the footwashing and the gift of life.[3] Jesus did not wash his disciples' feet until this point in his life immediately prior to his death. The footwashing somehow concludes his earthly ministry and initiates his departure. Lindars interprets v.3 by pointing to the heightened drama and paradoxical nature of the following verses. He sees this verse as introducing the "turning-point in the grand movement of redemption . . . . Jesus *had come from God . . . and now was going to God.*"[4]

Vv 14–15, however, explicitly state that Jesus behaved as a lowly δοῦλος to give his disciples an example. Here, then, we see the second impetus for Jesus' act. Jesus' words about giving his disciples an example reveal that as their Lord and Master, Jesus acts in order to encourage his disciples to do likewise. Jesus' own act is to be paradigmatic for those who would conform to his will. Just as Jesus has served his followers they are now compelled to serve each other. It is here that we must attempt to come to terms with the two interpretations of Jesus' act that are given in the Fourth gospel.

Scholarship has determined that vv 6–10 and 12–20 reflect two different ways of perceiving Jesus' behavior in vv 4–5. The most obvious interpretation is that Jesus washed the feet of his disciples to set an example of humble service that Christians should emulate. Bernard, in his commentary, says that "the simplest explanation is that provided in vv 13–16,"[5] and rejects the notion that the passage contains any connotation of spiritual atonement or baptismal symbolism.[6]

Brown responds to Bernard and others by reminding his readers that John "has several instances of two–fold symbolism." He believes that those who opt merely for the "moralizing" interpretation, as Boismard calls it, neglect the importance of vv 8 and 10, as well as glossing over the lack of harmony in this narrative concerning when understanding will come (after the resurrection [v.7] or now [vv 12 and 17]). Brown concludes this part of his discussion by saying, contra Boismard, that vv 6–10 are an earlier interpretation than vv 12–17.[7] This is because, while Boismard interprets vv 6–10 sacramentally, Brown understands them as prophetic: they symbolize Jesus' humiliation in death. "The foot-washing is an action of service for others, symbolic of the service he will render in laying down his life for others."[8]

Brown agrees with Boismard, however, that the entire passage reflects the combination of two separate interpretations of the footwashing. He notes, nevertheless, that while vv 6–10 can only refer to vv 4–5, vv 12–20 are more general and could fit with other episodes in Jesus' career. For Brown, vv 12–20 are derived from "a collection of miscellaneous material."[9]

In evaluating the two interpretive traditions within the text, scholars differ as to whether the two are compatible. Bultmann sees a way in which the two interpretations can be understood as congruous. He notes that both interpretations of the footwashing emphasize the importance of fellowship; first with Jesus (vv 6–10) and consequently amongst the disciples and Johannine Christians. Fellowship with Jesus can only exist if the latter is "made a reality through the disciples' action."[10]

Whatever the order of priority of the two interpretations, the passage, as it now stands, relates that the disciples are to be humble as Jesus was. This is the force of the word ὑπόδειγμα (example) in v.15. While the dialogue with Peter is an important aspect of the passage and can be interpreted in several ways, on the whole it is more significant in comprehending the Johannine view of Jesus' self-understanding and his relationship to his followers than their own service to each other. For the latter vv 14–16 are more important. Here the Johannine Jesus addresses the Johannine church. He instructs them to behave as he has. Emulating his example becomes the motive for their own acts of self-denying and loving service.[11]

The Requirements of Serving as Jesus Served

That the footwashing serves as an example to Jesus' followers is generally agreed upon. The requirements of how the disciples are to emulate that example are not, however. It cannot be over-emphasized that Jesus' act was one of complete humiliation and self-abnegation. Bernard, however, resists this by saying that it only seemed to be a great act of self-condescension to the disciples.[12] In his interpretation of v.13 he says, "Christ affirms his own dignity, even while stooping to what the disciples counted a menial office. He will not permit them to be in any doubt about this."[13] Barrett also cautions against exaggerating "the degrading character of the task" by pointing out that although Jewish slaves were not required to wash their masters' feet, "wives washed the feet of their husbands, and children of their parents."[14] Bernard, then, weakens the thrust of vv 4–5 by insisting that the act is only self-deprecating in the eyes of the disciples. One could argue, on the contrary, that Jesus' act was as lowly and as menial as possible. There were many ways the writer of John could have illustrated the point made in vv 14–17, without having Jesus stoop to such an act. Not only does Jesus wash the disciples' feet but he disrobes, and wipes their feet with a towel he has put on.[15] The text re-affirms the paradoxical nature of the servant-ethic, especially when Jesus himself becomes paradigmatic for its content. As we saw in our examination of the ethic in the Synoptic gospels the Son of Man comes not to be served but to serve (Mark 10:45 par.) and this is starkly illustrated in John 13.

Some scholars believe, however, that the nature of Jesus' act calls into question the entire tradition upon which this passage is based. They have been reluctant to acknowledge the tradition as authentic, often because of the degrading role it gives to Jesus.[16] Many suggest that the Fourth gospel incorporates in the footwashing account parts of the gospel of Luke, Luke's Passion account or at least some of the traditions used by Luke.[17] A final possibility is that the evangelist made up the story to illustrate the requirements of the humble service Jesus expects of disciples. W. L. Knox, however, believes that the details of vv 4–5 suggest a primitive tradition.[18]

We are concerned mainly with the significance of the passage for the intended audience of the gospel. What did it mean for them to do as Jesus had done to his disciples? Whatever the source of the episode, it illustrates in a dramatic and compelling way that the service to which Jesus' followers are called may require extreme self-abnegation. If the passage does indeed point forward to Jesus' death in some way, as many, including Brown, believe, then the footwashing presents a similar viewpoint to that found in the Synoptic saying that "the Son of Man came not to be served but to serve and to give his life as a ransom for many" (Mark 10:45 par.).[19] The gospel of John expresses the same viewpoint as that found in the Synoptic texts. Jesus' service unto and through death obliges his followers to behave in a similar way. Mark 10:35–45 par. make this point: such passages seek to arrest personal ambition by advocating service before others and pointing to Jesus as an example of such service.

Ecclesiastical practices, both in the past and present, generally have not required that such service be rendered in the sense of actual mutual footwashing amongst Christians. As Brown has pointed out, footwashing never became a sacrament or even a common practice except amongst some of the earliest Christians and some small sects.[20] Nevertheless there is nothing in vv 12–16 which suggests that these words of Jesus should be interpreted symbolically. That modern commentators almost universally understand them in this way reflects a desire perhaps to soften the distasteful connotations of this passage.[21] It is important, of course, to recognize that the gospel of John is full of symbolic deeds and words on the part of Jesus. Over and over again Jesus' hearers misinterpret the true import of his acts and admonitions because they cannot progress beyond a literal understanding of what they have heard and witnessed.

Jesus explicitly states, however, that καὶ ὑμεῖς ὀφείλετε ἀλλήλων νίπτειν τοὺς πόδας (v.14). The use of the verb ὀφείλω makes the saying tantamount to a direct command. John Christopher Thomas makes several important observations concerning the use of the verb here. He points out that it connotes obligation elsewhere in the Johannine literature (John 19:7; I John 2:6; I John 3:16; 4:11; 3 John 8). He also notes that the other instance of Jesus using this verb is "also in a context of mandatory service, that of slave to a master (Lk. 17.10)."[22]

In order for the disciples to have a part with Jesus they must carry out the same service amongst themselves to show that "a servant (slave [δοῦλος]) is not greater than his master" (v16). Thus while Jesus' act itself is symbolic, and may have the sacramental or prophetic connotations proposed by scholars, the command to the disciples, in a sense, goes beyond symbolism. They are to wash each others' feet; in a tangible way they are to become loving servants of each other, in order to honor Jesus' example. Thomas disputes the interpretation that reads the call to footwashing as a call to humble service in general. He bases his conclusions upon three reasons:

i)The fact that v.15 is so close to the direct command in v.14 makes the former a reinforcement of what Jesus charged in v.14.

ii)V.15 contains the only instance of ὑπόδειγμα on the lips of Jesus in the Fourth gospel.

iii)The combination of καθὼς . . . καὶ "emphasizes the intimate connection between Jesus' action (washing the disciples' feet) and the action of his disciples (washing one another's feet)." Thomas concludes:

> The instructions to wash one another's feet are rooted and grounded in the actions of Jesus in vv. 4–10. Therefore, the footwashing is far more than an example . . . .
> In all probability, the readers, as well as the disciples in the narrative, would take ὑπόδειγμα with reference to footwashing in particular, not to humble service generally.[23]

Footwashing was a common practice at this time and we shall briefly consider some of the pertinent data.[24] Within the New Testament itself the only other instances of footwashing are found at Luke 7:35–38, 44 and I Tim 5:10. The latter text lists the prerequisites for a woman to be enrolled in the order of widows. As well as having raised children, shown hospitality and relieved the afflicted, a widow must have "washed the feet of the saints." The verb used here is νίπτειν, which is the same word used in Jesus' exhortation in Jn 13:14. Bernard sees I Tim 5:10 as an aspect of ancient hospitality in which water was made available for guests to wash their own feet upon arrival. He also points to Luke 7:44 and Gen 18:4; 19:2; 24:32; 43:24; Jud 19:21; I Sam 25:41.[25] As Hultgren points out, only the last of these involves someone else washing an individual's feet.[26] In this case Abigail, upon being fetched by David's servants to become his wife, says, "Behold your handmaid is a servant to wash the feet of the servants of my lord." This fits in with all of the prior dealings between Abigail and David. She repeatedly presents herself as submissive and humble in order to sway David's judgment. Her offer to wash the feet of David's servants merely reinforces this characteristic. It emphasizes her humility and self-denial.

Although these are the only Biblical texts that describe an individual washing another's feet there is extra-canonical literature that describes this service. Often the context, as in the Biblical accounts is one of hospitality and of receiving guests and the act is usually performed by a woman. Whether or not women are understood to be present in John 13 is unknown from the text.[27]

Schrage points out that "Bultmann's statement that Jesus' washing of the disciples' feet is to be understood as a symbolic act . . . must not be allowed to spiritualize the exemplary concreteness of this service of love."[28] This assertion cannot be emphasized excessively. This passage calls believers to tangible acts of service on behalf of one another. Even when humiliation is involved they are to recall Jesus' example, for "the servant is not above the master." As Morris states, the disciples "should have a readiness to perform the lowliest service. Nothing was more menial than the washing of the feet . . . . . No act of service should be beneath them."[29] While chapter 13 may be interpreted as not requiring actual footwashing, it certainly demands a willingness to perform humble acts of service for others when the situation arises.[30] As in the Synoptic gospels, the reader who would follow Jesus must not seek to be first and must refrain from self-aggrandizement. Jesus' insistence that his disciples wash each others' feet recalls K. Thieme's observation that the willingness to perform lowly work is the characteristic of Christian love: it makes the Christian a 'servant' of his fellow.[31]

The Benefits of Mutual Service

Jesus performs the footwashing, we read, in order to set his disciples an example and to illustrate that he "loved them to the end" (13:1d). Jesus' service is paradigmatic for the type of love that the disciples are to extend to each other even when it may involve humiliation and degradation. Vv 15–18 describe the benefits of this mutual service. Jesus assures his disciples that if they understand that the servant is not greater than the master, then they are blessed if they carry out the type of loving service he has demonstrated.[32] Jesus' followers, assured of God's love and blessing, should be willing to serve and love each other even to the point of death. Bultmann, as we have noted above, says that the footwashing demonstrates how fellowship with Jesus and fellowship amongst the disciples are inextricably linked. For Bultmann "13.1–20 describes the founding of the community and the law of its being."[33] This law requires obedience to God, mutual love and service after the manner of Jesus amongst the members of the community. The primary benefit of fulfilling that law is to become one of the μακάριοι.

Relationship of the Footwashing to Johannine Ethics

The footwashing is, in some sense, illustrative of the new commandment of John 13:34, in which Jesus instructs his followers to love one another as he has loved them. Victor Paul Furnish points out that all the love-commands in the Fourth gospel occur in the Farewell Discourses of chapters 13–17 and that these commands to love one another "are at the very center of the moral and spiritual legacy" of these discourses.[34] The footwashing, of course, introduces this important section of the gospel, and Furnish calls this episode "an acted parable—or perhaps we should even say, an *actual instance*—of the divine mission of love for which the Father has sent him." Consequently, the disciples must not only receive that love, but also acknowldege "the *commission* it lays upon one to serve in love as the Son has served."[35]

This love for one another is a predominant theme throughout the Johannine literature. I John 3:17–18; 4:7-8 and 20–21 reveal that mutual love is to permeate the community, based on the example of Jesus as I John 3:16 asserts.[36] This love is self-sacrificing and is manifested in acts of service. The example of Christ, not only as the one who washed the disciples' feet, but also as the one who was crucified, who laid down his life for others, is the paradigm that is to direct the disciples' and the community's behavior.[37] This love, for the Johannine community, is the reflection of the glory of the Word made flesh. It derives much of its meaning from the concrete acts that often demand a degree of self-sacrifice.

Limitations upon Service in the Johannine Literature

Biblical scholars are divided as to whether the Johannine ethic and its requirement of sacrificial and loving service refers only to those members within the community addressed. J. T. Sanders, for example, is adamant that the Johannine love commandment implies that the Johannine Christians are compelled only to love other members of the community.[38] He and others believe that the Johannine literature reflects a narrowing of the apparent universal nature of the love found in the Sermon on the Mount and the parable of the Good Samaritan. Within that context, however, the love that Christians are to display toward one another, is to be limitless. This is illustrated by the extreme nature of the love described in I John. The love the Johannine

Christians have for one another is to be founded on the love God has displayed toward them in the death of his Son (I John 3:1,16). Like Jesus, they are to be prepared to sacrifice anything, including their lives, on behalf of each other. Sanders' evaluation of this love is negative. He sees its intensity as bordering on fanaticism:

> It is a crazy, dual way of behaving towards one's fellow men. The only concern with those outside the church is to bring them into the church, into the unity of faith and love that is the church; within the church, one gives everything for one's brother, whatever his need, willingly, selflessly, even to the giving up of life itself.[39]

While Sanders has overstated his case, it is true that for the Johannine community the commandment to love can be lived out exclusively within the Church. Distrust of outsiders is not unusual amongst sectarian groups; in fact it is often the over-riding characteristic of many religious minorities.[40] It is this attitude towards outsiders that perhaps explains the implicit restrictions upon the law of love within the Johannine literature.

Schrage also believes that the Johannine ethic reveals a tendency to restrict the law of love to the "brethren" rather than to one's neighbor.[41] He finds the explanation for this trend in the suggestion that the Johannine community faced severe persecution from without and their literature presents the results of attempts to "close ranks." He points out, however, that we do not find in John the "sectarian hatred of outsiders found at Qumran: others are not explicitly excluded from love or 'hated.'"[42]

Other scholars insist that the gospel and epistles of John do not limit the law of love simply to those within the community.[43] As Schrage himself points out, albeit somewhat casually, Jesus appears to have washed the feet of Judas, along with the others.[44] Thus while some suggest that the Johannine ethic of love is insular and less universal than that of the Synoptic gospels, there is little concrete textual evidence to demonstrate that this is the case. Serving the interests of others must not lead to disobeying God; but there are no explicit requirements against showing love to those outside the community if it does not lead to transgression.[45] It is only when serving others threatens to lead to disobedience that restrictions are explicitly delineated, as is the case with II John 10.[46]

Specific limitations, therefore, are rare, despite the so-called restrictive ethic of the Johannine community, and there are certainly no prohibitions upon aiding the wounded and dying, Christian or not. One's duty before God must be carefully maintained and the requirement of self-denial and service to others must not be allowed to violate it.

Nevertheless, it is somewhat disquieting to compare the expansive servant-ethic of the Synoptic gospels to the Johannine literature and to discover how explicit requirements of service seem to be limited to the Johannine community. Clearly these Christians' relationship with the outside world contained elements of tension that arise from the historical circumstances and theological agenda of the evangelist.

First, the community of the gospel is "neither Jew nor Greek" but one in Christ. Their self-understanding and identity come from their belief in Jesus as God incarnate, the bringer of eternal life. Membership is not limited, therefore, to ethnic origin. It is available to anyone who, like the Samaritan woman, believes that Jesus is the Messiah.

Second, the gospel appears to have been written for members of the community rather than as an evangelistic tool. Thus John 20:31 is interpreted as a call for increased belief or maintaining one's true belief. The evidence for this cuts both ways, however. Howard Clark Kee suggests that the gospel is a "book for the church, rather than an evangelistic appeal to the world." The final chapters confirm this evaluation for Kee, such as John 17:9.[47] A few passages, however, temper such an interpretation of John's purpose. The most notable is John 3:16–17. As Segovia says: "In Jn 3:16 one finds a relationship of love which is not mentioned elsewhere in the gospel and is, therefore, uncharacteristic of the author's thought: ἠγάπησεν ὁ θεὸς τὸν κόσμον." He notes that the gospel elsewhere insists that God loves believers and not the world.[48] Whatever its intended audience, the gospel presents the person of Jesus in order to encourage faith in him as the Messiah and λόγος of God incarnate. The important thing is to act upon this faith by displaying brotherly love.

Third, the Johannine literature as a whole is clearly the product of a community that saw separation from the world as imperative for salvation. The love God has for the world mentioned above is essentially disregarded in the remainder of the Johannine corpus. Although God is regarded as the creator of the world in the Prologue, it is important to note that a strict dualism cannot be maintained, because, as Schrage notes, "the idea expressed in 3:16 is not taken up or developed elsewhere, and nowhere are ethical consequences derived from it."[49] The world is the sphere of sin and ungodliness. John's world-view is dualistic in the sense that it contrasts good and evil, light and dark, belief and unbelief. This attitude to the world is perhaps born of the hostility of opponents towards the Johannine community but it leads inescapably to a suspicious, distrustful attitude to anything and anyone who is not a believer.[50]

Finally, within the community, composed of all who believe, the essence of love means serving the needs of one another. While this may be carried to the extreme of dying for another Christian, Schrage is correct when he expresses reservations about the "new" nature of Jesus' command to love in John and that "Nowhere does the Gospel make God's universal love a standard for the life of the Christian community."[51] Within the community, however, love and service to others do appear to be indiscriminate. The categories of believer/unbeliever are far more important to the community than rich/poor, Jew/Gentile, male/female and so on. The servant-ethic in John does appear to be insular and confined to the community, yet all who believe as the Johannine Christians do, are welcome to enter. In addition, it is an argument from silence to suggest that members of this community would ignore the needs of outsiders when confronted with them face to face. The life of the community in light of Jesus' incarnation, and the preservation of that life, is the primary interest of the writer. Ethical issues are only of interest insofar as they pertain to the Johannine circle. There is no room for compromise: the dangers that lurk in the κόσμος preclude any discussion of moral behavior outside the community. The *ideal* set before the Johannine community then, seems to be one of reciprocity in service and love. Verhey draws attention to the mutuality inherent in the love delineated in John.[52] This idea of ἀγάπη as somehow mutual is found in the writings of many scholars.[53] A relationship between the self and the other in which only one party serves the other is not one of love. Outka illustrates this with the more optimistic view that true ἀγάπη exists when the agent expects a response in kind from the other. "Agape unrequited appears not to be fully agape, and some mutuality is a necessary condition."[54] Stephen Post makes a similar point and insists that not only human love requires reciprocity but also divine love:

> Divine love . . . is mistakenly interpreted as containing no element of self-concern. This view is based on the false assumption that the divine neither needs nor seeks the mutual good of fellowship with humanity.[55]

Post believes that the life of Jesus reflects this deep love and desire for reciprocity. He rejects the ideas of those who see the cross and ἀγάπη as inexorably linked (he names Nygren, Yoder and Hauerwas) and argues that "the cross symbolizes the violation of love more than it does love itself."[56] In a similar vein, Sandra Schneiders also emphasizes that the service required in John is not because the "server" is in a subordinate position to the one served (i.e. a slave in relation to the master), nor is it service from "the top down" as in cases where a parent serves a child in need. In both of these cases service reflects or reinforces a "condition of inequality."[57] Rather she insists that the footwashing reveals "Jesus acting to abolish the inequality between" himself and the disciples,[58] by emphasizing the friendship that pertains between them.[59] Equality, reciprocity and mutuality become the motifs inherent in love and its consequent service. But this is paramount to saying that such service is not really service at all. The gospel does not suggest that service or love cease if it is not appreciated or reciprocated. It is a mistake to emphasize the reciprocity of the early Christian ethic as it is reflected in the gospels without also noting that self-sacrifice on behalf of others is a fixed principle throughout this literature. This latter dimension subverts love into one that is not primarily concerned with equality and reciprocity. James Gustafson notes the pervasiveness of this idea. The imperative to seek the good of one's neighbor and the accompanying diminishment of "the centrality that 'rational self-interest' often has in other forms of ethics" is for Gustafson the one distinctive aspect of Christian ethics.[60] As Furnish says, the New Testament, including the Johannine literature, sees that "love is present where it is 'active' in deeds of mercy and kindness, in the actuality of caring for and serving the neighbor."[61]

Relationship to the Synoptic Gospels

The principle of serving others in the Johannine literature is founded upon the duty to love one another (or "the brethren"). Although, as we have seen, the servant-ethic is limited to those within the community, it is clear that this ethic is fundamental to the self-understanding of the Johannine Christians, especially as it is acted out in the footwashing episode. The most remarkable aspect of the footwashing is that it serves as the counterpart to the institution of the Eucharist found in the Synoptic gospels. Despite this difference, the footwashing illustrates how the Johannine ethic of self-sacrifice on behalf of others corroborates the Synoptic tradition.

Barrett suggests that the footwashing is based upon Luke 22:27. Here Jesus refers to himself as ὁ διακονῶν, "the one who serves."[62] Brown notes an even more significant connection with Synoptic ideas suggested by J. A. T. Robinson. Brown agrees with Robinson that echoes of Mark 10:42–45 are found in the footwashing episode and notes that "it is interesting that Luke xxii 24–26, the parallel to Mark x 42–45, is part of the Last Supper scene."[63] Here Brown highlights how the footwashing confirms the principles of self-denial, self-sacrifice and service that spring up again and again in the Synoptic tradition and are most profoundly illustrated in the crucifixion. The stark portrayal of this principle in John 13 is startling. Although Jesus affirms his position as Lord and Master, his actions are self-abnegating, point forward to his crucifixion, and unquestionably reflect many of the teachings on selflessness that we find in the Synoptic gospels. While we cannot be sure that the writer of John knew any of the Synoptic gospels, we do know that the requirement of self-denial and routine service to others was widely known in the early Christian communities. Both the Synoptic gospels and the Johannine literature record that the cultivation of such an attitude was required by appealing to the words and actions of Jesus. That such behavior constituted a fundamental part of the earliest Christian ethic is apparent by these appeals to Jesus' authority or example in the traditions about his life. This is especially true when we examine how Christian love is illustrated by concrete acts in I and III John (e.g. I John 3:17–18; III John 5–7).

Conclusions Concerning the Ethic in John

The ethics of the Synoptic and Johannine traditions reflect different concerns and emphases. This is most apparent when we consider the idea of love and the universalist flavor found in the Synoptics as opposed to the more community-oriented accent in the Johannine literature. Despite this and other variations we should note that, like the Synoptics, the Johannine ethic also promotes the routine requirement to place the interests of others before one's own. Like the Synoptic tradition it uses the example of Jesus to encourage such behavior. Not only does the Fourth gospel confirm the Synoptic tradition in principle, it illustrates this principle with one of the most striking and compelling episodes in the entire New Testament.

It is largely unresolved as to whether the passage calls for actual footwashing amongst Christians (although it seems that the Johannine community as well as other churches probably did carry out this practice). It is obvious, however, that the passage functions to call Christians to emulate the loving service that Jesus rendered to his followers both during the Last Supper and at his crucifixion. The imitation of Jesus' humble service, even to the extent that one becomes willing to die on behalf of another (John 15:13; I John 3:16), helps to correct any inclinations towards pride or ambition (John 13:16), and also ensures God's favor (John 13:17; I John 3:22). These two themes also arise in the Synoptic treatments of the requirement to serve others' interests before one's own. The Johannine literature places few restrictions upon this requirement, provided that by responding to it one does not infringe upon one's duty to God.

The ethical principle of placing the interests of others first is clearly preserved in the literature of the Johannine community. The Johannine literature, as a reflection of a particular Christian community's self-understanding, acknowledges the importance of emulating Jesus' example of serving others. Again the emphasis is on how the believer should behave, not on any anticipated response. For the Johannine Christians such behavior was one of the characteristics of those who served God and kept his commandment to love as Jesus loved (John 13:36–7).

Chapter IV

THE UNDISPUTED LETTERS OF PAUL AND THE SERVANT-ETHIC

> The problem of Christian ethics continues to be discerning the obligations of walking according to the "desires of the Spirit" in very diverse, concrete situations. Paul presumes that one's judgments in such situations are molded by the gospel.[1]

In his epistles, Paul uses concrete examples to illustrate his assertion that Christians must adopt a stance that consistently places their own interests after those of others. These examples can be as mundane as calling for respect of the spouse's wishes concerning conjugal relations (I Cor 7:3–4), and as extraordinary as suffering wrong rather than bringing a lawsuit against a fellow Christian (I Cor 6:7). In addition there are some sayings, especially in Romans, that seem to echo the Synoptic Jesus. In Paul's writings, as in the gospels, love is intimately connected with seeking the best interests of others. Although this love is to be extended first to the members of the community of faith, Paul does not recommend that it be restricted to this group:

> The Christian's "slavery" to God finds concrete expression in his serving other men. Only in this one respect, but *always* in this one respect, is he to be in their "debt" (Rom 13:8). The neighbor to whom the Christian is bound in love is in the first instance the brother in Christ. Yet Paul's appeal to the Galatians to "do good . . . *especially* to those of the household of faith" (6:10b) defines only the minimum of love's responsibility, not its farthest extent.[2]

For Paul love is expressed in refraining from self-assertion and serving the interests of others whether they be within or outside the community.

The Content of the Servant-Ethic in Paul

Romans 12:1–13

Romans 12 contains a number of exhortations which are applicable to our study. As Morna D. Hooker says of Romans 12, "Here, the move from theological argument to ethical problems is plain."[3] Vv 1–2 contain the thematic impulse for Paul's advice here, as he encourages his readers to "stop allowing yourselves to be conformed to this age but continue to let yourselves be transformed by the renewing of your mind so that you may prove what is the will of God, that which is good and well-pleasing and perfect."⁴ Paul calls his readers to "be transformed" so that they might prove (δοκιμάζω) what constitutes the will of God.⁵ The result of such a transformation is outlined in 12:3 where Paul admonishes the Christian "not to think of himself more highly than he ought to think." As members of one body in Christ (here *not* the "body of Christ" [See I Cor 12:27]), "Christians, like the various members of a single body...are all necessary to each other and equally under an obligation to serve one another."⁶ Arrogance, therefore, is prohibited: each member has an important and necessary role.

The list of gifts that follows is interesting because of the seven gifts listed, at least three relate in some way to the servant-ethic: the ones who serve, contribute and show mercy. Each of these embody elements of what we may describe as the servant-ethic. The phrase ὁ προϊστάμενος can mean either the one who presides or the one who comforts, gives aid.⁷

The discussion of specific gifts is followed by general admonitions to all of the church. These ethical injunctions are terse and lacking in thematic connection, although Cranfield would group them under headings such as "Love in Action," or "The Marks of Love."⁸ In all there are thirteen phrases of which three are of an abstract nature (v.9), four describe relations between Christians (vv 10,13), three encourage appropriate behavior in relation to God (v.11), and three describe the unwavering faith of the Christian (v.12). While nothing in these verses specifically speaks of serving others, v.10 with its references to φιλαδελφία and showing honor recall our discussion of the Johannine literature. How can one honor one's brother without in some sense deferring to, i.e. serving, him?

Showing honor becomes paramount (προηγέομαι); love is to be without hypocrisy (ἀνυπόκριτος) and evil is to be hated (ἀποστυγέω).⁹ As Ernst Käsemann says of v.9: "[Ἀγάπη] is without illusions and ready for demonstrative action, involved in the good which is perceived as necessary and beneficial, and it abhors the evil. Compromising neutrality is excluded."¹⁰ If we substitute the phrase "the Christian" for "ἀγάπη" in these sentences we have a portrait of the nature of Christian character Paul is trying to promote in vv 1-13. The Christian is to be a living sacrifice to God; this requires a renewal of one's mind and an inner transformation. This is the ground of the ethical injunctions which follow. The self is to become a conduit for God's gifts and love towards others. This selflessness and other-directedness, one of the marks of the servant-ethic in the Synoptic gospels, is emphasized in the following verses.

Romans 12:14–21

Verses 14–21 turn the believers' attention outward from the one body in Christ to those who are indifferent or indeed hostile to Christians. These verses recall Jesus' exhortation to love one's enemies (Matt 5:44; Luke 6:28), although Paul never mentions Jesus explicitly. Persecutors are to be blessed not cursed (v. 14) and evil is not to be repaid with evil (v. 17). Between these two admonitions Paul encourages his readers to live in harmony with each other and not to be haughty. It is as if he is saying, "If you are willing to bless outsiders who persecute you, as you should, make sure that your own snobbishness and arrogance are not causing the animosity they feel." His insistence not to repay evil for evil could also refer to intra-church conflict, in that he does not want one member's unchristian act against another to be compounded by vengeance on the part of the aggrieved. To live peaceably with all (v. 18)— again the focus turns to those without as well as within the community—is a worthy goal and therefore vengeance is *always* precluded. Revenge is to be left to God and the Christian should therefore feed his enemy as recommended in Prov 25:21. This citation from Proverbs and its promise that by feeding one's enemy one will heap coals of fire upon his head has troubled many scholars. Scholarly opinion is divided on this issue. One line of thought believes the coals to represent the burning shame and contrition the enemy will suffer once the love of the Christian is experienced. Barrett, for example, calls the burning coals the "fire of remorse in light of v 21"[11] Käsemann mentions that the ἄνθρακας πυρὸς was part of an Egyptian penitential ritual involving a forced change of mind.[12] The other way of interpreting this passage reads the burning coals as representative of God's eschatological vengeance which is increased by the kindness of Christians. Piper prefers to see the coals as representative of eschatological judgment. He attempts to bring such an interpretation into harmony with the general principle of enemy love in three ways:

i)Although vv 19–20 appear to endorse kind acts in order to bring judgment upon the enemy, to call for blessings upon persecutors in v. 14 "excludes every motive that would desire our neighbour's destruction."[13]

ii)God must eventually avenge evil acts; otherwise faith in him is worthless. To think that God will not repay evil acts means that"faith and blasphemy are for him as good as equal....If this were true, the hope of the gospel which hangs on God's faithfulness would be shattered. And if the hope of the gospel is shattered, then the ground of enemy love...is lost."[14]

iii)Piper insists that Paul includes an unspoken conditional clause in 12:20 so that the individual who loves heaps the burning coals on the enemy's head "*if* the enemy is not moved to repentance by your love." Reliance upon God's righteousness assures believers that they are not ultimately responsible for the fate of the other: "The assurance that God will take vengeance justly on the evil of unrepentant animosity removes the last hindrance to enemy love."[15] Thus although Paul says that it is "*you*" who will heap the burning coals upon the enemy's head the matter actually resides with God. With this line of argument

Piper seeks to preserve the pristine nature of enemy love in Paul, while at the same time respecting the clearest understanding of the text (i.e. that the burning coals do in fact refer to eschatological judgment). For the most part he succeeds, especially when we cast our mind back to Paul's insistence that love be genuine (v. 9). Kind acts hardly constitute genuine love if the doer secretly wishes for the destruction of the recipient. William Klassen attempts to resolve the matter in a way similar to Käsemann by drawing attention to the importance of hospitality implicit in offers of food and drink. He notes that Livy stresses "the practice of hospitality as an alternative to war (Livy 21.2.5)."[16] Klassen insists that Piper's interpretation of God's "vengeance" is too narrow and that it should be understood as God's desire "to exert sovereignty over all."[17] The goal is to transform the enemy into a friend and thereby avoid conflict. The coals, then, are not signs of eschatological punishment, nor of remorse or contrition,[18] but are a sign of reconciliation.[19]

Although most scholars affirm the echoes of Matt 5:43–48 and Luke 6:27–36 in this passage, Paul's tone is much more triumphalist.[20] In those Synoptic passages the response and fate of the enemy is not even raised as an issue, and in Romans the command is not explicitly one of love as Krister Stendahl notes:

> the non-retaliation is undoubtedly based on and motivated by the deference to God's impending vengeance. It is not deduced from a principle of love....The issue is...how to act when all attempts to avoid conflicts with the enemies of God and of his church have failed (v.17).[21]

Stendahl calls attention here to the omission of love as a motivating factor for kindness to one's enemies. By offering hospitality to their enemies Christians overcome evil with good and are not themselves overcome. It is now that the strategic motivation of serving enemies may come into play since Paul understands such conduct as a way of advancing the gospel. This is a motive which we rejected in our examination of the Synoptic record.[22] Although these verses are reminiscent of Jesus' teaching about love of enemies there is a difference: Paul clearly sees the motive for serving/loving the enemy as one of overcoming evil through hospitality and service; as we saw above Jesus never used this rationale as impetus for the command.

Chapter 12 of Romans reflects in many ways how the process of being a Christian manifests itself in specific conduct. Much of this conduct is appropriate to the servant-ethic. In the present age, evil and vengeance are to be shunned in favor of fulfilling God's will. Social prestige is to be rejected. Service to others is to be paramount. In this way evil can be overcome, not necessarily by eliminating it completely, but by forestalling the escalation of enmity.[23] The enemy ceases to be an enemy because he is not hated. The believer who refuses to retaliate against the enemy advances the will of God:

"He will be sharing in the victory of the gospel over the world and setting up signs which point to the reality of God's love for sinners; he will be living as one who is being transformed by the renewing of the mind."[24]

Romans 13:8–10

Following a brief discussion of Christians' relations with civic authorities, Paul returns to a more personal level. In these verses we find his rendering of the commandment to love one's neighbor. Like Jesus (and R. Hillel[25]), Paul believes that the commandments of the Law are summed up in Lev 19:18. Love for others is the fulfillment of the Law.[26] Paul does not say, however, that love for neighbor is all that is required. It is through love for God that one discerns how to love one's neighbor. Knox calls such love a "concrete living spiritual reality" which "is the dynamic, outgoing reality of God himself . . . . In other words, the love of God is the presence of the spirit of God."[27] Thus when an individual becomes a Christian and undergoes the transformation described in 12:1-2, he or she passes from conformity to the world to obedience to God. Such obedience is expressed in love and the willingness to set aside one's own interests for the sake of others.

Romans 14:1-15:3

Following the short, succinct injunctions of chapters 12 and 13, Paul now enters into an extended discussion of inter-personal relations within the church. The first section (14:1–13) is devoted to warnings against judging one another on the basis of certain personal practices.[28] Paul seeks unity rather than divisions within the church. If someone is "injured" by another Christian eating a certain food love no longer reigns. Disputes about such things as food should never be permitted to interfere with God's work. Love is active when the interests of others are served. This is confirmed by vv 22–23 in which the dangers that threaten one who eats while in doubt amount to condemnation. The whole passage is summed up in 15:1–3. In these three verses three important elements of the servant-ethic are outlined:

i)Failings of others are to be borne: Christians do not seek to please themselves. The verb ἀρέσκω here has connotations of accommodation. Thus when the apprehensions of others lead to personal inconvenience one's own interests are to be put aside. Bauer also suggests that ἀρέσκω almost means to serve. Dale B. Martin takes up this connotation of the word and notes that the term ἀρέσκω often means to render service. "It therefore has status implications" and when used by authors from the higher social strata such as Aristotle, "it is a term or shame, referring to servile or fawning people." Martin says that Paul's use of the term challenges popular understanding concerning the social structure.[29] It should be noted that the idea of pleasing/serving the weak is not stated explicitly in 15:1: it is inferred, from the consequences of the strong not pleasing/serving themselves. The strong are "to bear with the failings of the weak" and each is to "please his neighbor" (v.2).

ii)One's neighbors are to be "pleased/served" for their own good and edification. This implies that there are situations in which mere accommodation is not to be undertaken—situations in which the neighbor would be harmed in some way by simply being pleased.

iii)The example of Christ is invoked as one who was not self-serving but bore reproaches on behalf of others. The scriptural quotation from Ps 69:9 perhaps is not entirely appropriate, although its context (Ps 69:6–12) may be applicable in some sense to the situation Paul is addressing, since in these verses the Psalmist prays that he might not be a source of shame or dishonor for others who seek God. It is a prayer for humility and righteousness in the face of opposition. The point of the quotation, of course, is to present Christ as the exemplar of humbly putting one's own interests aside.

In the ethical teachings of Romans, Paul devotes much attention to inter-personal relations. The unity and harmony of the church depends upon Christians putting the servant-ethic into practice: they are to please/serve others rather than themselves. In Romans, more than any other of his epistles, Paul presents an ethical ideal that is largely unencumbered by reference to particular problems within the congregation. This is not the case in his correspondence to the Corinthians and the Galatians.

I Corinthians 6:1-8

Paul faces much opposition and conflict amongst the Corinthian Christians. His letters to this community reflect his insistence, however, that no matter how "strong" or "wise" Christians may be, the interests of their fellows are to be paramount. One of the concrete examples that Paul gives of deferring one's rights is the challenge to "suffer wrong" rather than bring suit against a fellow Christian in pagan court (I Cor 6:7). Paul's argument becomes more radical as it develops. At first he encourages his readers to avoid bringing the matter before non-Christians by finding one within the church who is qualified to decide the matter (vv5–6). In v.7, however, he says that even to bring a suit against another Christian is a defeat, presumably on the part of the one who feels wronged. The word translated "lawsuit" in v.7 is κρίμα. This is not the word used in v.1 which is πρᾶγμα and more general. Κρίμα suggests judgment and condemnation of the other on the part of the court. These harsh connotations suggest why Paul sees such an action as a defeat: it is a sign that love has failed. In bringing a κρίμα against another there is no room for the love and conciliation that Paul seeks to kindle amongst his readers. He poses the questions, rhetorical in nature, but also able to cut to the heart of the matter:

"Why not rather suffer wrong? Why not rather be defrauded?" In this verse we hear echoes of Jesus' teaching found in Matt 5:39–42, although Paul does not refer to a "word of the Lord" here.[30]

Some suggest that Paul is offering two methods of resolving the problem. The first involves settling the dispute through some judicial mechanism within the community, while the second involves "turning the other cheek." If v.5 is understood as ironic, however, only the second option is available. It is possible that when Paul says, "Can it be that there is no man among you wise enough to decide between members of the brotherhood?" his implied answer is "Yes!" despite the Corinthians' high regard for their own wisdom and knowledge.[31]

In his discussion of this passage, Schrage takes a more discreet approach. He rejects the suggestion that Paul is calling for comprehensive self-denial and proposes that Paul is offering two solutions to the problem and insists that vv 1–6 juxtaposed with vv 7–8 show that "Paul is not demanding renunciation of all rights as a general rule, but is presenting a choice between two possible courses of Christian action." These two courses are the assertion of rights and the renunciation of rights, "a renunciation that...is intended to overcome evil with good."[32]

It is not so clear, however, that the juxtaposition Schrage speaks of does not demand renunciation of rights. If, as we have said, v.5 is ironic, then vv 7–8 offer the only course of action, which is, by implication, to take no action at all. In addition, there is clear support elsewhere in Paul for leaving judgment and vindication to God even if this means suffering at the hands of another (e.g. Rom 12:17–19). Ideally, Paul wishes the Corinthian Christians to be bound together in love so that lawsuits are not necessary. Rather than take a grievance against another Christian to court, one is to waive one's rights even though it means suffering wrong: "Love cares for others (I Cor 12:25); it does not go to court....It is not legal justice that love rules out, but the self-centred demand for justice as well as injustice."[33] This waiving of one's rights in favor of love is therefore concretely displayed when Christians refuse to get bound up in grievances against one another. It confirms the principles expounded by Jesus in the Sermon on the Mount, especially the principle of loving one's neighbor as oneself.[34]

I Corinthians 7:4–5; 33–34.

While Paul has some reservations about marriage (7:7–8), for those who do marry he insists that both parties respect the wishes of the other. In fact, this is one of the drawbacks to marriage since both husband and wife are anxious to please (ἀρέσκω) the other (7:33–34) rather than being concerned about the affairs of the Lord (μεριμνᾷ τὰ τοῦ κυρίου).[35] Marital relations, therefore, are to be marked with the same efforts to serve the other as are all the believers' personal relationships. While 7:3–4 are probably motivated by a desire to eliminate tendencies amongst certain Corinthian Christians, who call for sexual abstinence (v.5 seems to point to such an understanding), Paul clearly believes that the partner who would be celibate must surrender to the wishes of the other.[36]

I Corinthians 8 and 10

The issues in these chapters concerning meat-eating and idolatry are too complicated to investigate fully here. Some brief comments are appropriate however, insofar as these chapters are concerned with the believer's responsibility toward others.

In chapter 8 Paul recommends that his readers not participate in eating meat that is offered to idols since such practice can have a deleterious effect upon the believer's weaker brethren; those who have not yet come to the full realization that idols have "no real existence." Should these brethren eat such meat-offerings they engage in deliberate sin by violating the first of the Ten Commandments. Paul therefore insists that his readers who believe that idols are meaningless should not flaunt this belief if it might encourage others less secure in their faith to eat. Accordingly, the stronger believers should surrender their apparent right to eat food offered to idols for the sake of others' conscience, especially since they are "no better off if they do [eat]."

In chapter 10 Paul deals with a related problem. Should members of Paul's readership be invited to dine in an unbeliever's home and learn that the meat has been sacrificed they are not to eat out of consideration for the conscience of the one who informed them (10:28–29a). Somehow, according to Paul, this preserves the Christian's liberty, and avoids denunciation (vv29–30). Paul W. Gooch says of 10:29:

> In the objection "Why should my freedom be judged by someone else's *conscience?*" (v 29), there is no reference to the problem of competing moral consciences at all. Rather, Paul's problem is the legitimacy of exercising a right when it will harm other people.[37]

Verse 29 betrays a concern for the unbeliever, assuming this is the one who announces that the meat has been sacrificed, which is reinforced by v. 33. Paul concludes this section with a reminder that everything, including eating and drinking, is to be done to the glory of God (v. 31) and that offence is not to be given to Jews or to Greeks or to members of the church (v. 32). He then points to himself as one who does not seek his own advantage but that of many, and exhorts his readers to imitate him (10:33–11:1). Paul discusses similar concerns in Romans 14.[38] He seeks to avoid arguments and disputes amongst his readers by urging those who have no qualms in such matters to respect the principles of those who do. They are to do so out of love for their fellow-Christians, and to ensure that they build up rather than cause to fall. As Gooch has noted:

> The limits of freedom for Paul are grounded not in law or rules or regulations, but in relationships. As Christ's slave the Christian is freed from all else and everyone else, but he must have regard for his own good and the preservation of his freedom, *and above all he must look to the good of others rather than to his own advantage*.[39]

Thus while Paul agrees that the liberty one enjoys as a Christian brings the privilege of eating whatever one will, that privilege is to be surrendered in the interest of those who have not yet recognized that they too possess it. In essence Paul is calling upon "his" followers to adopt a conciliatory attitude towards those who disagree with his position. Personal rights and privileges are to be set aside.

I Corinthians 9:19–23

The requirement to become willing to serve the interests of others is especially illustrated by Paul's statement in I Cor 9:22 that he has "become all things to all men." Paul says that "though I am free from all men, I have made myself a slave to all, that I might win the more" (I Cor 9:19). This entire passage (9:19–23), serves to emphasize how Paul believes a Christian should behave. Paul's discussion in I Cor 8 and 10 brackets his "defence" of apostleship in chapter 9. The three chapters together outline in a concrete fashion how Paul applies the principles of the servant-ethic. On this view 9:19–23 is not strictly a defence of Paul's apostleship but an illustration of how the servant-ethic is operative in his own life. As Richard A. Horsley says:

> If a concept of "conscience" is emerging in I Corinthians 8–10 then its criterion is not inner freedom based on conviction at all, but the situation and self-consciousness of one's neighbor. Paul's autobiographical illustration in I Corinthians 9 has the same thrust.[40]

It is not completely clear from the passage whether Paul believes that such conduct is required of all Christians or whether it is part of Paul's self-understanding as an apostle. His vigorous defence of his authority which precedes this passage (I Cor 9:1–18), inclines one toward the latter understanding; but 9:24 suggests that he understands all Christians to be part of the race and that he Paul is but one example of a runner. Richardson believes that it refers only to the position of apostle.[41] He says that "Paul rarely advises his followers to adopt the same principle of behavior that he adopts in I Cor.9." Richardson also notes that the troubles within the congregations "arise either from obvious moral laxity or from a failure to be accommodating." He concludes that "the basic text on the question of accommodation does in fact provide evidence that Paul did not generally advise his constituency to adopt the same principle as he advocated for himself."[42]

Richardson points out that chapter 9 is concerned with Paul's defence of his apostleship and this is the context in which vv19–23 should be read. He admits that 10:31–11:1 extends "his principle of conduct to his congregation, but in a weaker and more passive form." He suggests that Paul's invitation to accomondation was not well-received and insists that Paul "is much more comfortable with the application of a principle of accommodation to himself than to others."[43] For Richardson, then, Paul's adaptability to the demands of others is a mark of his apostleship which he does not expect others to adopt.[44]

In an article written in response to Richardson, David Carson approaches the problem quite differently but in a way that also bears on our discussion.[45] Carson understands I Cor 9:19–23 to be exemplary rather than a direct call to similar actions on the part of the Corinthian Christians. I Cor 9:19–23 demonstrates how a fundamental principle operates in Paul's own life. That principle is not one of accommodation but of self-denial and servanthood. In Paul's own life this principle is reflected by his practice of accommodation. Although chapter 9 may well be a defence of his apostleship, in the larger context of 8–10 it functions as a further illustration of Christians' responsibility to surrender personal rights: "Paul's principle of accommodation is an expression of his commitment in his apostolic ministry not to use all his *Exousia*." The question in chapter 8, then is not a call for accomodation but rather a "willingness to abandon personal rights, of which Paul's principle of accommodation is a prime example."[46]

Carson's argument is compelling here, especially in his insistence that these verses offer an example of fulfilling a principle (not of accommodation but of self-denial), and not an example of normative conduct: "Paul is simply providing a personal example of the principle of self-denial which he *does* enjoin on the Corinthian readership."[47] For Paul there are limitations on how far this principle should be extended, but *all* Christians are bound to practice self-denial and surrender their own rights, a responsibility which is partly, but not completely, demonstrated by Paul's practice of accommodation. The aim of the Christian is to fulfill God's will. While I Cor 9:19–23 illustrates how flexible Paul can become on behalf of the gospel, if such behavior repels rather than attracts others to Christ it is not only redundant but evil.[48] As we have noted above, and as Richardson points out, there are certain practices that Paul is unwilling to accommodate unrestrictedly including the role of women, prophecy and tongues in worship.[49] With Carson we have to iterate, however, that the accommodation illustrated by I Cor 9:19–23 is not, in and of itself, a principle, but merely the demonstration of the principle of self-denial in Paul's own life.

Paul does not allow personal scruples or reservations to prevent fellowship with those who will not listen to him. He puts himself at the gospel's disposal, so to speak, and willingly adapts to his neighbor. This precludes the type of division that Paul sees at Corinth, and the way is clear for the preaching of the gospel. Paul also makes explicit his hope of bringing "enemies" into the community through a strategy of accommodation and charitableness towards non-Christian opponents.

The use of the verb δουλόω, however, suggests something more radical than considerate accommodation to the scruples of others. Paul considers himself a slave to everyone in order that he might serve to win more to the Gospel. Thus one should read 9:19 in the context of 9:1–18. Although Paul is free (the answer to his rhetorical question of v.1), he has deliberately become a slave to everyone for the sake of the gospel.

II Corinthians 4:5

In II Cor 4:5 Paul again speaks of becoming a slave to, or abasing himself before, his readers for the sake of the gospel. In v. 2 he asserts that he and his cohorts do not preach the gospel for their own gain. Rather they become slaves of the reader, for Jesus' sake, while they preach Christ as Lord. A similar idea is found in 11:7, where Paul asks: "Did I commit a sin in abasing myself so that you might be exalted, because I preached God's gospel without cost to you?" Because Paul was not paid for his preaching he is a slave to those he serves: not only to the gospel and Christ, but also to his listeners who benefit by receiving the hope of salvation and exaltation. Thus Paul's abasement results in others' exaltation. This is an echo of the idea we saw in I Cor 9:19 in which Paul's willingness to put others first (accommodation) and himself last (abasement) demonstrates his desire to bring the truth without cost to others.

Paul, by his own estimation, has authority over his readers, because he claims full apostleship despite those who believe to the contrary (eg I Cor 9:2). He manifests this authority, however, by becoming a slave, even a slave to the Corinthian Christians. Paul sees his role as an apostle in terms of service to others. In his commentary on II Cor 4:5 Barrett says, "Paul has already renounced the thought of being himself a lord over the Corinthians' faith (i.24, using the verb κυριεύω cognate with the noun κύριος, lord); here he expresses his relation to them positively." (Barrett wryly remarks that, "Paul was doubtless wise to add that he served them not because they were such pleasing masters, or had in themselves any claim upon him, but *for Jesus' sake*.")[50]

II Corinthians 8:1–15

Concerning the question of alms and personal wealth Paul does not suggest that believers should surrender all that they have to give to the poor (II Cor

8:13). He expects his readers to contribute to the collection for the saints, but not to the point of personal impoverishment. This seems to reflect a shift from the Synoptic (especially the Lukan) attitude towards wealth. Those in the community who are unable to support themselves should be able to rely upon the generosity of their fellow-Christians; but Paul insists that each is to earn a living as far as possible (I Thess 4:9–12). Christian love requires that the believer not only not inflict an undue burden on others but also stand ready to relieve the financial affliction of those in need.[51] Nevertheless, there is in Paul no general exhortation to relieve those in need who stand outside the community: "Paul obviously did not espouse or undertake social action for the benefit of unbelievers on the basis of the fundamentally unrestricted law of love."[52] It is likely, however, that Paul would respond in love to a non-believer who confronted him in abject material need, and would expect other Christians to do likewise (Gal 6:10). In addition, Paul saw all his evangelistic activity as a means of service toward those outside the community. Concerning financial well-being, however, his primary concern is to ensure that all the saints have their own needs met (I Cor 8:13–14).[53] Paul himself has apparently surrendered material wealth for the sake of the gospel and chooses in some instances at least not to earn his living from his preaching (I Cor 9:1–18). He does not, however, extend this idea of deliberate impoverishment into a general principle that all his readers should adopt. Again, the principle of self-denial on behalf of others is to be operative in the life of every believer; but this is manifested in different ways, of which Paul's (and the Macedonians') own practice is only one example.

Galatians 5:13

In his letter to the Galatians Paul speaks of how Christians were once enslaved to the στοιχεῖα. Now that they have found freedom in Christ and walk in the Spirit, the servant-ethic is to become operative. In his book *The Ethics of Paul*, Morton Scott Enslin notes:

> Paul, though free, was ready to sacrifice his freedom to the claims of brotherhood; so must the other Christians. Christianity consummated the ethics of self-realization by the ethics of self-sacrifice . . . . Freedom must never be at the expense of a brother; it found itself only in service.[54]

While the gospels, especially the Synoptic gospels, place the ethical emphasis upon behavior appropriate to discipleship and following Jesus, Paul's ethical concerns are bound up with instilling the values of the Christian community within his readers who are one in the Spirit. In Paul's writings, becoming a member of the body of Christ is akin to the decision to become a disciple in the gospels, and is the primary impetus for his ethics. Although free in Christ, Paul insists that Christians must "become as slaves to one another" (δουλεύετε ἀλλήλοις, Gal 5:13). The freedom one finds as a member of the body of Christ is expressed through service to others in love.[55] One's own rights and interests are to be subjugated to those of others in a way that recalls many of the gospel passages examined above.

Gal 5:13 functions as a central text when examining the idea of service to others in the Pauline literature. Its context includes many themes found throughout the writings that bear his name, including law, unity, freedom and love, while the text itself is one of the clearest expressions of the principle to place the interests of others above one's own.[56] In Gal 6:2 he urges readers to bear one another's burdens and thereby fulfil the law of Christ. Both Gal 5:13 and 6:2 illustrate the principle of walking in the Spirit (Gal 5:25). While 5:13 is paralleled by the injunction to "love your neighbor as yourself" which is, in fact, the fulfillment of the whole law (5:14), Paul suggests that the Galatians are having difficulty within the Church controlling their interpersonal relations (5:15).

Richard B. Hays, in his essay "Christology and Ethics in Galatians: The Law of Christ," has shown that Gal 5:13 fundamentally illustrates how Paul's ethics proceed from his theology. He reminds his readers that Paul wrote his letter for a *community* but that contemporary interpretation of the epistle is colored by post-reformation scholars who read "the text through a hermeneutical filter that highlights the relation of the human individual subject to God."[57] Hays seeks to balance this tendency by recalling that Paul addresses the Galatians corporately and that this is illustrated by 5:13 which constitutes "an integral part of his theological vision...set forth in opposition to the prospect of using freedom 'as an opportunity for the flesh,' which means, in Galatians, as a cause of division in the community." For Hays the vice and virtue lists of 5:16–24 emphasize the need for unity especially since they are bracketed by 5:13–15 and 5:25–6:5 which are "clear directives against conflict in the church." The interests of the community are always to be placed before the interests of the individual. "The conformity of the Galatians to Christ is to be expressed in their communal practice of loving mutual service. It is in *this* context that the exhortation of 6:2 occurs: 'Bear one another's burdens and so fulfill the law of Christ.'"[58]

In Gal 5:13 Paul tells his readers that although they were called to freedom they are not to use their freedom as an opportunity for the flesh. They are to be servants of one another. Paul uses the verb δουλεύω to express this thought, which literally means "to be a slave" or "to be subject." F. F. Bruce describes this slavery as completely different "from that against which he otherwise warns them." Bruce paraphrases Paul: "If you must live in slavery, here is a form of slavery in which you may safely indulge—the slavery of practical love for one another."[59]

The question remains, however, what exactly Paul envisions when he tells the Galatians to be as slaves to one another through love. Clearly, they are to express their love by being of service rather than harming each other, but how are they to become each other's slaves?

In chapter 4 of Galatians Paul has spoken of how the Galatian Christians were once slaves to the "elemental spirits of the universe" but have since become sons and heirs of God; they are no longer slaves (4:7). Before the work of Christ people were enslaved in ignorance of God and his grace. Now Christians are free, liberated by Christ, and must "not submit again to a yoke of slavery" (Gal 5:1). In all this passage (4:1–5:12) the emphasis lies upon preserving the freedom found in Christ. The words δοῦλοι, δουλεία and δουλεύω describe the state of those who have not yet become Christians. Yet in 5:13 the verb is used to describe the state of Christians toward each other "through love." The freedom received from Christ is not to take the form of licentiousness but is to become yet another form of slavery. Christians are now to bear one another's burdens (Gal 6:2) and thereby fulfill the law of Christ. This law is summed up in the entreaty to love one's neighbor as oneself, which Paul uses to justify the mutual service he insists upon in 5:13. Ernest De Witt Burton's comments on the phrase "but through love be servants of one another" are important to note here. He sees 5:13 as a means of overcoming "the harmful restrictions of legalism and the dangers of freedom from law." Love, in the form of mutual service typifies the Christian's freedom and mind-set: "The present tense of δουλεύετε reflects the fact that what Paul enjoins is not a single act of service, nor an entrance into service, but a continuous attitude and activity."[60] Burton also points to Mark 9:35; 10:43 as expressing a similar idea and observes that there διάκονος rather than δοῦλος, is used.

Rengstorf, in his article for *TDNT*, suggests that Paul uses the term ἐλευθερία "freedom" only in contrast to Christians' former state of δουλεία. That Christians are now sons and heirs of God does not mean that they are totally independent. "The attainment of υἱοθεσία does not mean the attainment of autonomy in every sphere of life, in relation to God as well as to sin." The freedom achieved is reconciliation rather than the previous state of separation. This new relationship finds expression in the demonstration of ΄υπακοή towards God by those who are liberated through Christ. "Thus the new state of the Christian comes under the thought of service, though in a very different sense from the earlier usage."[61]

Thus when Paul tells the Galatians to "become slaves to one another" through love, he means that they are to be willing to serve each other with no thought for themselves. By so doing they will respond appropriately to their call to freedom and also clear up the divisiveness within the community.

The language Paul uses here is, however, even more radical. Despite Burton's attempts to interpret δουλεύω in this passage as having less to do with subjection and more to do with rendering service, the verb is extreme. Hans Dieter Betz suggests that this has to do with the paradox that Paul is intentionally creating in this passage. On the question of why Paul calls this new state of mutual love a state of slavery Betz says:

> Love is voluntary and reciprocal, but it involves commitments to be maintained even under difficult and strained circumstances. It is the necessity of commitment and the difficulties of maintaining human relationships that cause Paul to describe the free exercise of love as a form of mutual enslavement.[62]

Although this verse does speak of reciprocity as part of the paradox of becoming a slave to others in love and freedom, I think Betz emphasizes the mutual aspect too much, although I do believe that Paul uses the verb δουλεύω because of the "difficulties of human relationships." The freedom that Christians have been called to is new life in Christ: a life of selflessness and other-directedness, which automatically places them at the disposal of others. A community of Christians, therefore, is ideally made up of persons "enslaved" to each other, but even if some relationships are not fully reciprocal the attitude should be maintained.

Philippians 2:1–5

Paul encourages his Philippian readers to "unity of mind" several times in his epistle to them. Again, they are to look to the interests of others in order to maintain this unity. The inclusion of the christological hymn (vv 6–11), plays a role in underlining the viewpoint put forward in vv 1–5. Paul calls the Philippians to work out their salvation (v. 12) by maintaining their unity "being in full accord and of one mind" (v. 2). Verses 3 and 4 tell them to "do nothing from selfishness or conceit, but in humility count others better than yourselves. Let each of you look not only to his own interests, but also to the interests of others."[63] He continues the thought with v. 5 (τοῦτο φρονεῖτε ἐν ὑμιν ὅ καὶ Χριστῷ Ἰησοῦ) which has caused many exegetical headaches because the interpretation of the hymn that follows depends, in large part, upon one's understanding of this verse. The first four verses, however, clearly encourage Paul's readers to practice the servant-ethic because they are Christians. This is the implication of verses 1 and 2. If the work of Christ is operative in Philippi, Paul's joy will be "complete" when the Philippian Christians are of the same mind (τὸ αὐτὸ φρονῆτε), have the same love, are in full accord and of one mind (τὸ ἐν φρονοῦντες) (v. 2).[64] This will be evident because of the Philippian Christians' humble regard for each other.

The Motives for the Pauline Servant-Ethic

We can identify at least four motives for the Pauline call to serve others and to place their interests first. One of the most important of these is to maintain unity within the Pauline communities and also within the Christian movement as a whole. Often this motive is cited in the face of a specific conflict that has arisen, either internally or as opposition from outside the community. A second motive is the promise of reward, although this is rarely the only incentive given in any passage. A third reason is the challenge to imitate Christ in his humility and service on behalf of others. Finally, and perhaps most important for Paul, is the desire to display appropriate behavior "for the sake of the gospel," or Jesus. Behind all these inducements, however, is the Christian experience of new life in the Spirit. The old ways and customs are discarded and replaced by the new reality of life in Christ.

Service to Others for the Sake of Christian Unity

For Paul, the unity of the Church is one of the most critical issues faced by the early Christians. It is clear from his letters, especially those to the Galatians and Corinthians, that he himself has become a focal point for certain divisions within the church. In I Corinthians 9 he seeks to overcome his opponents' denunciation of him both by asserting his apostolic authority (9:1–18), and by reminding his readers of his conciliatory attitude towards the views of others (9:19–27), even the views of those outside the community.

Graham Shaw observes that "calls for unity are often most vigorously made by those whose activity is peculiarly divisive." He believes that Paul himself must take responsibility for much of the problem: "He cannot, for instance, resist distinguishing himself from all the rest of God's workers in the Corinthian vineyard....Even in his exhortation to unity, Paul draws attention to his own special position."[65] We must remember, however, that Paul faced opposition in Corinth, which manifested itself, at least in part, as an attack on the authenticity of his apostleship. These attacks seem to have been made subsequent to Paul's initial mission to Corinth. Paul is convinced that he carries the true gospel-message. He is not so much concerned with attacks upon himself (if he were he would have abandoned his mission long before), but rather the dangers inherent if the Corinthians abandon the truth.

Ben Meyer explains I Cor 9:19–23 as an illustration of how Paul reconciled the demands of various factions within the Christian community. He overcame factionalism by distinguishing between unity and uniformity. Meyer portrays Paul as one who recognized that full uniformity between Jews and Gentiles was impossible although Paul himself could accommodate both groups (I Cor 9:23). Ultimately "Christian identity—obviously more fundamental in Paul's view than the diverse self-understanding that qualified it—was correlative to 'the gospel' in whose name Paul accommodated himself to all."[66] This question of unity versus uniformity is important because we need to determine how far diversity could extend without compromising unity. As Meyer says, the New Testament writers "recoiled from division." Christian unity was sought by all of them and was promoted through baptism and the eucharist. "Christian identity, rooted in the experience of salvation, correlative to the gospel, susceptible of diverse self-definitions, open to progress as to regress and collapse, grounded the possibility of the unity passionately sought by Paul."[67] It is by acceptance of the gospel, as preached by Paul, that one enters new life in Christ. Upon experiencing this new existence Christians, according to Paul, discover the freedom in Christ that leads to serving others. There is room for diversity (in practices such as eating meat, celebrating holy days, female dress), but only if such matters do not compromise the truth of the gospel. When the servant-ethic is practised such diversity should not threaten the unity of the community because each will seek to serve the interests of others.

It is also clear that while Paul realizes that his mission caused a certain degree of tension in his relationship with other apostles, he is careful not to speak of such strain as decisively affecting the unity of the church. When discussing his visit to Jerusalem in Gal 2:1–10 he emphasizes the cordiality between himself and the Christian authorities in Jerusalem. They were in full agreement on the substance of his message, the legitimacy of his message, and that he should remember the poor (v. 10). In his other letters Paul gives the impression that he was extremely conscientious in fulfilling this latter obligation, and concerning the collection for the saints, the passages from Romans and I Corinthians are most intriguing because they speak of Paul travelling to Jerusalem personally to deliver the money. In Romans he acknowledges that he risks endangering himself if he appears in Jerusalem (Rom 15:31), while in I Cor 16:3–4 he contemplates sending delegates but promises to go himself if necessary.[68] While the other passages we have cited reveal Paul's concern for the poor his insistence on going to Jerusalem himself is puzzling. Longenecker believes that the solution to the problem lies in Paul's desire to act as a unifying force in a Christianity that is becoming more and more fractured. For Longenecker, "In [Paul's] determination to present the contribution personally, we see his willingness to sacrifice himself, if need be, for the unity and welfare of the Church."[69]

This concern for unity is especially apparent in Paul's insistence that Christians place the interests of others first and act toward others in love. In this regard certain issues and principles sometimes should be discarded in order to prevent disputes and divisions amongst Christians. This is clearly illustrated in the discussion of eating sacrificed meat. One is not to flaunt one's own convictions if by so doing one damages the faith or conscience of another. For Paul each member of the body of Christ is responsible for the well-being of the others.[70] In I Cor 12:12–26 Paul underscores this mutual dependence by emphasizing the inter-relatedness of all parts of the body (12:24b–26).

In Paul's view the church is a community of disparate but united elements who depend upon and care for each other. There is no room for self-assertion or personal ambition. Nevertheless, the unity of the community also depends upon a degree of selflessness that is not hindered by a lack of positive response. In other words, while mutuality is clearly the ideal after which Paul encourages his readers to strive, he recognizes that often acts of personal service and self-denial on behalf of others were scorned or rejected even by those within the community. The hymn to love in I Cor 13 underscores that such rejection is to be borne patiently, for love bears, believes, hopes and endures all things (13:7). Within the community this love is expressed in acts which continually seek the edification of the church as a whole. Anything which could undermine the community is to be forsaken, even if this means forsaking one's own rights and privileges. To reiterate: Paul is an example of this (I Cor 9:12–15a). While Paul encourages a reciprocal attitude among Christians he contends that when reciprocity fails it is the task of each Christian to continue to act out of love:

> [Love] expresses itself not in mere feeling or inclination but in concrete acts of service. While it delights in reciprocation, love gives itself to others irrespective of the reaction it receives.[71]

I Cor 6:1–8 illustrates how far Paul believed this principle should be carried within the Christian communities.

Phil 2:1–5 is also an important text for considering Paul's efforts to maintain church unity by means of the servant-ethic. J. Paul Sampley speaks of this unity in terms of Roman law and calls the relationship Paul maintains with the Philippian Christians a *societas*, or legal partnership, which has become *societas Christi*, or partnership in Christ. Phil 2:1–5 is for Sampley a prime example of how Paul incorporates *societas* language into his paranesis. He examines the structure and content of each verse to demonstrate how they point to the Roman concept of *societas*.[72] Although Sampley's goals differ from ours, he understands Paul's challenge to the Philippians to lead to the same result: a community (or partnership) of Christians who have renounced self-interest in favor of maintaining harmony within the community.[73]

For Paul, diversity in and of itself, is not to be rejected in favor of uniformity. Unity, however, is of paramount importance. Gal 3:28 perhaps captures this aspect of his thought. Social status, race and sex are no longer grounds for making claims upon God, and therefore have no inherent significance. They do not have to be ignored, however, and Paul nowhere insists that they ever should be. Being in Christ overcomes any diversity and provides the bond of unity.

The Promise of Reward as a Motive for Service to Others

The entire Biblical tradition has a legacy of looking to the humiliated and lowly and identifying them as God's own people. This trend is especially pronounced in the wisdom literature but is evident from Genesis through to the end of the New Testament. In his book on humility, Klaus Wengst gives a succinct if less than exhaustive view on the role of the oppressed in the "Old Testament-Jewish Tradition."[74] One of the most powerful themes in the Hebrew Bible is that God favors the cause of the oppressed and the poor. This motif is also used by Paul as he seeks to encourage the "servant-ethic" amongst his readers.

For Paul the element of reward—God's exaltation of the lowly—is also a prominent theme, although Paul himself never quotes verses such as Prov 3:34 directly. In terms of the servant-ethic the hope of eschatological reward is cited as a motive in such passages as Rom 12:12; I Cor 6:2–3, 9–11; 9:23–27; Gal 6:6–10; Phil 2:1–12. As Furnish says, "The Jewish doctrine of recompense is by no means absent from Pauline teaching," and he cites as evidence Rom 2:6–10; I Cor 3:13–15 and II Cor 5:9–10 which are not explicitly related to the servant-ethic.[75] Furnish seeks to overcome the inherent tension between recompense and the doctrine of "justification by faith" by noting that "the good works Paul commends are not regarded as having a value in and of themselves. They have value only as responsible acts of obedience to the sovereign Lord." Eternal life is not the "wages" of obedience. "Rather, eternal life, participation in the Lord's victorious reign over all things, inheritance of his kingdom, is bestowed as a *free gift* from God himself" (Rom 6:23).[76] I am not sure that a non-Christian Jewish contemporary of Paul would not speak in a similar fashion. E.P. Sanders notes that, "the concern that, in doing the law, one do so with the right attitude of devotion to God was doubtless present in the synagogues of the first century"[77] and that, "surely non-Christian Jews saw themselves as remaining in the grace of God by remaining loyal to the covenant." He continues:

> For a modern theologian to say that *in fact* the fault of the Jews was that they were self-righteous he must not only share Paul's assumption that rejection of Christ *is* rejection of grace, he must then add the assumption that Jews rejected grace *because* they preferred righteousness by merit.[78]

In Rom 12:12 Paul tells his readers to rejoice in their hope amidst his general ethical exhortations. In Cor 6:2–3 and 9–11 he reminds his readers of their future role in an attempt to overcome the divisiveness of their lawsuits. In I Cor 9:23–27 Paul says that he has become all things to all men so that he might share in the blessings of the gospel and follows this with the analogy of the race and the sacrifices that must be made to win. In Gal 6:9 Paul concludes his paranesis with the assurance that "we shall reap [eternal life v. 8], if we do not grow weary." The hope of God's approval is interwoven in Paul's calls to put aside the interests of the self. The idea of the exaltation of the humble is prevalent throughout Paul's writings. Whether or not specific biblical texts are used to support his assertion of this principle, it is clear that the early Christians were exhorted to service, sacrifice and humility because this would guarantee them God's favor.

Serving Others as Imitation of Christ

The question of how, and indeed if, Jesus as the Christ plays a paradigmatic role in the writings of Paul has engendered much scholarly debate.[79] Texts such as Phil 2:5–11, I Cor 11:1 and Rom 15:1–3a seem to give Christ the role of exemplar. Many scholars, however, dispute that Paul was actually suggesting that the figure of Jesus somehow provides an ethical pattern. Paul's supposed disinterest in the earthly Jesus is the reason that some hold that the idea of *imitatio Christi* is not really operative in his writings.[80] Hays notes that the position of Davies and C.H. Dodd on the meaning of the "law of Christ" in Gal 6:2, which understands the phrase to mean a new messianic Torah, has led to a backlash. This backlash "has caused many interpreters to reject altogether the possibility that Paul might intend to suggest in this phrase some distinct normative function of the figure of Jesus Christ for Christian ethical behaviour."[81] Schrage tends towards the middle path on this issue: although he rejects the notion that the historical life of Jesus is paradigmatic for Paul the incarnation and crucifixion do provide a call to conformity. The usual examples (Phil 2:5–11; II Cor 8:9; I Cor 11:1; I Thess 1:6; Gal 2:20; Rom 15:1–7) "demonstrate that Christ's humbling himself in the incarnation or his self-sacrifice on the cross not only establishes a formal purpose and intention but defines a fundamental orientation of Christian living."[82] Hays, however, sees the imitation of Christ as an important motif in Paul's writings, including Galatians.[83]

That Paul regards Christ as paradigmatic is also the view of W. P. de Boer. Of Rom 15:1–3a he says that in the self-denial of Christ and the "foregoing of his claims, rights and pleasures," which was revealed in his suffering and humiliation during life and death, "there is the indication of how Christians are to give themselves in seeking the well-being of their neighbours."[84] It is the pattern of Christ's life that is to be paradigmatic rather than specific actions, words or events as Paul's pattern of self-denial is to be paradigmatic rather than his specific practice of accomodation outlined in I Cor 9:19–23. Repeatedly Paul offers his own behavior to illustrate his calls to serve, which also highlights that self-confidence, at least in his case, accompanies his self-denial. His invitations to his readers to "become imitators of me" (I Cor 4:16; 11:1; as well as Phil 3:17 and I Thess 1:7) reflect his proclivity to exhibit his confidence in the rightness of his own approach to whatever is at issue. I Cor 11:1 reveals that Paul wants the Corinthians to imitate him because he imitates Christ. This is especially apparent with regard to suffering wrong and accommodating oneself to the wishes and interests of others in the first epistle to the Corinthians. In I Cor 4:8–13 Paul contrasts his own position with that of the Corinthians who appear to believe that their membership in the Church has left them "filled," "rich" and "kings" (4:8). While the Corinthians are wise, strong and held in honor, Paul (and Apollos) are fools, weak and held in disrepute (v. 10). More importantly, "when reviled, we (Paul and Apollos) bless; when persecuted, we endure; when slandered, we try to conciliate; we have become, and are now, as the refuse of the world, the offscouring of all things" (vv12–13). Paul assures the Corinthians that he does not seek to shame them but rather to encourage them to recognize him as their father in Christ Jesus and "to become imitators of me" (vv14–16). Part of this imitation is to disavow any claims, for the present at least, to "kingship," wisdom, honor and the like, and to become "fools for Christ's sake," suffering reviling, persecution and slander, without seeking vengeance.

I Cor 11:1 follows on his discussion of eating sacrificed meat and his insistence that the Corinthians should follow his example in trying "to please all men in everything." Here Paul explicitly states that part of his imitation of Christ is his deliberate forsaking of his own interests. This is how he wishes his Corinthian readers to behave. The fact that they do not, has led to the problems and disputes over eating sacrificed food, and to litigation. Despite their apparent wisdom and knowledge they have failed to grasp that the essence of the Christian life lies in self-giving and service to others. The needs and interests of the other are to be paramount, not one's own prestige, comfort or religious principles.[85]

It is well-known that Paul does not recall specific incidents in Jesus' earthly life that should be exemplary for believers. But he does insist that his readers should try to conform to the nature of Christ as it was revealed in the general pattern of his life. Harvey suggests that the lack of calls to imitate the specific content of Christ's ethical conduct in Paul and other New Testament epistles can be explained by the slant put on the life of Jesus by the earliest Christian interpretations of his death and resurrection: "We might say, the inspiration for our loving is not the moral example afforded by Jesus in his life, but the theological imperative implied by his death."[86] Thus Harvey sees the meaning of Jesus' death as overwhelming the ethical content of Jesus' life from the very first so that it became the basis for arguing (or explaining) matters both theological and ethical. Morna D. Hooker sees Paul, in his Corinthian correspondence, as calling for a change in "life-style" by summoning Christians to become like Christ which necessarily involves a "concern for other people." The Corinthians' problem is that they understand themselves to be simply recipients of grace and have not sought to be like Christ in their own lives. "They think of the interchange between Christ and themselves in terms of simple exchange—he gives, we take—instead of in terms of mutual give and take . . . . It is not so much a case of giving *to* Christ but giving *in* Christ—that is, sharing in *his* giving."[87] Hooker also says that Paul "did not consider Christian ethics to be simply a matter of imitating the example of Christ" since Paul knows that the relationship between salvation through Christ and appropriate conduct for Christians is profound. She notes that the principle of not appealing to the pattern of Jesus' life for Christian ethics arises only because of "dogma that the Jesus of History and the Christ of Faith belong in separate compartments."[88] Hooker acknowledges that Paul does not often explicitly call Christians to imitate Christ. She points out, however, that in II Cor 8:9 a summary of the Gospel message similar to Phil 2:6–11 is made and that its context also concerns Christian behavior.[89]

We have to ask whether Phil 2:5–11 actually calls Christians to imitate Christ. Several scholars, such as A. Dihle, believe that there is no doubt that the text in question calls Christians to imitate Christ in his humility and self-sacrifice and thereby constitutes a call to fulfill the servant-ethic.[90] Those who oppose this understanding of the passage claim that it makes vv 9–11 of the Christological hymn irrelevant.[91]

While the debate over the correct interpretation of vv 5–11 is intense, it is clear that Paul called the Philippians to humility because of their relationship to Christ. Christ plays a paradigmatic role in this passage. His self-humbling and "taking the form of a slave" serves as an example of the humility the Philippian Christians should practice.

Paul formulates his appeal to the Philippians for humility and the subordination of one's own interests to those of others in these terms: τοῦτο φρονεῖτε ἐν ὑμῖν ὃ καὶ ἐν Χριστῷ Ἰησοῦ. Upon this verse turns much of the interpretation of 2:1–11. It is the connecting link which determines how the Christological hymn is to be interpreted in light of verses 1–4. Beare translates this verse, "Let this be the disposition that governs in your common life, as is fitting in Christ Jesus."[92] The verb φρονέω links verses 2 and 5 so that the disposition (to use Beare's word) that exists amongst Christians is founded upon the truth of Jesus Christ's own experience. What was that experience? It was a surrendering, an emptying; it was the act of becoming a slave (vv6–7). Stephen E. Fowl, therefore, understands the hymn to have the function of presenting Christ as an exemplar.[93] He does not explicitly connect Christ taking the form of a δοῦλος with this observation, however; rather he concentrates on trying to interpret whether Christ appearing as a servant refers to becoming human or obeying God. "By not explicitly resolving this ambiguity the passage is able to draw on both possibilities."[94] A third ambiguity can be added: Christ's "appearance" as a slave/servant is manifested in his willingness to look to the interests of others—his undeterred readiness to serve and to love. This, perhaps is the form of slavery that Paul wants to convey Christ as taking: not only standing in obedience rather than equality with God, nor simply becoming human and thereby somehow enslaved, but unreservedly taking on the role of a servant of others and confirming the principle reflected in Mark 10:45. On this reading of the passage the disposition or likemindedness spoken of in verses 2 and 5 is ultimately a readiness to serve—a state of mind that is found in Christ and in believers to stand ready to serve the interests of others whatever the cost. Where does this leave the remainder of the hymn? For Christ such a disposition led ultimately to death, "even death on a cross," an ignoble, dishonorable death. But God, of course, was faithful so that Jesus Christ was ultimately exalted. The passage implies, but does not specifically state, that Christians have the same hope.

As we have noted, the main drawback to this interpretation suggested by those who oppose any attempt to claim the hymn as illustrative of some ethical interpretation is that it tends to render the second half of the hymn to Christ irrelevant. At the end of his discussion on this issue, Martin offers what he considers to be the most compelling piece of evidence against the theory that the hymn offers Christ as an example. We learn that Martin is, above all, squeamish about the idea of reward: "In fact the teaching of 'reward' is a positive hindrance to disinterested ethical endeavour."[95] So, rather than an objective view of the text, in the context of Pauline and New Testament teaching as a whole, we see that what worries Martin about the ethical interpretation of the christological hymn is that it might remind Christians that a heavenly reward awaits them if they seek to be humble as Christ was. Martin prefers to believe that Christians in Philippi pursued the good for its own sake and had no thought about the personal consequences of such a quest.[96] At the same time, however, we should note that both Paul and the four gospels do not primarily depend upon the promise of heavenly reward as a motivating factor for appropriate conduct, but upon the experience of God's grace as already manifested in the life and death of Jesus. It is only because of this experience that Christian moral injunctions have any foundation or appeal. Reminders of Christ's exaltation following his humiliation and enslavement do not seek to make Christians humble and self-effacing by promising a heavenly reward; it is assumed that believers already seek to serve others based on their experience of Christ. The various claims that exaltation does indeed await them are promises not bribes.

Thus the Philippians' humility and willingness to serve the interests of others

have a direct bearing on their relationship to Christ. Like Mark 10:45 the role
and person of Jesus Christ gives shape to the call to servanthood and humility:
"Whatever else it may be, Christ's action is more than vicarious: it is evocative,
it constitutes a summons to a properly derivative mimesis."[97] But we can go
beyond the idea of mimesis here and claim that the point of the passage is to
emphasize to the Philippians that their new life in Christ gives rise to this: "It
would be better, perhaps, to use . . . 'conformity' . . . when speaking of the
appeal Paul makes in 2.5–11 . . . . One cannot separate the Christian character
from the character of Christ himself."[98]

Christian Wolff summarizes Paul's attitude to the role of Christ as exemplar
in his own life. He points to I Cor 10:33 and even II Cor 4:5 as instances in
which Paul deliberately invokes Jesus' example as the motive for his own
conduct: "In the service of this Κυρίος, who brought about salvation through
lowliness, the apostle works selflessly for the church."[99] Salvation has come
through selflessness. The self-denial and service of Jesus therefore becomes
paradigmatic for the attitude of believers toward others.

Serving Others for the Sake of the Gospel

There are two passages in the Corinthian correspondence in which Paul
speaks of serving others for the sake of the gospel or of Jesus (I Cor 9:19; II
Cor 4:5). These verses refer to Paul's commitment to the spread of the gospel
and his desire to bring others into the community of believers. To do this he is
willing to serve others and become like a slave to them ("For what we preach is
not ourselves, but Jesus Christ as Lord, with ourselves as your servants [or
slaves] for Jesus' sake"). The very act of preaching the gospel is for Paul an act
of service to others.

The Limitations of the Pauline Servant-Ethic

It is as difficult in Paul as in the Synoptic texts to find limits to the servant-
ethic. If we look to the example of Paul himself we can see that he placed no
explicit limits on his role of servant to others while carrying out his apostolic
responsibilities and even set aside his rights as an apostle for the sake of the
gospel (e.g. I Cor 9:1–18). Paul's limitations upon the servant-ethic are, like the
Synoptic writers', implied rather than baldly stated. There are no limits to the
lengths a Christian should go to serve others unless he or she risks violating the
will of God. If serving others by surrendering one's rights and conceding to the
requirements of others does not violate God's will it constitutes service to God
and should be undertaken.

As in the Synoptic texts, questions of prudence and justice as they relate to
the interests of the self are not primary. Prudence is perhaps required in

discerning the will of God, but only to the extent that acts of service be in accord with it. Justice, in the sense of vindicating one's rights, is to be set aside (I Cor 6:7). The main problem for Paul is not discovering the limits of the servant-ethic but encouraging his readers to implement it in their lives: the divisions and squabbles within the churches are evidence that believers are not serving the interests of others but are still seeking self-aggrandizement. Rather than looking to Christ and his example of self-denial and humble service, they are trying to assert their own interests, whether out of simple misunderstanding or wilfull disobedience. Many of Paul's readers are not yet free to serve.

Freedom in Christ and Serving Others

Allen Verhey identifies freedom (informed by love) as the most fundamental value for Paul's discernment in matters pertaining to God's will.[100] Nevertheless, Paul warns the Galatians not to use the freedom to which they have been called as "an opportunity for the flesh." Rather they are to become as slaves to one another through love (Gal 5:13). Barrett understands love to be the opposite of flesh and "Flesh . . . means self-centred existence, egocentric existence; not specifically a proclivity to carnal sins (as we call them), but a concern focused upon oneself."[101] The freedom to which Christians have been called is the freedom from self demonstrated in the crucifixion of Christ on behalf of others. This awareness has a profound impact on Paul's ethical view because it is the basis for all his thought. Christian ethics become, therefore, the ethics of grace.

For Paul freedom in Christ and the love of Christ become the final arbiters in resolving moral dilemmas. Love and freedom together recognize the flux and change of the human situation. Freedom recognizes the vast number of courses of action that may be taken by one justified by faith in Christ, while love identifies the potential consequences for others. If harm to another results from a specific act then the Christian who performs that act is not free in Christ. The tyranny of the self has triumphed over the pursuit of God's will. It is faith in God's saving mercy which makes this freedom from self possible.[102]

Based on these observations we might suggest that Enslin misses the mark when he says, "Paul, though free, was ready to sacrifice his freedom to the claims of brotherhood; so must the other Christians. Christianity consummated the ethics of self-realization by the ethics of self-sacrifice."[103] Paul never suggests that one sacrificed one's freedom in Christ by responding to the claims of brotherhood. Temporal rights and privileges may be surrendered but these are not the stuff of self-realization or of Christian freedom. Freedom without service is merely the tyranny of the self and cannot be Christian. Service without love born of Christian freedom risks becoming redundant and irrelevant (I Cor 13:3).

The willingness to serve others reflects the truth of self-realization in Christ: the paradox of Christian selflessness.

This paradox is reflected in Paul's own experience and self-understanding. He "boasted in his infirmities" and clearly saw himself as an exemplar of self-denial. Nevertheless, he asserted his apostolic authority whenever necessary and also understood this as part of his service to others for the sake of the gospel. Thus the undercurrent of arrogance and even authoritarianism in his writings is overcome by his endorsement of the principles of selflessness and "other-directedness" which he sees as essential to authentic Christian existence. This is most apparent in his writings to the Galatians and the Corinthians, less so in Romans, which is directed to a community with whom he had no personal contact. Despite this ambivalence, we discern in Paul a genuine concern to place the interests of others first, often at significant personal cost to himself. There is no hint that he strives after selfish gain even in the defence of his apostolic authority. The dilemma of Paul is to practice self-denial, *and* at the same time encourage it in others. He strives to maintain both his authoritative position within the community and his role as a servant of the gospel and of others. His epistles clearly illustrate the importance of the servant-ethic as characteristic of the early Christians' self-understanding.

According to Paul, then, when believers understand themselves to be "free in Christ" this liberty is ideally manifested in self-conscious and voluntary "other-directedness." The interests of the self are subordinated to the interests of others. To behave as a δοῦλος reveals that one has placed oneself in God's hands and is totally reliant upon him.[104] It is for him, and him alone, to decide who deserves honor. Christians are called to serve through their love and freedom in Christ. As Pheme Perkins points out in the quotation at the beginning of this chapter, the problem for Paul, and Christians in general, is determining how to walk according to the Spirit in specific situations. The freedom Christians have achieved in Christ, according to Paul, liberates them for service on behalf of others. While there are no rules of conduct that can be applied in every situation, the principle that the interests of others rather than of the self are to be paramount guides every ethical decision. Freedom in Christ is liberation from self.

Chapter V

THE SERVANT-ETHIC IN OTHER NEW TESTAMENT WRITINGS

The servant-ethic points to a strong ethical link between the Synoptic gospels, the Johannine writings, and the undisputed Pauline epistles. We shall now turn to the remainder of the New Testament to see if the chain is as secure in those texts, and if it is not, what elements of the servant-ethic, if any, are evident.

The Servant-Ethic in Acts

As we have noted above, the servant-ethic proceeds from a radical transformation of the heart, a μετάνοια. In Acts there are two passages which illustrate both the success and failure of such a transformation and the consequences in terms of the servant-ethic. The first passage is found in Acts 8:9–24 and describes Simon Magus' conversion and subsequent encounter with Peter. This passage is important for two reasons: it illustrates how submitting to the wishes of others must never contradict the will of God, and also how God does not require money and possessions but the heart and will of an individual.

Simon's request to receive the power to bestow the Holy Spirit is bluntly rebuffed by Peter. Peter understands the limits of his ability to serve Simon. Even to suggest that it is possible for Simon to receive such power in return for money would constitute disobedience to God. The fact that Simon believes such ἐξουσία can be bought leads to the second point. Peter admonishes Simon to repent so that he might be forgiven. Simon has not yet learnt what it truly means to repent and therefore what it means to be a Christian. He has been too dazzled by apostolic power, and the desire to have it for himself, to be able to come to an understanding that his own self must be abandoned to God. His ambition and self-will have not been surrendered. He seeks to be served rather than to serve. Peter's words "Your silver perish with you" reminds the reader that it is folly to think that money and possessions have real value in the context of God's kingdom (Cf. Matt 6:19–21; Mark 10:21; Luke 12:33–34; Jas 5:1–3; I Tim 6:17–19).[1] Despite his apparent belief and baptism, Simon has yet to yield absolutely to God. And it is there that Luke leaves the reader. The story of Simon recalls the episode about the ruler in Luke 18:18–25. While the ruler could not abandon his material wealth for the sake of eternal life, Simon believes that the riches of the Kingdom can be bought with his money. Possessions and the hunger for status have overpowered both individuals, making it almost impossible for them to yield to the will of God. The reader never learns whether either man finally acquiesces. The fact that Peter does not respond to Simon's request for prayer reflects, according to Conzelmann, Luke's uneasiness about the situation: "Luke does not report Simon's apostasy, nor could he make the well-known rival into a Christian."[2]

The second passage is found in Acts 16:25–34 and describes the conversion of Paul and Silas' jailer. The response of the jailer to the pair's refusal to escape his custody following the earthquake is a prime example of how the transformation of one's heart following repentance makes the servant-ethic integral to the Christian life. The jailer's conversion is a six step process of inquiry (v. 30), hearing the gospel (vv 31–32), service (he washed their wounds, v. 33), acceptance (he was baptized, v. 33), service (he brought them up to his house and set food before them, v. 34) and rejoicing (v. 34). This is the clearest instance in Acts of how an affirmative reaction to the gospel brings about an ethical response in turn. While it is certainly possible that the jailer could have been moved by gratitude and compassion to wash and feed Paul and Silas, it is important that in this passage such service is intimately linked with his conversion. His baptism is bracketed by his acts of service to the two prisoners. The jailer's behavior is similar to that of Lydia in Acts 16:15 who invites Paul and his company to stay at her home following her baptism (16:14–15). Such service to others is highlighted by the sharing of goods practised by Christians in Acts 2:43–45 and 4:32–37. Here, those who are in need benefit as the wealthier believers relinquish property and goods to be distributed by the apostles.

In Acts, the gospel spreads outwards from Jerusalem to capture the hearts of the Gentiles and the world. It is this story that Luke recounts and, therefore, explicit ethical instruction is sparse. The statement that "It is more blessed to give than to receive" in Paul's speech to Christians at Miletus is one notable exception (Acts 20:35). Nevertheless hints of the servant–ethic are discernable that go beyond the Hebrews' willingness to make arrangements for the Hellenist widows to be included in the daily food distribution (Acts 6). This is, however, an interesting incident because the apostles show a certain unwillingness to perform the more mundane tasks of service within the community. Thus seven are appointed to take responsibility for the disposition of community goods. Luke T. Johnson points out that once their selection is complete we hear no more of them performing such tasks—they too, like the Twelve, become "ministers of the Word." Johnson explains this discrepancy because Luke relates spiritual authority to power over possessions which is transferred from the Twelve to the Hellenistic missionaries. "It is awkward; once the image is established, he forgets it and talks about the reality of spiritual power."[3] Here, if nothing else, we see a clear example within the tradition of how the ideal of servanthood remains unrealized as community members bicker over authority and service.

The Servant-Ethic in Colossians

The authorship of the epistle to the Colossians is disputed by many (e.g. Eduard Schweizer),[4] and accepted unreservedly by others (e.g. C.F.D. Moule).[5] The vocabulary, style and theology of Colossians differs from that of the Pauline epistles discussed above, but it is not inconceivable that Paul is indeed the author; early Christians certainly believed this to be the case.[6]

In Col 1:24–29, Paul describes how his suffering is on behalf of the Colossian Christians and reflects his role as a servant (διάκονος) of the church.[7] More remarkably, Paul characterizes his suffering as completing "what is lacking in Christ's afflictions" (1:24). F.F. Bruce explicitly relates this verse with the portrayal of the Suffering Servant in Isaiah, who, in the "history of interpretation" first represents corporate Israel, then the individual Jesus Christ, and then the body of the Church. "The Servant's sufferings are...to be carried on by the disciples of Christ—at least by one of them, Paul himself."[8] For Bruce, the suffering of Paul (and any other Christian), insofar as he is part of one body, the Church, of which Christ is the head, means that Christ himself suffers. "And as Christ Himself suffers in His members, this suffering of theirs may be regarded as a filling up of Christ's personal suffering."[9]

Bruce also draws attention to another possible interpretation which, if it can be maintained, is more pertinent to our study. He points out that Paul might be suggesting that his own suffering fulfills more of the quota of hardship to be endured so that his fellow Christians in Colossae will not have to endure so much.[10] Paul understands his sufferings to be for the sake of his fellow Christians, the Church, the body of Christ. He has become a διάκονος of the Church (v. 25), so as "to make the word of God fully known." Schweizer believes Paul's designation of himself as διάκονος of the church tells against the authenticity of the epistle.[11] Paul, however, as we have seen above, is very conscious of the role of Christians as διάκονοι and δοῦλοι, and it may be that the use of the word office (οἰκονομία) has led Schweizer to understand διάκονος as an ecclesiastical position, rather than a description of Paul's role as he serves his fellows in his suffering. Paul's "office" is not διάκονος but to "make the word of God fully known." He undertakes this office as a servant of the church.[12] Paul makes sense of his sufferings in prison by seeing them as part of his service to his fellow-Christians.

Paul describes the service his readers should render others in Col 3:12–15. They are to be compassionate, kind, humble, meek, patient and forgiving. Above all they are to love one another in order to preserve harmony. The Colossian Christians are to put off the old nature (3:10) and put on that which is fitting for God's elect.

Much of the epistle to the Colossians involves polemic against what Meeks terms a "deviant form of Christianity."[13]   The epistle is concerned with encouraging its readers to close ranks against heretical tendencies and to maintain a unified community. Colossians also illustrates the idea of freedom from old ways of thinking about religious principles and ideas (Col 2:20–23). This pursuit of unity and the transforming liberation in Christ are illustrated in the two different uses of the word ταπεινοφροσύνη (humility), which in 2:18 and 23 refers to heretics and in 3:12 to Christians.[14] We shall examine this more closely, because most commentators agree that in the first two instances the word is a technical term.

In his article on "Humility and Angelic Worship in Col 2:18," Fred O. Francis points out that most scholars and commentators are satisfied with suggesting that the ταπεινοφροσύνη of 2:18, 23 cannot be the same as that in 3:12 and the reference in the first two verses is to false humility.[15] Francis concludes that in 2:18,23 the word is a technical term of the writer's opponents and offers much evidence from various texts, primarily Hermas and Tertullian, where the word is used for ascetic devotion. He also points to other texts where fasting is accompanied by divine visions.[16] The main problem with this evidence is that it tends to be late, much later than any would date Colossians. That does not of course mean that the term is not technical in 2:18, 23. We have to consider, however, its relationship with the same term in 3:12, where we assume it is used in the everyday sense. The possibility remains that the word means the same thing in all three verses; that is, general self-abasement, but that the distinguishing feature of 3:12 is the readers' status as ἐκλεκτοὶ τοῦ θεοῦ. The ταπεινοφροσύνη of 2:18 and 23 is of no avail because it is not done with reference to the κεφαλή, to Christ, and is, therefore, self-indulgent (2:23b).[17]

In 3:12 the word is used in a list of things a Christian is to "put on." The context reveals both the need for mutual service within the community, and for forgiveness toward others "as the Lord has forgiven you" (v. 13).   The relationship between the readers and God and Christ points the way. To be holy and elect one must be humble, compassionate, meek and kind to others, especially fellow-Christians.   Toward outsiders Christians should conduct themselves "wisely," although there is no direct admonition to love or serve them. The important thing is to maintain unity within the church, especially in the face of heretical opposition.

The Servant-Ethic in Ephesians

In Ephesians concerns about unity in the community are also paramount and again readers are exhorted to display appropriate behavior towards each other.

Eph 4:1–3 calls believers to lead a life of lowliness (ταπεινοφροσύνη), meekness, patience, forbearance, unity and peace. It is almost certain that the author of Ephesians has used Col 3:12–15 as a basis for these verses.[18] As Wengst says, these verses encourage ecumenical unity by admonishing Christians to strive after harmony within the community.[19] By "forbearing one another in love" they practice the servant-ethic by "putting up with" each other. The use of the verb ἀνήκω has connotations of endurance. The Ephesian Christians are to tolerate each other rather than seeking to rebuff or repudiate others. The construction in Ephesians also recalls the inversion of the traditional order that the gospel brings about. To be worthy of one's election one must be lowly. The context of the verse not only encourages unity but also reminds readers of the work of Christ.

Eph 5:21 also reminds readers of Christ when the writer tells them to submit to one another. This verse directly precedes the Ephesian *Haustafel*, a block of traditional paranesis that serves primarily in Ephesians to illustrate the relationship between Christ and the Church (23–33). Thus, after the author tells readers to submit to one another "out of reverence for Christ," he seeks to remind them that Christ gave himself up for the Church (v. 25). While Christ is the κεφαλή, he is also the one who gave surrendered himself on behalf of the Church.[20] Christians, therefore, are called to mutual submission out of reverence for Christ, because they should demonstrate the love that leads to self-sacrifice on behalf of others. Thus the placement of v. 21 immediately before the expanded *Haustafel* links it with the comparison between marriage and Christ and the Church.

Eph 4:32–5:2 perhaps echoes the servant-ethic most clearly. Here the readers are called to mutual kindness, imitating God in his forgiveness and remembering the love that Christ displayed in his sacrifice on their behalf. It is this element of self-sacrifice that is most pertinent to our theme and it is notable that in Ephesians it also occurs in a discussion of household relationships and calls the dominant partner to be willing to practice self-sacrifice on behalf of the other (5:25–28). It would be dangerous to push the analogy too far here. It seems that the author is more interested, based on the overall thrust of the letter, in explaining Christ's relationship to the Church than in sketching the ideal marriage.

The Servant-Ethic in the Pastoral Epistles

In the Pastoral epistles little is said of serving the interests of others. Moral and ethical concerns are addressed generally using exhortations which are considered normative and are to be applied universally.[21] The ethics described is primarily one of individual godliness and much is made of the moral qualifications of those seeking ecclesiastical office (I Tim 3:1–13; 5:9–22; Tit 1:7–9). Interestingly, little is made of these officers' responsibilities to serve the interests of others, although widows who seek to be enrolled should have performed "good deeds"—demonstrated, in part, by their hospitality and the act of washing the feet of the saints (I Tim 5:10). As Furnish points out, the nature of Christian love is somewhat diminished in these letters and that love appears most frequently in lists of virtues: "In these lists 'love' invariably stands as simply one among several desirable characteristics of the Christian life."[22] Quarrelsomeness and anger are forbidden, nevertheless, but more on the grounds that such behavior is unseemly and inappropriate than out of genuine concern and empathy for one's fellows (I Tim 2:8; 3:3; Tit 3:2–3).

Nevertheless, as Barrett says, "truly Christian motives do underlie the ethical teaching of the Pastorals, though it must be admitted that these are sometimes far from evident."[23] The pastoral epistles reflect some traces of the servant-ethic. Much is made, for example, of the responsibility of the community for the poor, especially widows. As far as possible families are to care for their own but the church can be called upon to provide for widows. Schrage deplores the fact that moral judgment is involved in this process and it is true that certain conditions are applied in I Tim 5:3–16 to distinguish those who are eligible to receive benefits from the church and those who are not.[24]

I Timothy also cautions against making too much of personal wealth. The wealthy are to be "rich in good deeds, liberal and generous" mindful that true riches come from God (6:17–19). Likewise, the epistle to Titus concludes with the exhortation to "do good deeds so as to help cases of urgent need" (3:14).[25] While the Pastorals epistles do not reflect the servant-ethic as clearly as we would perhaps expect, this concluding admonition brings the Pastoral epistles into the realm of the Christian servant-ethic.

The Servant-Ethic in Hebrews

As Leonhard Goppelt says, the paranesis of Hebrews concentrates "on the warning against irreversible apostasy."[26] In terms of the servant-ethic, however, the pertinent passages in Hebrews look forward to the rewards of the faithful rather than the judgment of those who deliberately forfeit the grace of God. Scattered throughout the latter chapters of Hebrews we find those texts which bespeak an attitude of "other-directedness" and its consequences (6:10–12; 10:32–39; 11:24–26; 12:14; 13:1–3, 16). The servant-ethic, to be sure, is not paramount in the writer's mind; there is much greater attention paid to the need for faithfulness.[27] Nevertheless, especially as the epistle enters its final chapters, elements of the servant-ethic filter through as the writer seeks to encourage Christians in faithfulness, obedience and endurance.

In Hebrews, then, service to God is paramount rather than service to others. There are traces of ethical content in Hebrews, however, many of which have a bearing on our discussion. Chapter 13 of Hebrews is filled with ethical exhortation and consequently is considered an appendix by many. But we also find an explicit reference to serving the saints in 6:10, encouragement about mutual love and good works (10:24) and concern for imprisoned brethren (10:34) in the earlier chapters. The servant-ethic is implicit in each of these texts. In 6:10 the readers are assured that the just nature of God implies that he will not forget their "service for the saints." Despite this, Jack Sanders finds little ethical content in Hebrews that is exemplary, beyond general summonses to good citizenship. He concludes that the lack of eschatological urgency in Hebrews leads, in chapter 13, to a simple recitation of examples of behavior that "everybody knows is right and good."[28] Sanders' overall thesis relies heavily upon the extent to which eschatological expectations provoke the ethical discussion of the New Testament writers. When a particular writer does not display a keen sense of eschatological urgency Sanders usually finds nothing notable in that individual's ethical reflection. When eschatological expectations are heightened (as in the Synoptic accounts of Jesus' teaching), the ethics are "invalid."[29]

Sanders says that the "ethical concern" Hebrews is "strictly religious": the concern "that the congregation 'hold fast' to its 'confession.'"[30] He goes on to say that "the author of Hebrews thinks of 'love and good works' . . . as a subdivision of the broader category of keeping the faith." This is exactly the point of the servant-ethic. Subordinating one's own interests to those of others is not undertaken because such a stance is somehow "good and right" in itself but because one is a Christian. Becoming a Christian adds a new dimension to ethical behavior. Certain aspects of ethics, of which the servant-ethic is perhaps the most notable, become paramount. Faith is seen as the foundation for doing what is "right and good" and points to a more demanding ethics than would be required by "good citizenship."

Sanders recognizes this in his discussion of chapter 13 and disputes that the requirements listed there are the natural ethical outcome of the author's theological reflections:

> The individual items of chapter 13 are there, not because the author has reflected on the ethical implications of his theological argument and come up with them, but rather because he already knows they are the right thing to do, already knows this because they are stock Christian teaching.[31]

This is, of course, exactly true, and as such should not be presented as an indictment of Hebrews' ethics. The purpose of paranesis and exhortation is not to promote and justify new and extreme behavior but rather to encourage others to do the mundane, the difficult and the self-sacrificing, often by citing motives that are guaranteed a certain appeal to one's audience. To please God, to seek his approval in faith and hope in light of the new covenant, is the ostensible motive of the echoes of the servant-ethic we hear in Hebrews. This is true even if these echoes do not directly radiate from the theological argument the author of Hebrews has presented prior to chapter 13.[32] The focus of the motive in Hebrews shifts from Jesus as paradigmatic of self-denial and other-directedness, as we find in the gospels and in Paul, to one of fulfilling the terms of the new covenant God has established through Christ. This is not to imply that Christ does not fulfill a paradigmatic role in Hebrews, for he undoubtedly does. As Schrage says, "[Christ] is not only the 'pioneer' or source of eternal salvation (2:10; 5:9–10), but also its model."[33] In addition, of those named in chapter 11, who "died in faith," both Moses "who chose to share the ill-treatment of the people of God" (11:25)[34] and Rahab, who "gave friendly welcome to the spies," conduct themselves in ways which may recall the servant-ethic. By this I mean that they willingly put aside their own interests in favor of those of others. Their conduct, moreover, does not serve as ethical motivation, but rather as an illustration of faith. It is this faithfulness, however, as it manifests itself in the Christians addressed by Hebrews, which gives rise to brotherly love, hospitality, and concern for those in prison.[35]

Likewise, there is no explicit missionary impetus for the ethic as it appears in Hebrews, unlike I Peter. The Christians Hebrews addresses are not explicitly told to fulfill the ethical obligations set out in the epistle in order to promote the gospel outside the church. In fact, in Hebrews, missionary activity seems particularly muted. 13:2 may encourage a willingness to be open to strangers on missionary grounds but the second half of the verse seems to militate against such an interpretation. Nevertheless, in 12:14 readers are encouraged to "strive for peace with all men," an admonition which is linked in the second part of the verse with "holiness." Peace is a worthy goal in itself and there is no explicit missionary motive; however, such behavior may be encouraged to moderate the suffering the readers face at the hands of non-Christians or to overcome divisiveness within the community.[36]

Hebrews concentrates on theological themes rather than ethical exhortation. What ethical instruction there is, however, is "other-directed" and includes brotherly love and hospitality. In addition, the faithful endurance of the addressees often involves the foregoing of retaliation and vengeance in the hope of receiving a greater reward in the future (10:32–36; 11:25; 12:2–3).

The ethical horizon of Hebrews tends to extend only to the limits of the community. Beyond that there is no instruction other than to endure hostility and to strive for peace with others (12:14). Within the community there is to be special concern for those in prison. In two places the author reminds the readers of their solidarity with those in prison (10:34a; 13:3) In the first instance the author calls for compassion (συνεπαθήσατε) toward the imprisoned, and in the second, the need for total empathy with the incarcerated (ὡς συνδεδεμένοι). In the context of the letter these verses serve to place the suffering and endurance of the readers into a larger perspective: not only should one joyfully and faithfully accept one's own hardships but one should also be acutely aware of and respond to the suffering of others. These two verses alone lift the ethical concerns of Hebrews from the realm of deportment "equated with good citizenship," to use a phrase of Jack T. Sanders, to a moral scheme which understands "other-directedness" and empathy as paramount.

The Servant-Ethic in James

The epistle of James is one of the most controversial books of the New Testament. Its canonicity was questioned throughout the early Church and Luther's famous verdict—an epistle of "straw"—still finds echoes in scholarship today.[37] James stands in tension with Paul primarily because he links "works" with justification, but also because the epistle lacks any explicit—and many would say implicit—christological statements. Leander E. Keck, for example, says that despite James's insistence on faith *and* works, the moral obligation in Paul is stronger because it is grounded in Christ's death and resurrection.[38] Some have questioned whether James is in fact a Christian document, suggesting that it is rather a Hellenistic Jewish text that has undergone interpolation at 1:1 and 2:1.[39] Whether or not this is true—and scholarship now seems to lean away from this possibility—the epistle was understood by some Christians to have value and authority. Dibelius' characterization of James as paranesis seems sensible even if this leads him to the conclusion that the letter is late, despite the "Jewish" character of the epistle.[40]

The words δοῦλος and διάκονος do not occur in the epistle, except at 1:1, where the author styles himself a "slave of God." Nevertheless the epistle contains many exhortations to selflessness and service to others that resonate with the servant-ethic already delineated in the gospels and Pauline writings.

One possible example of the servant-ethic is the exhortation in 2:8 to fulfill the love commandment, which James describes as the royal law. This royal law forbids partiality to the rich. This prohibition is illustrated by 2:1–7 and James's condemnation of those who favor the rich and disregard the poor in the συναγωγή. James opposes these practices not by claiming the impartiality of God as a paradigm—as we find in Matt 5:43–48—but by picturing God as actively on the side of the poor. Jouette M. Bassler understands 2:5 differently. She says, "He grounds this exhortation (2:1–4) in Deuteronomic fashion by pointing to God's own impartiality in choosing 'the poor of this world to be rich in faith and heirs of the kingdom which he has promised to those who love him.'"[41] I would argue however that God serves here as a model, not of impartiality, but of favoring and honoring the poor. For James partiality means honoring the rich because they are rich. The opposite idea of impartiality then becomes displaying respect to the poor. In other words, the poor are to receive equal respect and their needs are to be cared for. This is confirmed by 2:14–17, in which James reminds his readers of their responsibility to the naked and hungry in their community, and also in 1:27 in his description of "true religion." Again we hear echoes of Matthew and the judgment on those who fail to respond to others' needs (Matt 25:31–46).

James's call to impartiality then becomes a summons to serve, or at least to honor, the poor in order to counter apparent mistreatment of the poor. Some believers have made the church into a tool of persecution.[42] James reminds his readers in 2:6 that not only have they dishonored the poor but actively have furthered the ambitions of the rich who are their oppressors. It is difficult to accept that 2:1–7 is not addressed to a specific tendency with which James is familiar. Thus, although the epistle may be characterized as general paranesis these verses seem to apply to a specific situation. James Adamson, for example, who dates the epistle very early, sees in the reference to courts "habitual harassment" of Christians by Jews, the same sort Paul engaged in prior to his conversion.[43] Dibelius expressly cautions against such a reading. He says that 2:2–4 is an example "and not a special case which has motivated the introductory admonition."[44] This would be easy to accept were it not for v. 6 and the reference to the readers being dragged into court. While I, like Dibelius, do not believe that the reference is to systematic persecution of Christians by either Jews or Gentiles, the inclusion of court-action with the vaguer references to oppression and blasphemy points to a more specific situation than Dibelius allows.

James seeks to address a community in which wealth, social status and prestige determine one's position in the eyes of others. This is not only partiality but is against God's law, and the author reminds his readers that such activity renders them liable for judgment (2:13). While Dibelius is correct in cautioning against inferring a crisis in the community or communities on the basis of Jas 2:2–7, it is clear that James sees the true Christian community as one that rejects, or rather should reject, "worldly" standards of honor and prestige. Such a picture of the church does not constitute an explicit call to the servant-ethic. It is indicative, however, of the attitude that usual perspectives concerning status and esteem are to be rejected. It is the attitude which insists that social status and wealth are not evidence of God's approval: the more lowly position should be deliberately sought.

In James the figure of Christ is not mentioned as paradigmatic, an incentive found in Paul and the Gospels for the servant-ethic. The readers are to serve the poor in order to practice true religion and thereby incur God's favor (e.g. 1:27; 2:15–17). For James the coming of the Lord is at hand (5:7–8), but this expectation is to be tempered with patience. Practically every section of paranesis in the epistle points to the judgment, blessing or reward from God as a consequence of action (e.g. 1:12. 15, 25; 2:13; 3:1; 4:10–12; 5:1, 9, 19–20).[45]

The emphasis upon honoring and helping the poor while eschewing snobbery shifts the focus of the servant-ethic in James. James's readers are called upon to meet the temptation to disdain the poor with compassion and concrete aid. The limitations of James in terms of "other-directedness" are reflected in his uncompromising opposition to the rich and his implicit requirement of serving the poor. For James, on one level at least, salvation is achieved only through "enmity with the world" or, to put it more accurately, *not* through friendship with the world (4:4). James makes no mention that his readers should attempt to welcome more rich oppressors into the community. Piety, in James's view, manifests itself in rigorous regard for the welfare of others. James encourages his readers to feed and clothe the poor. Within the community, righteous action, born of wisdom, is to be the order of the day.[46] Conventional standards of those outside the community are to be eschewed when they serve to promote selfish gain, ambition and jealousy. The poor are to be served. In James, therefore, the limitations of what we have termed the servant-ethic are more sharply defined than in either Paul or the Gospels. James does not advocate submitting to and loving one's enemy unreservedly. James may be said to strike a cautionary note in taking the servant-ethic and the principle of other-directedness too far. The rich are not to be served and honored at the expense of the poor. The epistle points out how the servant-ethic may be abused should it become abject servility towards the rich for the sake of satisfying one's own snobbish instincts.

3:13–18 gives the foundation for James's ethic. Anyone who is wise will reveal his or her wisdom by works (3:13). True wisdom, the wisdom from above, precludes selfishness and ambition, and is manifested in peaceableness, mercy and reasonableness. Those who are wise, who seek to do God's will, are not jealous or ambitious; they seek to make peace. It is in these verses that the servant-ethic, or at least the underlying attitude of the ethic, is most clearly expounded in James. The word ἐριθεία (3:14), which is translated "selfish ambition" in the RSV, points, as Mitton says, to conduct that is clearly contrary to the servant-ethic. ᾿Εριθεία "is the determination to get what one wants in position and power, no matter what bitterness and ill-will are caused."[47] Such an attitude recalls that which Jesus opposed in his rebuke of James and John (Mark 10:42–45). True wisdom is the way to overcome the disorder and vile practises born of earthly or unspiritual wisdom. In his discussion of 3:17, Mitton says that "God's wisdom as bestowed on man reveals itself in conduct which is *pure* (ἀγνή). This means that it is free from self-interest and selfish ambition." While Mitton may be pushing the limits of the meaning of the Greek ἀγνή here it is clear that the overriding thrust of the passage in James is to promote a manner of conduct that bespeaks the servant-ethic. Thus Mitton has grounds to define "gentle" (ἐπιεικής) in the same verse as applying to the one who "does not stand on his own rights," which again recalls the servant-ethic.[48] James is a call to put into practise the consequences of faith in Christ, even if this is not explicitly stated in the letter. His emphasis upon the just treatment of the poor has made the epistle especially appealing in the context of liberation theology.[49]

The Servant-Ethic in I Peter

"Reading the first epistle of Peter immediately after the epistle of James...one suddenly gains the impression of being enveloped in a much more ardent glow of faith."[50] Schnackenburg continues, however, that like James "this writer's principal concern too is with religious moral exhortation."[51] I Peter encourages its readers to display appropriate behavior before others. Much of this behavior is constitutive of the servant-ethic.

The writer of I Peter is especially concerned with his readers' behavior in the sight of outsiders. At 2:12 he beseeches them to "maintain good conduct among the Gentiles."[52] Based on his examination of the literary structure of I Peter, David Kendall notes that doing good includes being submissive and honoring all persons (2:13–17; 3:1–2, 7, 8), suffering unjustly (2:18–19; 3:9–14; 4:1–6), repudiating vengeance (2:19–23; 3:9, 15–16; 4:1) and loving fellow believers (3:8; 4:7–11). "When believers 'do good' they prepare themselves for the consummation at the revelation of Christ and, in the process, their lives bear witness to God's grace before non-believers (2:12; 3:1–2)."[53] Part of this bearing witness, this conduct, involves respecting human institutions. In addition, when any of the readers are reviled or slandered, the abuse is to be suffered quietly (3:9, 13–16; 4:4–5, 14–16). Amongst themselves the readers are to have "unity of spirit, sympathy, love of the brethren, a tender heart and a humble mind" (3:8). They are to practice hospitality ungrudgingly (4:9), and the elders are not to domineer the group but are to be examples (5:1–3).

I Peter calls Christians to love one another and to behave appropriately towards those outside the fellowship, although there is no explicit reference to Lev 19:18 in the epistle.[54] Schrage believes there is no particular emphasis upon the law of love although φιλαδελφία is invoked repeatedly (1:22; 2:17; 3:8).[55] In I Peter "ungrudging" hospitality towards one's brothers and sisters is an expression of φιλαδελφία. As Schrage says, "'ungrudgingly' reminds us that hospitality can be... burdensome, costing both time and money and requiring selfless love."[56]

2:16–17 sums up the ethical content of the epistle. Furnish notes that 2:16 is the only reference to freedom in the epistle and, like Gal 5:13, it is paradoxically aligned with bondage.[57] In addition, the command πάντας τιμήσατε (honor everyone) shows that not only are the brethren to be loved but that believers have an ethical responsibility to all people.[58] As well as showing love to their brethren, believers are to show honor to all in their role as servants of God. As Allen Verhey says, "Faith exists as obedience, and obedience exists as love no less for Peter than for Paul."[59]

The emphasis upon enduring unjust suffering is part of the Petrine ethic. The motives for such suffering are varied but they have to do with the obedience to God which permeates the paranesis of the author (1:14,22). As Schnackenburg says, "The epistle puts forward an abundance of truly Christian motives for readiness to suffer and trial by suffering." In addition, Schnackenburg notes that the author tells slaves that "with God suffering is a grace (2:20)" and that at 3:17-18 the same argument applies to all believers.[60] The example of Christ's sufferings, however, is also allied with his ultimate vindication and glorification, which inspires hope (1:21; 4:13–14). There is, moreover, the implicit sense that Christians should endure suffering as Christ did as a means of honoring or revering him (3:14–15).[61]

Finally, the selfless conduct of Christians no matter what abuse they may face, and their rigorous refusal to disrupt the institutions of society, including the patriarchal household and government, would, the author believes, bring others into the community of Christians.[62] I Peter, then, is more compromising than James in accepting the social structure of society at large. Established human authority in the domestic and political spheres is to be respected even if believers incur unjust suffering. The self-interest of individuals is to be surrendered in the interest of bearing witness to the truth of the Gospel, which in the long run will serve the interests of society as a whole.[63]

This strategic, missionary motivation for self-denial in I Peter does, however, have some drawbacks. While the focus for ethics in I Peter is much broader than, say in James, there are dangers inherent in I Peter's approach. Being subject to every human institution, for example, leads to an especially notable development in the Petrine *Haustafel*. The *Haustafeln* texts in the New Testament have often been criticized as examples of how early Christianity capitulated to social institutions and mores that were burdensome for many people. I Peter is perhaps most susceptible to such a critique.[64] In I Peter there is no address to masters to balance the one to slaves and in the address to slaves Christ is seen as paradigmatic of the suffering slaves are counselled to accept with equanimity. While this does not actually give approval to the institution of slavery, some argue that it accords it connotations of nobility since patient endurance of suffering is advocated. Some find this distressing, although others are able to infer from this text a subversion of slavery:

> Subordination now signifies submission to *God's will* and solidarity with the obedient servant Lord (2:18–25). In this brotherhood all members are co-heirs and household stewards of God's grace (3:7; 4:10). While this represents no frontal assault on the institution of the Hellenistic household, it also constitutes no case of total capitulation to pagan values.[65]

Jack Sanders, however, criticizes the *Haustafeln* for corrupting the *agape* ethic found in Paul. For Sanders, the "other-directedness" of Paul's ethic disappears in the *Haustafeln*: "All interest in one's fellow man is out, concern for living up to a standard of personal submission *for one's own sake*, is in."[66] Sanders is correct that the slave's patience in suffering, according to I Peter, will ultimately bring God's approval and that there is no explicit benefit for the unjust master, but he is too harsh when he suggests that "all interest in one's fellow-man is out." This is revealed in two ways: First, the role of Christ as paradigmatic is the role of one who suffers unjustly on behalf of others (2:21; 3:18). Believers who endure slander and other sufferings at the hands of outsiders are promised that these very opponents will come to a realization of the truth (2:12). Second, the address to wives explicitly calls for submission before husbands in the hope that some of them at least "may be won without a word." This emphasizes the insistence throughout I Peter that the truth of the gospel is to be made evident through the behavior of Christians rather than merely through their speech.

The idea that it is especially the unjust suffering and submissive behavior of Christians that illustrates God's will and glory to non-believers is evident elsewhere in I Peter (1:12, 15; 3:1–2; 4:4–6). This could, and does, lead to the acceptance of injustice. This, however, is the price that must be paid, according to I Peter. Such suffering finds its paradigm in the one who paid a far greater price for the sake of many. It is one of the scandals of Christian history that I Pet 3:1–6 and its parallels (Col 3:18; Eph 5:22) have been used many times to induce a woman to remain in an abusive marriage "as is fitting in the Lord." That such marriages existed in the time I Peter was written is likely, if only because a woman had defied her pagan husband in becoming a Christian.[67] We cannot tell how much suffering a Christian woman would have to endure at the hands of her pagan husband before the early church would relieve her of her role as a "missionary." Even Paul, in I Cor 7:10–16, leaves the dissolution of the marriage in the hands of the unbeliever, although v. 11 seems to offer a woman a way out if necessary.

John Howard Yoder understands the calls to voluntary subordination in such texts as the *Haustafeln* to reflect how the messianic ethic preached by Jesus and taken up in the later apostolic tradition undermines the normative social order.[68] In cases that call for the submission of subordinate classes such as slaves, women and children it is not enough to point to the converse requirements of love and patience on the part of masters, husbands and parents. These texts have been used to justify cruelty and even hold the victim responsible for brutality suffered. There is no way to subdue this dimension of the text. All believers are called to serve others including those who find themselves already in the subordinate position, even if this involves unjust suffering. At the same time it would be wrong to suggest that the *Haustafeln* simply rationalize a hierarchical social order by lending it theological and christological support. The critique of the world as it is, the affirmation that social structures fail to reflect what God requires, is implied on every page of the New Testament. The self-understanding that calls for consistent service to others, whether they be pagan husbands or fellow Christians, undercuts the general human tendency of self-serving ambition. I Peter, then, with its emphasis on maintaining good conduct in society no matter what the cost in unjust suffering, endeavors to encourage believers to be living witnesses to the gospel in the hope that this will lead others to obey God.[69] According to I Peter, Christians in submission to God, yet also in freedom, must face, even suffer from, social injustice, in order to witness to the truth of the gospel.[70]

The author of I Peter, despite his emphasis upon φιλαδελφία, believes that selflessness transcends the boundaries of the community, as is evident in his insistence that the lives of Christians bear witness to the truth of the gospel. Commenting on 3:9, Schrage points out that in I Peter, "contrary to all common sense and logic, evil is to be answered with good, cursing with blessing."[71] Verhey summarizes the goal of such an approach as doing what is right "in terms of the Christian paranetic tradition and in terms of what is universally acknowledged as responsible conduct" rather than the Mosaic law. He asserts that:

> Indeed, to be freed for the service of God is to be freed to "be subject for the Lord's sake to every human institution" (2:13). It is God's will that Christians should live lives beyond any possible reproach. Such lives will silence their detractors and be serviceable to the missionary enterprise of the church.[72]

The servant-ethic in I Peter, then, is strategic. In essence, it seeks to turn enemies into friends.

Conclusions on the Remaining Books and the Servant-Ethic

As we move away from the Gospels and the undisputed letters of Paul we can see that the boundaries of the servant-ethic tend to turn inward towards others within the Christian community. Nevertheless, important aspects of the ethic continue to radiate out to the world at large. Even the Pastoral Epistles reveal echoes of the servant-ethic. Colossians and Ephesians, with their emphasis upon the transformation of human nature through belief in Christ, also show the particular foundation of New Testament ethics. This foundation is illustrated in Acts by the jailer and Simon Magus. The former responds to the truth of the gospel-message and his response is manifested in service. The latter seeks personal glory and therefore risks judgement. The most significant aspect of the ethic in the remaining texts is the call to endure unjust suffering at the hands of others. In I Peter such behavior has an explicit missionary impetus, while in Hebrews and James it is undertaken in the hope of future exaltation by God. We should remember that such a motive is also offered in the Gospels and we need not shirk from concluding that the promise of future reward encouraged many early Christians to endure injustice patiently. This is a testament to their faith and is described most explicitly in Hebrews, but also occurs in I Peter and even (!) James.

It is apparent that the writers of these three epistles found that their experience as Christians alienated them from the world at large. Their ethics reflect this alienation in their emphasis upon enduring injustice. For James the alienation is mirrored in a retreat from the values of the world (by eschewing snobbery and championing the poor), while Hebrews insists on special compassion for those who suffer in prison. I Peter is also aware of the need for faithful endurance of injustice but understands this as an opportunity for missionary activity. All three of these writers understand the Christian life to be one of personal sacrifice. They encourage their readers to continue to take up their crosses secure in the faith that "whoever loses his life" for the sake of the gospel will save it.

A Note on II Peter and Jude

In our investigation we have found at least traces of the servant-ethic in all parts of the New Testament, with the exception of II Peter and Jude. In these two epistles the sparse ethical content yields little concerning the servant-ethic. In II Peter the only text which is pertinent is 1:7 which encourages readers to supplement their "godliness with brotherly affection and brotherly affection with love." This is standard Christian paranesis and reflects how much such ideas permeate the consciousness of the writers of the New Testament. Likewise, in Jude 12 those who "boldly carouse together, looking after themselves" are obviously engaging in behavior inappropriate for Christians. They serve as an example of how not to behave, apparently because they satisfy selfish desires (follow their own passions, v. 16), rather than looking to the interests of others. In both these epistles the emphasis is upon avoiding the wicked ways of others and preserving the Christian life from worldly corruption. In essence they are the exceptions that prove the rule: The servant-ethic characterizes early

Christian paranesis, encouraging an extreme degree of self-denial and other-directedness.

Chapter VI

CONCLUSIONS AND IMPLICATIONS

The call to . . . service we find only in the presence of another, whose need is often the very occasion of our freedom. For it is through the need of another that the greatest hindrance to my freedom, namely my own self-absorption, is finally not so much overcome as rendered irrelevant.[1]

The sense that the interests of the self must be overcome or set aside if a believer is to abide as a Christian and in the will of God permeates the early Christian documents that we have covered. For many scholars this selflessness manifests itself as love (ἀγάπη). Scholars who seek to find a unifying ethical theme in the New Testament often focus on this. Love, however, has to be put into practice; it has to be expressed. Invariably these scholars come to the conclusion that to love largely means to serve others.

It is important to recognize also that the idea of love is not the most important element in the New Testament writings. While love is a significant theme in the New Testament, it does not constitute the central message. The person and message of Jesus do not provoke a call first to love, according to the New Testament, but rather a call to a fundamentally new orientation. Only after repentance (or conversion) has occurred can love become constitutive for Christian action: "The programmatic centre of Jesus' ministry was not the concept of love, but that of God's rule"[2] A similar viewpoint is found in Paul and John. According to the New Testament writers, Christian love does not and cannot proceed from a person unless he or she has come to an affirmative decision about the person of Jesus and his role in God's scheme. The ethics of the New Testament are worked out in light of the person of Jesus and the believer's response to him. The question is not how one should act but how the *believer* should act. Often, the believer should act in ways that any other person should act, whether they be Stoic, Jewish, or atheist. It is the grounds of this action that differs—for the earliest Christians it proceeded from a profound self-awareness of the requirement to serve others because of the reconciliation God achieved with humanity through Christ. Scholars such as John Howard Yoder speak of this reconciliation in terms of revolution and understand it to have profound implications for Christian ethics, even when those ethics do not greatly vary from those found in other traditions. Although the early Christians accepted the requirements of living up to one's role in society, "the meaning of that role was changed in substance by the stance of servanthood derived from the example and the teaching of Jesus himself." For Yoder the "revolution" occurs not in visible social reform but in the transformation that occurs in believers' self-understanding. Jesus' "motto of revolutionary subordination, of willing servanthood in the place of domination," achieves two ends while essentially leaving the social strata untouched. First, it allows those in subordinate social roles to accept their position without resentment and second, it persuades the person with more status to "forsake or renounce all domineering use of his status." Yoder says that now the subordinate person "becomes a free ethical agent when he voluntarily accedes to this subordination in the power of Christ instead of bowing to it either fatalistically or resentfully."[3] Eduard Lohse also acknowledges that the ethics of the New Testament writings include moral maxims found in other sources. It is how these maxims can be fitted in with service that makes them adaptable to the early Christian view of ethics. Lohse notes that love becomes the grounds for embracing moral principles: "That love that does not seek its own advantage, but the good of the other, places itself as the critical orientation point for evaluating the variety of traditional ethical maxims in circulation."[4]

The earliest believers, as their views are expressed throughout the New Testament, then, saw service to others as the predominant characteristic of the Christian life. While the content, motives and limitations of this characteristic vary from book to book, there is an inherent coherence in each which can be demonstrated.

The Content of the Servant-Ethic in the New Testament

There are four primary elements that constitute the servant-ethic in the New Testament writings. We shall consider each in turn before identifying the underlying connection.

1. The Call to Love Others

In the Synoptic gospels the neighbor is the other person. That person may be friend or enemy but in every case the believer is called to show love unrestrictedly. The Synoptic gospels are forthright in their portrayal of the stance of the self before others. Following Jesus requires extreme self-denial. The interests and even the demands of others are to come first.

In the Johannine writings the neighbor is primarily restricted to those within the Christian community. Loving service takes place above all within this context and is exemplified by the footwashing episode.

In Paul love of neighbor refers most often to the believer's Christian fellows, but he also insists that it must extend beyond the community. Paul's ethic includes accommodation to the scruples and claims of others. For Paul the Christian life requires that one stand ready to serve others.

In I Peter Christians are called to honor all people and to love the brotherhood. In I Pet 3:9 they are called to return evil and reviling with blessings. Likewise in James believers are called upon to offer practical assistance to those in need (1:27; 2:14–17), which is a mark of a living faith and true religion.

2. The Call to Serve the Poor

Related to the call to love others is the requirement to take on a special responsibility towards the poor. (Of all ethical injunctions, almsgiving seems to have a common emphasis in all religious traditions. It is one area in particular where the human religious impulse strikes a universal note.) As we have noted above, the poor play an important role throughout the biblical literature, in revealing the mercy of God. Service to the poor becomes service to God because it manifests his mercy. There is also a sense that Christians are to identify with the impoverished, at least in the sense of living without reference to material wealth. Luke gives this injunction special prominence with, for example, the emphases in the story of Zaccheus (19:1–10) and the accounts in Acts 2:44–47 and 4:32–35 of the distribution of surplus possessions to those in need. The other two Synoptic gospels also reflect a concern for those who are without money, often in the context of alerting the believer to the danger of wealth that is not distributed (e.g., Mark 10:21). I John 3:17 and its insistence that love is expressed in concrete help towards one in need reflects a similar view, and that the practice is a primary focus of James hardly needs to be mentioned. Even I Timothy and its so-called bourgeois ethic insists that the wealthy must be generous (εὐμετάδοτος) and liberal (κοινωνικός) (6:17–19). Material wealth is no longer a means of security. The willingness to give, rather than to retain, one's possessions is a mark of the servant-ethic.

3. The Call to Surrender One's Rights

In the Bible justice becomes the manifestation of God's righteousness and mercy.[5] The servant-ethic advances justice by calling one into conformity with the will of God, the God of justice. Curiously but necessarily this means that on some occasions justice forbids that one's own rights should be asserted in its name. The New Testament writings frequently call their readers to go beyond an understanding of justice based on external dictates of equity between persons, at least insofar as the self is concerned.

There is also a sense, then, in which justice as equity becomes as it were a non-issue, rather than being superseded, especially as manifested in the servant-ethic. Here rights and formal duties fade from view. Believers ignore the claims of justice insofar as they no longer seek their own *rights* but look to the *interests* of others. Justice remains with the one alone who is just—God. The only "rights" that a Christian has are those granted by God. But the believer can make no claim on God. The gift of the truth as manifested in Jesus Christ demands reception or rejection. If the gift is acknowledged the believer stands in the realization that every act must now be conducted in light of divine grace. There is no room now for selfish ambition or arrogance. The claims of others supersede the claims of self even when the former are unfair. Thus the believer is sometimes called to go the second mile (Matt 5:41), relinquish the right to sue (I Cor 6:1–7), and even abandon the opportunity to escape unfair imprisonment (Acts 16:25–34).

The limitations of justice spring from within. Justice exists to determine the validity of competing claims within a community. In his discussion on "The Human Good," Bernard Lonergan notes that egoism is in conflict with the good of order and that the legal and judiciary systems can never fully contain the assertion of self. In his view the law becomes more tolerant since not every infraction can be dealt with. This leads not only to the deterioration of the good of order but it also means that justice is compromised and in "all likelihood it becomes to a greater or lesser extent the instrument of a class."[6] After a brief discussion of how such limitations in the application of justice eventually lead to cultural decline, Lonergan concludes:

> Finally, we may note that a religion that promotes self-transcendence to the point, not merely of justice, but of self-sacrificing love, will have a redemptive role in human society inasmuch as such love can undo the mischief of decline and restore the cumulative process of progress.[7]

For the earliest believers God alone is perfectly just. At the same time, as Josef Pieper explains, human beings can never make a claim on God because they owe their very existence to him. This is a debt that can never be fully discharged.[8] In his conclusion to his essay on justice he asserts that because injustice prevails it is necessary for the just person to give beyond what is strictly due.[9]

4. Rejection of Social Rank and Selfish Ambition

For those who would serve God by serving others there is no room for considerations of social position and rank. The fact that one is assured a place in the coming βασιλεία makes status and class in this age irrelevant. Pursuit of social recognition is rejected out of hand as contrary to God's will. This, of course, has implications for the status of Christian slaves in society as a whole, but it also underlines the basic equality of all Christians within the community. As far as the κοινωνία is concerned, mutual service and respect is to be practised. Attempts to bring worldly considerations of rank to bear within the community are rejected (e.g Mark 10:42–45; Matt 23:1–12; Rom 12:3,16; I Cor 4:6–13; II Cor 10:18; Phil 2:3; Jas 3:14). This is not to say that there was no consideration of rank or authority within the church as a whole. Paul, obviously because of pressure from opponents within the community, constantly asserts his authority as an apostle. The *Haustafeln* texts clearly do not reject social hierarchy even within the community. It is the preoccupation with rank and the seeking after it for selfish reasons rather than for the interests of others that is rejected throughout the New Testament.

5. Unifying Motif: Placing One's Interests Last

The underlying aspect of each of these four elements, love for others, service to the poor, surrender of rights and the rejection of selfish ambition, is the consistent requirement to subordinate one's own interests to those of others. Such self-subordination can be carried out in the confidence that the believer's own interests have already been taken care of by God. The interests of the self may thus be considered secondary to those of the other person. It is evident that the implications of such a requirement—self-abnegation, humility, forebearance and sacrifice—are least onerous for those who have full trust in God to provide and vindicate. Such trust arises from the motives for the servant-ethic.

The Motive to Place One's Interests Last

Although we have identified a consistent call to self-subordination throughout the New Testament writings it is the motives for this ethic and its consistency that makes it characteristic of the early Christian self-understanding. These motives number at least four, but again there is one pervasive element that unites them all.

1. Jesus Christ as Paradigm

Jesus is seen as paradigmatic for the servant-ethic in the sense that his ministry and death illustrate the supreme service he practised on behalf of others. Discipleship is the context for the servant-ethic—to follow Jesus is to become a servant of others. This does not mean, of course, that the disciples (or the earliest believers) understood themselves to be equal with Jesus in serving others. His role as a servant is pre-eminent and can never be emulated completely: "It could never occur to anyone that the way of a disciple was on the same level with that of Jesus. For they had all been taken by him on *his* way; they all merely shared *his* way."[10]   Believers are not to attempt to duplicate Jesus' service exactly, for this is obviously impossible, but they are to look to him for the example of how others are to be served (Matt 20:28; Mark 10:45; Luke 22:27; John 13:15; I Pet 2:21–24).   Paul sees such emulation in a particularly astute way and calls upon his readers to practise imitation (E.g., I Thess 1:5–6, 2:14; I Cor 4:16–17; 10:32–11:1; Phil 3:17).

2. The Preservation of Unity

The earliest believers were called to faith in Jesus Christ in community. From the inception of Jesus' religious movement the idea of fellowship, of κοινωνία, was central. When Paul tells the Corinthian Christians about their counterparts in Macedonia who gave beyond their means willingly and liberally, he is illustrating how the Macedonians' self-understanding as servants of others promotes the unity of the church. Such an act is a manifestation of God's grace (II Cor 8:1), and follows the example of Christ (II Cor 8:9). The Macedonians want to share in the ministry (διακονία) to the saints (v.4). L.S. Thornton notes that the significance of the contribution was not simply social but "was in harmony with God's will and was a direct product of his grace." It was an illustration of the "essence of κοινωνία" which involves mutual self-giving.[11]

3. To Ensure the Spread of the Gospel

When Paul speaks of accommodating himself to all in I Cor 9:19–23, his stated motive is not to make the situation more comfortable for himself but to ensure that the Gospel gets a sympathetic hearing. When Paul says that for the sake of the Gospel he becomes all things to all men he illustrates his principle of accommodating the interests, scruples and wishes of others, so far as possible. A similar sentiment is expressed in the Petrine call for wifely submission (I Pet 3:1–6) in which the motive is not to relieve the awkwardness (or suffering) of women married to unbelievers, but rather to induce the husbands to see the truth of the Gospel. For a community whose self-awareness was founded upon the truth that it believed resided in the Gospel, it is hardly surprising that sacrifice was called for in order to disseminate the good news as much as possible. (It is interesting to note that in the Synoptic writings this motive is not offered for the servant-ethic. This may well have much to do with the person of Jesus and the transition from the messenger to the message in the post-Easter community. One would hesitate, however, to contend that the separation between the two is as wide as some scholars maintain.)

4. Reward

The New Testament speaks frankly, as we have seen, of the reward for the believer who practises the servant-ethic. The self-understanding of the earliest Christians was based upon the belief that somehow their self-sacrifice would be vindicated by God, even in the most unjust situations. Those who are prepared to surrender their life will gain it. Those who give liberally store up treasure for themselves. Those who abandon their rights, who do not retaliate, can expect vindication from God. This idea of reward, however, does not proceed from somehow "making a deal" with God. God himself has acted decisively in history through Jesus. Upon the response to this turning-point, repentance or rejection, hangs the final outcome. The reminders of reward are, in fact, reminders of grace.

5. Unifying Motif: Responding to God's Grace

It is this awareness of divine grace that permeates the motives offered for the servant-ethic. All the New Testament writers are responding either explicitly (as Paul) or implicitly (as the Gospel writers) to situations within Christian communities. These circumstances influence their directives for moral action. Their belief in the death and resurrection of Jesus as salvific and in the future culmination of history as revealing God's glory also impel them. Motivations for moral action reflect these dual beliefs. Often the New Testament writers appeal to the example of Jesus or to the Christian's future reward. The calls to servanthood before others reflect this dual concern.

It is clear, for example, that Paul believes that once an individual has become a Christian, the in-dwelling of the Spirit causes a moral transformation in the believer's heart (E.g., Gal 5:24–25; Phil 3:7–14). This leads to a corresponding change in one's moral behavior since, to use Paul's words, it is "no longer I who live, but Christ who lives in me" (Gal 2:20). Consequently, the reminders of heavenly reward, the example of Jesus, the promotion of church unity, or the desire to act in certain ways to promote the Gospel, are all seen as secondary, in terms of motive, to the natural consequences of becoming a Christian. It is God's will that Christians are mindful of Christ as a paradigm, prevent schisms within their fellowship, and bring the gospel to those who have not heard the good news. More importantly, however, as heirs by grace (Gal 4:7), Christians walk by the Spirit and have crucified the flesh (Gal 5:22–26). It is the indwelling of the Spirit which is the primary impetus for Christian moral behavior.[12] Such conduct is marked both by freedom in Christ and by its fruit which is, in part, the "love which seeks not its own" (I Cor 13:5).

Given that it is the indwelling of the Holy Spirit (to use Paul's language), or the transformation of μετάνοια (to echo the Synoptic gospel writers), or new birth in the Spirit (to iterate John's terms), that leads to the fulfillment of God's will, the motive for the servant-ethic is essentially the desire to respond to God's will, because of the experience of his love and grace. According to the writers of the New Testament, the freedom achieved in Christ inclines the Christian to seek the good of the other since there can be no greater self-fulfilment. The ethics of the New Testament embody an extreme impulse to other-directedness.

Limitations upon the Servant-Ethic

1. Questions of Prudence and Common Sense

For the most part, the requirement to serve, to put aside one's own interests is enjoined in the face of considerations of prudence and common sense. It is folly, in terms of common sense, to offer one's left cheek if the right has already been struck. It is certainly imprudent not to seize the opportunity to escape captivity should an earthquake shatter one's fetters. Common sense dictates that one should seek redress for fraud rather than simply revoke one's legal rights. It seems appropriate to respect a compassionate master but unreasonable to honor the demands of a domineering one in a like manner (I Pet 2:18). The servant-ethic does not find its limitations, however, in prudence and common sense. Any ethic grounded in the response to God's grace made known cannot seek its limits in common sense.[13]   The primary limitation is found not in human reason but in God's will. The freedom Christians find in Christ renders questions of prudence, common sense, and even justice subordinate to seeking the will of God in a given situation. The New Testament, then, is not a call to "situation ethics" in the sense that ethicists such as Joseph Fletcher have advocated.[14]   For Fletcher, the aim of all Christian ethical decisions is love. Only love is always good, and love is the only norm.[15]   Fletcher's "non-systematic" approach resembles the ethics of the New Testament, but cannot be said to parallel the approach found there, since he virtually abandons the principle of seeking God's will and makes the rule of love paramount. What appears to be the action "love" demands in a given situation may, in fact, be at odds with what God requires. As Dodd says the statment "God is love" must not become "Love is God" thereby "making the ethical primary and subordinating the religious to it."[16]   Once love becomes absolute, God is in danger of being relativised. Although others have recognized the context of a situation as important for ethical decision-making, most do not extend this principle to the extreme, as Fletcher does. C.H. Dodd also invokes the reality of Christian experience as constitutive for ethical-decision making in the thought of Paul: "The Christian if he has truly entered into the new life, is able to 'ascertain by experience what is the will of God' and to judge for himself what kind of conduct conforms to that will"(Rom 12:2; Phil 1:10 and Eph 5:10,17).[17]

2. The Primary Limitation—Violating God's Will

All moral exhortations in the New Testament are grounded in the will of God. Right conduct depends not upon prudence, or upon common sense, but rather upon the very experience of his grace. Paul refers to "conscience" as a means of determining ethical limitations or guidelines as do the writers of the Pastoral epistles, I Peter and Hebrews.[18]   Refraining from violating God's will is the only ostensible limitation placed upon the servant-ethic in the New Testament. The only time a believer should not place his or her interests last is in circumstances that would constitute resistance to God's will. This is made especially clear in James which insists that the rich are not to be served at the expense of the poor. Essentially the servant-ethic is without limitations. The self-awareness of the believer as servant of God and others by grace imparts a sense of freedom to Christian conduct as expressed in the New Testament. The inner transformation that occurs in response to divine grace is manifested as freedom—the freedom to serve.

The Freedom to Serve

The idea of Christian freedom is the key to the servant-ethic in the New Testament. As Heinrich Schlier says in his article on ἐλεύθερος:

> By the Spirit and power of the life of Jesus Christ radically offered up in love there is brought into being in our lives an existence which is unselfish and self-forgetting because it is dynamically hidden in love and can no longer be self-seeking or self-willed. In the Spirit of the freedom of Jesus Christ, there arises our freedom.[19]

For Luther the freedom found in Christ leads to joyful service of others. He asserts, "A Christian is a perfectly free lord, subject to none. A Christian is a perfectly dutiful servant of all, subject to all."[20] This is a paradox which arises directly from the Christian belief in the crucifixion and resurrection of Jesus. For the New Testament writers this act of God in history has broken the bonds which enslaved human beings and offered them true freedom (e.g., Gal 4:8–9). At the same time, however, the spontaneous response to this act of grace is to seek the good of others rather than oneself. Paul represents this paradox most clearly (Gal 5:13). In the Synoptic gospels the acceptance of discipleship implies a liberation from concerns about the self in that true discipleship requires the willingness to lay down one's life (Mark 8:38). Personal ambition is incompatible with such a decision, for "the Son of Man came not to be served but to serve," and his behavior is paradigmatic for his disciples. This aspect of Jesus' self-understanding, as depicted in the gospels, implies a movement away from concerns about prestige, social status or personal gain. The true disciple is "other-directed." Authentic freedom is freedom from self.

The Self and the Other and the New Testament Servant-Ethic

The words of Jesus and the writings of Paul early on became normative as *guides* for ethical reflection in the early Christian communities, but the primary principles for moral action were derived from the experience of God's love as

manifested in Christ. Modern Christian ethicists continue to seek the answer to
how the Christian should go about acting ethically, but most agree that love is
one principle that needs to be discerned and applied if ethics are to be Christian.
This love is applied when others are served. The New Testament idea of
freedom in Christ demands that Christians meet the needs and act in the interest
of others. The New Testament in all its diversity consistently reflects this
requirement, even if it is not systematic in describing how one should go about
this. The servant-ethic is a consistent and unifying characteristic of the earliest
Christians' self-understanding. It consists of self-subordination in response to
the grace of God. It is the manifestation of God's grace and is limited only by
his will. The other is the one who is in need or the one who enjoys abundance.
He is a friend or he is the enemy. She participates in the community of Christ
or she rejects the truth of the Gospel.

Ever since the ancient Greeks inscribed "know thyself" at Delphi, it seems
that the aim and goal of human endeavor, at least in the West, has been the quest
for self-understanding. Such a quest is carried out in the community of others;
however, it is a community in which the alienation of the self is a perennial
dilemma. It is only in the encounter with others that the self can become human.
Lonergan claims:

> Just as it is one's own self-transcendence that enables one to know others accurately
> and to judge them fairly, so inversely it is through knowledge and appreciation of
> others that we come to know ourselves and to fill out and refine our apprehension of
> values.[21]

Lonergan speaks in a context of attempting to overcome conflict through
dialectic. On a more basic level the encounter with another person, in every
instance, brings greater self-knowledge and also opportunities to serve. One of
the most radical articulations of this found in some of the more accessible work
of the Jewish philosopher Emmanuel Levinas. He captures the spirit of the New
Testament servant-ethic in a way that many contemporary Christian ethicists fail
to do.

For example, Levinas says:

> I am responsible for the Other without waiting for his reciprocity, were I to die for it.
> Reciprocity is *his* affair. It is precisely insofar as the relationship between the Other
> and me is not reciprocal that I am [in] subjection to the Other.[22]

For Levinas, the Other makes absolute claims upon the self that can only be
responded to by self-transformation: "To recognize the Other is to recognize a
hunger. To recognize the Other is to give. But it is to give to the master, to the
lord, to him whom one approaches as 'You [*Vous*]' in a dimension of height."[23]

In a sense the self becomes a servant of the Other, especially since Levinas sees freedom contingent upon the Other. Only the Other who, in a sense, limits freedom, can also justify it. Thomas Ogletree comments that Levinas' work "is likely to be irresistible to those nurtured in Biblical faith" because of "the infinite enlargement of responsibility" found therein. Ogletree says, however, that Levinas' call for self-sacrifice before the other need not be in fundamental contradiction to egoistic satisfaction. He says that the freedom of self "always embraces the possibility that moral sacrifice, rather than negating egoistic enjoyment, will transfigure and ennoble it—that life will be discovered and embraced in the power to give it up for the sake of the other."[24]

Christian ethical reflection, whether it arises from the earliest communities or contemporary theologians, demands that the other, the neighbor, even the enemy, is to be served simply because he or she is there.[25] God's will, in and of itself, effectively abrogates any other principle for ethics on the part of those who seek to fulfill his will. For the New Testament writers to "know thyself" was important, but to "know God" was paramount. The work of Christ and the subsequent continuation of that work through serving others both fulfills God's will and reveals his just, merciful and loving nature in human encounters according to the ethical schema of the New Testament. This was the freedom the early Christians believed was achieved in Christ—the freedom to serve because of the manifestation of God's grace. "Wherever one person regards another more highly than self and is concerned to be of service to the other person, there God's will is done and the law of Christ is fulfilled."[26]

The existence of the other is constitutive for defining the self. The servant-ethic emphasizes the responsibility of the Christian to the other that goes beyond mutuality and reciprocity and makes the interests of the other paramount. Thomas Ogletree pursues the question of the other in his essay subtitled "The Role of the 'Other' in Moral Experience." Ogletree points out that Western ethics is "self-centred" in the sense that the "other" is largely instrumental in the ethical development of the moral actor.[27] This is essentially true in the servant-ethic. The emphasis is placed firmly on the conduct of the believer. A specific response to service is never explicitly looked for. The believer serves others not primarily for their own good but in order to do what God requires. Thus evil may be overcome with good, pagan husbands may become Christians, but such considerations are never paramount. Seeking the good of others is a way ultimately to serve God. Christians are, by and large, not responsible for how their service is received (or rejected) by others.

It is this dimension of self-understanding of the servant-ethic that distinguishes it most clearly from the ideal of love (αγάπη). Αγάπη is articulated differently throughout the New Testament. In recent years the trend has been upon emphasizing the mutual and reciprocal nature of love. Love looks for a response. The servant-ethic resists such considerations. Its most radical articulation, therefore, may well be the call to enemy-love in Matthew and Luke since no response is anticipated and the accent is on the conduct of the believer.

Almost all of the writers of the New Testament, whatever their differences in their expressions of kerygma and ethics, seem to agree that the Christian life is one of self-subordination and service to others. Pursuit of personal interests, selfish ambition and self-assertion are to be replaced by "other-directedness" and "self-forgetfulness." Belief in the Son of Man who came "not to be served but to serve," requires that the Christian also serve. The paradox, of course, is that the New Testament consistently affirms that such "self-forgetfulness" leads to authentic "self-realization" as a servant of God. This servant-ethic is a fundamental characteristic of the Christian life as it is presented in the New Testament. It permeates this early collection of Christian writings and is emblematic, therefore, of the earliest phase of Christian ethical thought.

NOTES

Chapter I: Introduction

1   E.g. Jack T. Sanders, *Ethics in the New Testament* (Philadelphia: Fortress, 1975) and
    James Dunn, *Unity and Diversity in the New Testament* (Philadelphia: Trinity Press
    International, 1990). Eugene E. Lemcio argues that "contrary to the prevailing view,
    there is a central, discrete kerygmatic core that integrates the manifold plurality of the
    New Testament" ("The Unifying Kerygma of the New Testament," *JSNT* 33 [1988],
    3). While our investigation is not primarily concerned with kerygma, Lemcio's article
    is important because his procedure involves "a study of the New Testament *per se*,
    which is first and foremost a body of literature. Such textual examination has an
    integrity in its own right, so that it may be conducted separately from and indeed prior
    to the historical" (Ibid., 5). The state of the quest for thematic unity in the New
    Testament documents has been summarized and the quest itself pursued by John
    Reumann (*Variety and Unity in New Testament Thought* [Oxford: Oxford University
    Press, 1991]).

2   See, for example, Gene Outka, "Character, Conduct and the Love Commandment,"
    Norm and Context in Christian Ethics, ed G. Outka and Paul Ramsey (New York:
    Charles Scribner's Sons, 1968), 40. There also exists today the problem of defining
    love in ways that are acceptable to all. Traditionally understood as sacrificial in
    nature, many Christian thinkers are now interpreting ἀγάπη in terms of mutuality and
    reciprocity. (E.g. Gene Outka, *Agape: An Ethical Analysis* [New Haven: Yale
    University Press, 1972], 52–53, and for a general discussion, Barbara Hilkert
    Andolsen, "*Agape* in Feminist Ethics," in *Journal of Religious Ethics* [Spring, 1981],
    62–83.)

3   *Christian Neighbor-Love* (Washington D.C.: Georgetown University Press, 1989),
    47–62.

4   Ibid., 5, emphasis his.

5   Ibid., 47.

6   *Biblical Ethics and Social Change* (New York: Oxford University Press, 1982),
    59–62.

7   Ibid., 63.

8   Ibid., 64.

9   *Love and Conflict: A Covenantal Mode of Christian Ethics* (Nashville: Abingdon,
    1984), 105.

10 Ibid., 107.

11 Ibid., 114.

12 Ibid., 114, emphasis his. Allen's discussion is compelling here in that the right to
    sacrifice somehow is subordinated to the inclination to sacrifice. Allen quotes Luther
    to support his view that Christian faith liberates and thereby inclines one to sacrifice
    on behalf of others. Lambert's translation reads:

> Although I am an unworthy and condemned man, my God has given me in
> Christ all the riches of righteousness and salvation without merit on my part
> . . . so that from now on I need nothing except faith which believes that this
> is true . . . . I will therefore give myself as a Christ to my neighbour, just as

> Christ offered himself to me; I will do nothing in this life except what I see is necessary, profitable and salutary to my neighbour, since through faith I have an abundance of all good things in Christ ("A treatise on Christian Liberty" in *Luther's Works* 31 [Philadelphia: Muhlenberg Press, 1957], 367).

13 *Love and Conflict*, 116, emphasis his.

14 Ibid., 117. Allen points to Matt 10:38–39; 16:24–26; 25:31–46; Mark 8:34–36; Luke 9:23–24; 10:29–37; 14:27; 17:33; John 12:25; and I Cor 10:24.

15 Ibid., 118–119.

16 Ibid., 122–125. In his book *Jesus on Social Institutions* (Philadelphia: Fortress, 1971), Shailer Mathews suggests that the sacrificial love to which Jesus calls his disciples is in a sense strategic because it ensures the welfare of the individual by promoting the welfare of the group. He describes Jesus' call for love as a call for social cooperation. "The welfare of the individual is furthered by the cooperation of all those who are members of the group. They can act egotistically only at the cost of suffering in the group" (55). There is, however, no evidence in the texts to support such an evaluation of Jesus' teaching. The calls to the servant-ethic and love for the other do not function as insurance of one's own well-being, although they may have that effect, but rather as the natural manifestation of the disciple's faith in God. It is perhaps important to note that while the New Testament text may advocate a position that is different from that held by modern scholars, most notably Christian theologians and ethicists, we are not suggesting that their arguments are thereby invalid. The role of scripture in modern theology and ethics is part of an on-going debate and modern ethical discussions take place in a social context that is far different from that of the early Christians.

17 In his discussion of how Christians discern the way in which they ought to conduct themselves James Gustafson tries to identify what kinds of considerations are brought to bear. The correct application of the love-command in some situations is self-evident. In other circumstances he notes that moral reflection requires a greater degree of sophistication ("Moral Discernment in the Christian Life" in *Norm and Context in Christian Ethics* [New York: Charles Scribner's Sons, 1968], 33–34). While I do not want to depict the early Christians as unreflective, the New Testament does not seem to encourage the conviction that much consideration is required of the Christians to act appropriately. The early Christians undoubtedly faced situations in which it was not clear how one might express love of neighbor. One senses that it was not sophistication that was required so much as ingenuousness: a belief that God's will would prevail in one's own self-forgetfulness and "other-directedness."

18 *Ethics in the New Testament* (Philadelphia: Fortress, 1975), 28–29.

19 For a sober analysis of the impact of eschatology upon Christian ethics, see C.H. Dodd, *Gospel and Law* (New York: Columbia University Press, 1951), 25–32.

20 *First Century Slavery* (Atlanta: Scholars Press, 1971), 67–70.

21 See Bartchy, 73–78, Dale B. Martin, *Slavery as Salvation* (New Haven: Yale University Press, 1990), 11–22. Also see Wayne Meeks, *The First Urban Christians* (New Haven: Yale University Press, 1983), 20–22.

22 Eg. *Nichomachean Ethics*. III.i.2–8, concerning behavior under compulsion; III.vii.5, concerning the courageous man; and V.ix.1–3, 8 on the belief that one should not suffer injustice voluntarily. (George F. Thomas offers a decidedly negative summary of Aristotle's ethics in comparison with those of Christianity in "Aristotle's Theory of

Moral Virtue" in *Christian Ethics and Moral Philosophy* [New York: Charles Scribner's Sons, 1955].)

23   We might note, however, the surrendering of rights that is found in Genesis 13 in which Abram defers to Lot for the sake of peace, and in Gen 26:17–22 in which Isaac follows a similar course to avoid contention.

24   "The Laws Regarding Slavery as a Source for Social History of the Period of the Second Temple, the Mishnah and Talmud," *Papers of the Institute of Jewish Studies, London* I (Jerusalem: Magnes Press, 1964), 8.

25   *Oxen, Women or Citizens? Slaves in the System of the Mishnah* (Atlanta: Scholars Press, 1988), xii.

26   Flescher, xi–xii. The institution of slavery was a political, social, and economic reality in the first century C.E. It was apparently rejected only by the Therapeutae and the Essenes. (See Philo, "The Contemplative Life," 70 and "Every Good Man is Free," 75–78.), Philo, himself, shows no discomfort with the social division of human beings into slave and free. For him and his contemporaries such a division was as natural as that of male and female. As Barclay says: "In the normal run of life, where the time-honoured structures of society seemed unchangeable, it was impossible to imagine a slaveless society, except in a utopian dream-world where food cooked itself and doors opened of their own accord" ("Paul, Philemon and Christian Slave-Ownership," in *NTS* 37/ [April 1991], 177).

27   *Oxen*, 37.

28   Urbach, "Laws," 34–35.

29   Martin, *Slavery*, 1–49.

30   *TDNT* II, 266–67.

31   Examples and discussions abound but for a brief summary see Clarice J. Martin, "Womanist Interpretations of the New Testament" *JFSR* 6 (1990), 55–59. See also the first part of Willard M. Swartley's book, *Slavery, Sabbath, War, and Women* (Kitchener, Ontario: Herald Press, 1983), 31–53), for a concise summary of 19th century pro-slavery and abolitionist arguments based on biblical texts.

32   Emil Brunner notes that "duty and genuine goodness are mutually exclusive" (*The Divine Imperative: A Study in Christian Ethics*, trans. Olive Wynon [London: Lutterworth, 1937], 74) He continues:

> Above all, freedom means being free from the obligation to seek one's own good. Freedom is utter dependence upon God, and this means the absolute renunciation of all claims to independence, of all illusory independence over against God (78).

At the same time, however, the requirement to serve others because an individual is a Christian can be described in terms of duty and obligation. Fulfilling the servant-ethic does not make an individual a Christian, however. It is the result of becoming a Christian not the cause or prerequisite.

33   The literature has multiplied in the last decade, but the work of Elisabeth Schüssler Fiorenza is especially representative. *In Memory of Her: A Feminist Theological Reconstruction of Christian Origins* (New York: Crossroad, 1983), has become a classic in the field as an attempt to develop an adequate "hermeneutic of suspicion" to lay bare the patriarchal nature of the text and expose its androcentrism in order to attempt an imaginative historical reconstruction that reveals the participation of women in the earliest ἐκκλησία.

34   This does not mean, of course, that the contents of the New Testament are not

informed by the experience and social situation of the writers and their communities. For an account of this as it explicitly relates to the moral disposition of the earliest Christians see Wayne A. Meeks, *The Origins of Christian Morality* (New Haven: YaleUniversity Press, 1993).

35   Paul's Ethic of Freedom (Philadelphia: Westminster, 1979), 56.

36   See Stephen Post, *A Theory of Agape* (Lewisburg: Bucknell University Press, 1990), 106–108, who notes that the ideal of individual freedom so extolled in the West has not been pursued so enthusiastically by all cultures. The idea is absolutely foreign to the New Testament communities. As Dodd says, "The New Testament gives no encouragement to the idea that the individual is self-determining or is an end in himself. He does not exist for himself" (*Gospel and Law*, 35).

37   Dodd, *Gospel and Law*, 10.

Chapter II: The Servant-Ethic in the Synoptic Gospels

1   C. G. Montefiore, *The Synoptic Gospels*, I (London: Macmillan, 1927), 217–218.

2   Gunther Bornkamm, *Jesus of Nazareth* (New York: Harper and Row, 1975), 82–84. Or, as Ben Meyer puts it, "Repentance did not prompt God's mercy but attested it. It was joy and thanks as well as tears, remorse, resolution" (*The Aims of Jesus* [London: SCM Press, 1979], 132).

3   See William Lillie,"The Christian Conception of Self-Denial" in *Studies in New Testament Ethics* (Edinburgh and London: Oliver and Boyd, 1961), 162.

4   A. E. Harvey, *Strenuous Commands: The Ethic of Jesus* (London: SCM Press, 1990), 64.

5   See Furnish, *The Love Command in the New Testament* (New York: Abingdon, 1972), 24–45.

6   Robert Funk highlights the paradoxical nature of this parable and asserts that it cannot be classified as an example story because the listener is not necessarily led to comport oneself as the Samaritan but can also be cast in the role of the victim (*Parables and Presence* [Philadelphia: Fortress, 1982], 29–34). Nevertheless, the context of the parable makes clear that one should emulate the Samaritan's conduct.

7   Kierkegaard concludes that it is incumbent upon the believer to become the neighbor. The Samaritan's compassion does not show that the assault victim was his neighbor but that he was a neighbor of the one assaulted (*Works of Love,* trans. Howard and Edna Hong [New York: Harper Torchbooks, 1962], 38). Love commanded is required to view each neighbor equally without pausing to consider the worth of a person as an object of love. The command is the requirement to ensure that the interests of others are served impartially. See also, Bruce Chilton and J. I. H. McDonald, *Jesus and the Ethics of the Kingdom* (Grand Rapids: Eerdmans, 1987), 94–95; L. H. Marshall, *The Challenge of New Testament Ethics* (London: Macmillan, 1946), 105; Hans Windisch, *The Meaning of the Sermon on the Mount,* trans S. Maclean Gilmour (Philadelphia: Westminster, 1951), 69–70. Windisch dismisses the question of whether love can "be prescribed" as irrelevant.

8   Part of the irony of this parable, of course, is that it is a Samaritan who represents the ideal, and who recognizes his neighbor in the victim. The original saying about loving one's neighbor in Lev 19:18 makes the reader's fellow Israelite the object of the love.

The Samaritan, often scorned by many Jews in Jesus' time, replaces the Israelite in the familiar triad of priest, levite, Israelite, as Jeremias says (*New Testament Theology* [London: SCM Press, 1971], 213). The Samaritan understands the assaulted Jew as *his* neighbor. Also see Fitzmyer, *The Gospel According to Luke I–IX* (Garden City, New York: Doubleday, 1981), 878. In his interpretation of the parable Funk makes the inherent irony and paradoxes especially clear. Jesus' listeners undoubtedly "identify" with the robbers' victim initially until they become aware that it is a Samaritan who offers them aid—it is the enemy who serves (*Parables and Presence*, 29–34). For the victim, the enemy becomes the neighbor because of circumstance and the Samaritan's human compassion. The victim, therefore, is in no position to refuse to be served.

9   Kierkegaard, *Works of Love*, 72.

10   Scholars have pointed out that since striking the right cheek suggests a back-handed blow, it is doubly offensive. Manson, *The Sayings of Jesus* (London: SCM Press, 1949), 51. Also Jeremias, *New Testament Theology*, 239.

11   See Manson, *Sayings*, 51. He cites Exod 22:25–27 and Deut 24:12–13 as examples in Jewish law which forbid forcing individuals to surrender their outer mantle, which also served as a blanket at night, if they failed to honor a pledge. Jesus, employing characteristic hyperbole, however, insists that one's cloak also be given up, despite one's intrinsic right to its return at dusk. If followed literally, as scholars have observed, such a command condones nakedness. This is surely not, therefore, the intent of the passage. Since the text perhaps also hints, in light of 5:39, that the suit for the coat is itself unjustified, the issue is one of personal rights. As Davies and Allison affirm: "Jesus' hearers are being asked to give up their lawful rights" (*The Gospel According to Saint Matthew*, I [Edinburgh: T and T Clark, 1988], 544). See also Ulrich Luz, *Matthew 1–7* (Minneapolis: Augsburg Fortress, 1989), 326.

12   See Manson, *Sayings*160; Davies and Allison, *Matthew* I, 547.

13   Furnish, *Love Command*, 85 and 90.

14   For the meaning of τέλειος in Matt 5:48 see Davies and Allison. They conclude that "without doubt 'moral perfection' is the meaning" in 5:48a (*Matthew* I, 561).

15   [The] "deeper the revolution, the more the distinction between mine and yours disappears, and the more perfect the love . . . . The deeper the revolution is, the more justice shudders; the deeper the revolution the more perfect the love." (*Works of Love*, 248–9.) Also see C. Spicq, (*Agape in the New Testament* I [St. Louis: Herder, 1963], 81). Outka defends the view that the two are often compatible depending upon the way in which one defines "justice" (*Agape: An Ethical Analysis*, 75–92).

16   Similar attitudes are also found in Jewish texts from the turn of the era; for example, *Joseph and Asenath* (23:9; 28:4; 12; 29:3) prohibits rendering evil for evil.

17   *Matthew* I, 540.

18   *The Theology of Liberation* (Maryknoll, New York: Orbis, 1988), xxxvii.

19   E.g. Wis 15:1–2; m 'Abod. Zar. 4.7; and also Ta'an. 7a, which reads:
     R. Abbahu said:
     The day when rain falls is greater than [the day of] the Revival of the Dead, for the Revival of the Dead is for the righteous only, whereas rain is both for the righteous and for the wicked. (J. Rabbinowitz, trans.)
     Also see H. Windisch, *Meaning*, 82–85, and G. Friedlander, *Jewish Sources of the Sermon on the Mount* (New York: Ktav, 1969), 83.

20   See Davies and Allison, *Matthew*, I, 508–09.

21   *The Ethos of the Bible* (Philadelphia: Fortress, 1981), 48.

22   See Harvey, *Strenuous Commands*, 188.

23   Harvey explicitly rejects this latter interpretation. The suffering individuals whose need the Christian is to respond to are themselves believers. In their need they have become agents of Christ (Ibid., 188).

24   The possibility exists that the "goats" are simply outsiders to the Christian community and that this passage illustrates that believers are always found to be engaged in serving the destitute. Such an interpretation stretches the limits of credulity since Matthew himself recognizes that outsiders are capable of alms-giving (e.g. Matt 6:2), and that some who call Jesus "Lord" will not enter the βασιλεία (kingdom) (7:21–23).

25   *Luke X–XXIV*, 1045.

26   This also offers a clue to explain Jesus' apparent "repudiation" of Martha's service and hospitality in Luke 10:38–42.

27   *Luke X–XXIV*, 1128.

28   See Luke T. Johnson, *The Literary Function of Possessions in Luke–Acts* (Chico: Scholars Press), 158.

29   See Joachim Gnilka *Das Evangelium nach Markus* II (Köln: Benziger Verlag, 1979), 58.

30   Matt 26:11 is much more brusque than the Markan account, but also suggests that the disciples will have plenty of opportunity to serve the poor. The irony of the passage in Mark, of course, is that immediately following this episode we read of the betrayal of Jesus by Judas (Mark 14:10–11): the woman's loyalty and loving extravagance become foils for Judas' treachery and greed (Wolfgang Schrage, *The Ethics of the New Testament*, trans. David E. Green [Philadelphia: Fortress, 1988], 72–73). Luke, however, has edited the passage considerably, most notably by omitting the saying about the poor and changing the setting. Instead of a harbinger of Jesus' burial, the passage becomes an illustration of Jesus' power to forgive. Luke has attempted to completely eradicate any traces of indifference to the poor on the part of Jesus. Fitzmyer believes that Luke was using a completely different tradition for this episode than either Matthew or Mark (*Luke I–IX*, 686). Raymond E. Brown suggests with others, that two incidents in fact took place, one in Bethany and one in Galilee, and that the two stories have been conflated by oral tradition reflected in the Lukan account (*The Gospel According to John I–XII* [New York: Doubleday, 1970], 449–54). Whatever his source, and assuming Luke knew Mark at least, his account reflects a desire to prevent his readers from inferring that Jesus was indifferent to the sufferings of the impoverished.

31   Jeremias helps to explain the attitude of Jesus in Mark 14:3–9 by recalling the distinction early Judaism made between almsgiving and "works of love" in "Die Salbungsgeschichte Mk 14:3–9" in *Abba* (Göttingen: Vandenhoeck and Ruprecht, 1966), 109–115).

32   In Matthew the man asks "What do I still lack?" Jesus responds, "If you would be perfect, go sell what you possess and give to the poor and you will have treasure in heaven; and come, follow me." This recalls earlier episodes in Matthew that we have considered. First, the reference to being perfect reminds the reader of Matt 5:48, and the challenge to be like God (Rudolf Schnackenburg, *The Moral Teaching of the New Testament*, trans. J. Holland-Smith and W. J. O'Hara [London: Burns and Oates, 1975], 108–109). Luz notes that Matt 19:20–21 may be seen to stand in tension with 5:48 since in the former simple renunciation of possessions may be seen to lead to

perfection. He rightly asserts, however, "that perfection is for Matthew a *task* which all Christians face and which motivates all" (*Matthew 1–7*, 347). Second, the demand to "follow me" parallels Matt 16:24, so that denying oneself and taking up one's cross can be read as equivalent to surrendering one's possessions on behalf of the poor. The Lukan parallel also reflects special interests. In Luke 18:18 the man is referred to as a ruler (ἄρχων), one who is not only rich, but also enjoys political power.

33   But note Harvey's comment: "The motivation of giving alms is always the good of the donor, never the relief of poverty" (*Strenuous Commands*, 136). Jeremias insists that total surrender of one's possessions is restricted to those who actually accompany Jesus. Zacchaeus, for example, only gives away half of what he owns (222–223). (The Essenes also called for individuals to surrender their material goods upon entering the community [IQS 6:19–20; 22; 24–25]. See Schnackenburg, *Moral Teaching*, 124, concerning attitudes at Qumran towards property and the title "the poor.")

34   *New Testament Theology*, 223.

35   Ben Meyer has kindly pointed out that the original German text of Jeremias' work uses Nietzsche's phrase *Unwertung der Werte*, better translated perhaps as the "transvaluation" or "revaluation of values."

36   *The Great Reversal* (Grand Rapids: Eerdmans, 1984), 17.

37   See Schnackenburg, *Moral Teaching*, 115–117.

38   See Gerhard Lohfink, *Jesus and Community* trans. John P. Galvin (Philadelphia: Fortress, 1984), 49; and Luz, *Matthew 1–7*, 327–28.

39   Chilton and McDonald see much affinity between the two models of παιδίον (child) and διάκονος (servant). (See *Jesus and the Ethics of the Kingdom*, 88–89).

40   *Love Command*, 69. It is significant that the disciples, those in the inner circle, persistently fail in this regard. As noted above the verb διακονέω is never used of the (male) disciples but it is clearly the ideal to which the disciples of Jesus should aspire. As P. H. Boulton notes the apostles are especially adverse to serving in Acts 6:2 since they see here tension between evangelism and service. But their evangelism is expressed in terms of service ("Διακονέω and its Cognates in the Four Gospels," *SE*, I, ed. K. Aland, *et al* [Berlin: 1959], 419).

41   While some have suggested that the child here represents the "weaker members of the community" (e.g. Vincent Taylor, *The Gospel According to Mark* [London: Macmillan, 1953], 405, or personal emissaries of Jesus, (e.g. William Lane, *The Gospel of Mark* [Grand Rapids: Eerdmans, 1974], 341), it makes more sense for the παιδίον to be understood simply as a child, who, in the kingdom proclaimed by Jesus, represents an ideal (e.g., Mark 10:14–16). All children, all people, are to be welcomed as if they were Jesus himself (not simply children or "weaker disciples" who come in his name). See M.-J. Lagrange who notes that the text does not say that the believer should receive others who come in the name of Christ, but that they should be received in his name. In other words by welcoming others the believer honors Christ. (*L'Évangile de St Marc* [Paris: Librarie Lecoffre, 1966], 246).

42   *The Ethics of Mark's Gospel: In the Middle of Time* (Philadelphia: Fortress, 1985), 158–59.

43   *Markus*, II, 103.

44   On διάκονος and its occurrence in Mark 10:45, see Gnilka, *Markus*, II, 103. Jesus' exemplary role constitutes a large part of the motive for the servant-ethic throughout the New Testament. For a discussion on this point with specific reference to the gospel of Matthew see Birger Gerhardsson, "Sacrificial Service and Atonement in the Gospel

of Matthew" in *Reconciliation and Hope* (Grand Rapids: Eerdmans, 1974), 25–35.

45   It is perhaps important to note here that there is no mention of glory in this passage until v.38c, and that there is no explicit mention of reward (unlike the Matthean parallel in 16:27).

46   See Ernest Best, *Following Jesus: Discipleship in the Gospel of Mark* (Sheffield: JSOT, 1981), 50, n.67. Also see: Lane, *The Gospel According to Mark*, 308–9.

47   Best, *Following Jesus*, 39. He also notes that Luke definitely understands the saying to be metaphorical because he inserts the word "daily" at Luke 9:23.

48   Ibid., 39.

49   *The Charismatic Leader and his Followers* (Edinburgh: T and T Clark, 1981), 61.

50   *Jesus of Nazareth*, 147.

51   *Charismatic Leader*, 62.

52   "Sacrificial Service,"

53   Ibid., 30.

54   See A. Nygren, *Agape and Eros* (Chicago: University of Chicago Press, 1953), 100–101, 217; Outka, *Agape*, 55–74; Schnackenburg, *Moral Teaching*, 103–104; Schrage, *Ethics*, 79; Marshall, *Challenge*, 106–7 and R. Bultmann, *Jesus and the Word* (New York: Charles Scribner's Sons, 1958), 115–120 for the meaning of loving one's neighbor as oneself.

55   This inversion is illustrated, for example, by Mark 10:14–15 in which Jesus welcomes the little children and encourages his followers to receive the kingdom ὡς παιδίον.

56   E.g., Jack T. Sanders, *Ethics*, 33.

57   *The Great Reversal*, 77.

58   Schrage, *Ethics*, 141.

59   "Silent Voices: Women in the Gospel of Mark." *Semeia*, 54 (1991), 153. Antoinette Clark Wire makes a similar point concerning Matthew ("Gender Roles in a Scribal Community" in *Social History of the Matthean Community*, ed., David Balch [Minneapolis: Fortress, 1991], 104).

60   Larry Hurtado notes that in Mark 1:30–31 the woman's response to her healing is illustrative of the appropriate response to the kerygma on the part of Mark's readers (*Mark*, [San Francisco: Harper and Row, 1983], 15).

61   But see Mark 12:38–39. I do not want to suggest that Mark is innocent of condemnation of the Jewish religious establishment.

62   *Ethics*, 151.

63   It is interesting to note that Mark, which many consider to be devoid of any real ethics, also is far less interested in notions of reward. For example the Markan parallel to Matt 16:27 (Mark 8:38) is less explicit concerning how the Son of Man will "repay every man for what he has done." Verhey notes that Matthew "sometimes makes 'entering the kingdom' (a phrase used more often by Matthew than by any other New Testament author) contingent on doing the righteousness required in the Sermon (5:20; 7:21; but see 21:31)" (*The Great Reversal*, 90). Throughout the New Testament a standard of righteousness is required of those who would remain within the community. The servant-ethic stands as a primary characteristic of that standard. This does not mean that fulfillment of the servant-ethic alone is adequate to practice true righteousness.

64   Mark does not explicitly refer to the command to love one's enemies. John Piper, however, sees a correlation between the call to serve in Mark and the love commanded in Matt 5:43–48 (*Love Your Enemies: Jesus' Love Command in the Synoptic Gospels*

and in the Early Christian Paranesis [Cambridge: Cambridge University Press, 1979], 87).

65 Schrage, *Ethics*, 148.

66 *JAAR* 56 (1988), 223.

67 "Non-Violence and the Love of One's Enemies," in *Essays on the Love Commandment* (Philadelphia: Fortress, 1978), 23.

68 *Love Command*, 67, emphasis his.

69 *Love Your Enemies*, 143–44. Also see F.W. Beare, *The Gospel According to Matthew* (Oxford: Basil Blackwell, 1981), 162.

70 *An Interpretation of Christian Ethics* (New York: Meridian Books, 1956), 46).

71 *Jesus and Community*, 55.

72 *Strenuous Commands*, 107.

73 *Matthew 1–7*, 351.

74 Ibid., 350.

75 *Strenuous Commands*, 104.

76 Davies and Allison find this call to be part of a paranetic pattern found in Matt 5, Eph 5, I Pet 1 and I John 4 that is derived from Jesus' teachings (*Matthew* I, 554).

77 Ibid., 556.

78 Schrage points out that Matthew is concerned with "fulfillment of the law as expounded authoritatively by Jesus." It is this, rather than the suffering, humility and service of discipleship that is most important for Matthew according to Schrage (*Ethics*, 145).

79 *Matthew* I, 565.

80 Furnish, *Love Command*, 81.

81 Antoinette Clark Wire suggests that the gospel of Matthew offers a critique of social structures that emphasize prestige and authoritarianism because of "its central emphasis on figures without social power, including women, as models of faith in God and as the challenge to service." Wire, "Gender Roles," 107-108. Jesus' words and actions call for a response and the only appropriate response is service to him.

82 Schrage, *Ethics*, 156. For a feminist view of the Magnificat that insists while it represents "traditional" Jewish messianic hopes concerning divine intervention on behalf of the oppressed, the overall thrust of the gospel "articulates instead Christian identity as grounded in Luke's depoliticization of 'the good news for the poor" (E. Schüssler Fiorenza, *But She Said* [Boston: Beacon, 1992], 210–13).

83 It seems likely that the reference to the cup in the Markan and Matthean accounts inspired Luke to place this episode at the Last Supper. He omits the details of the dispute, including the involvement of James and John and their request to sit next to Jesus "in glory."

84 Gnilka describes Luke as giving Jesus' words a Hellenistic shape or form (*Gestalt*) here (*Markus* II, 100). Also see: David J. Lull, "The Servant-Benefactor as a Model of Greatness (Luke 22:24–30)" in *NovT* 28 (1986), 289–305, for a different, albeit uncovincing, approach to the text which understands ἐνεργέται in a positive light.

85 See Fitzmyer, *Luke X–XXIV*, 1413–1414.

86 Luke perhaps avoids using the noun διάκονος in v.27 because it had already become a technical term for an office in the Christian church. Fitzmyer, however, thinks that the participle διακονῶν might itself "represent the service of the church in Luke's day" (*Luke X–XXIV*, 1417). Turid Karlsen Seim notes that, in fact, Luke "avoids the substantive completely, even in cases where the already existing Markan text uses it"

(*The Double Message.* trans. Brian McNeil. [Nashville: Abingdon, 1994, 59).

87   For Luke's attitude towards wealth see   Johnson, *Literary Function.* Most
       commentators and writers on New Testament ethics also include sections on this
       emphasis of the third evangelist (e.g., Fitzmyer, *Luke I–IX,* 247–251; Schnackenburg,
       Moral Teaching, 127–131).

88   *The Great Reversal,* 94, emphasis his.

89   The parable of the Good Samaritan also exemplifies this aspect of the Lukan ethic
       (Luke 10:30–35). The passage serves to illustrate the command to love one's neighbor
       as oneself by explaining who is one's neighbor. Part of the parable, however, tells how
       the Samaritan assisted the traveller by paying for his keep at the inn. See Fitzmyer,
       who, while admitting that the parable was told for another purpose, notes that it
       "exemplifies a right use of material possessions to aid an unfortunate human being"
       (*Luke I–IX,* 249).

90   *Ethics,* 106–107.

91   For a summary see Fitzmyer, *Luke X–XXIV,* 1144–1146.

92   *The Great Reversal,* 95.

93   Windisch, while insisting that the imperatives in Matthew 5 are indeed commands, also
       recognizes that the spiritual condition of the hearers of the Sermon on the Mount must
       be such that each individual can respond to the challenge that these commands present
       (*The Meaning of the Sermon on the Mount,* 88–89). Also see Schnackenburg, *Moral
       Teaching,* 114–167, concerning Jesus' motives for his moral imperatives, and the ideas
       of reward, *imitatio dei,* and *imitatio christi.*

94   *New Testament Theology,* 217.

95   *Jesus and the Word,* 112.

96   *New Testament Theology,* 216.

97   See Eric Osborn, *Ethical Patterns in Early Christian Thought* (Cambridge:
       Cambridge University Press, 1976), 23.

98   *New Testament Theology,* 217, emphasis his.

99   *Jesus of Nazareth,* trans. Herbert Danby (New York: Menorah Publishing, 1925),
       394–95.

100   *Matthew* I, 563–64.

101   *The Challenge,* 35.

102   See Joseph L. Allen, *Love and Conflict,* 198–217, for examples of such resistance.

103   *An Interpretation of Christian Ethics,* 49–50.

104   See William Klassen, *Love of Enemies: The Way to Peace* (Philadelphia: Fortress,
       1984).

105   *An Interpretation of Christian Ethics,* 52.

106   *Lydia's Impatient Sisters* (Louisville: Westminster John Knox, 1995), 209–211.

107   See: Klausner, *Jesus of Nazareth,* 392–397; Montefiore, *Synoptic Gospels* II, 86–91;
       John Knox, *The Ethics of Jesus in the Teaching of the Church* (New York: Abingdon,
       1961), 18–23. C.H. Dodd in his discussion of this point reflects upon the "unlimited
       scope of God's demands." They lead to an acute realization in the hearer of the need
       for repentance (*Gospel and Law,* 60–63). Windisch, however, contra Montefiore,
       Klausner, Knox et al, defends the position that the antitheses are not only commands
       but are also practicable. He quotes *Slavonic Enoch* 50:3–4 which encourages one to
       endure ill-treatment, not to retaliate, and to wait upon the Lord to avenge on the day
       of Judgment, as an example of a similar ethic in Judaism. He concludes that the
       individual sayings of the Sermon on the Mount are to be understood and interpreted

literally (*Meaning*, 95–123). Thomas Ogletree calls for a middle path that takes into account the eschatological emphasis of Matthew (*The Use of the Bible in Christian Ethics* [Oxford: Basil Blackwell, 1983], 108). For Ogletree, however, the eschatology of Matthew's gospel does not render his ethics invalid since they offer a "realistic assessment of what is entailed if we are to break the structures of destruction which presently order human life" (ibid., 109). Davies and Allison insist that Matt 5:21–48 is not a moral code but a stimulus to the "moral imagination." It is a "challenging moral ideal" (*Matthew* I, 566). The challenge can only be taken up by those who respond to the central call for repentance in the Synoptic texts.

108   *Love of Enemies*, 77.

109   Goppelt notes that Mark 10:42–45 par. illustrates this principle (*Theology of the New Testament* I, trans., John E. Alsup [Grand Rapids: Eerdmans, 1982], 114).

110   There is perhaps one exception to this. In Matt 5:25–26 (par Luke 12:57–59) Jesus' hearers are advised to "settle out of court" with their accusers in order to avoid going to prison. Fitzmyer describes this as "Jesus challenging his audience to timely and prudent reconciliation with one's opponent" (*Luke X–XXIV*, 1001).

111   P.H. Boulton, "Διακόνεω," 415. For an argument for the historicity of the entire verse see Peter Stuhlmacher, *Reconciliation, Law and Righteousness*, trans., E. R. Kalin (Philadelphia: Fortress, 1986), 22.

112   Furnish, *Love Command*, 63.

113   It is interesting to recall the response of Peter's mother-in-law following her healing (Mark 1:29–31; Matt 8:14–15; Luke 4:38–39). The point of the account is to show that her recovery was so complete that she was able to serve Jesus (Matthew) or Jesus and his disciples (Mark, Luke) immediately, presumably by providing food and other essentials of hospitality. The verb διακόνεω also has broader connotations, however. Upon experiencing the benefits of Jesus' ministry the woman stands able to serve others. She parallels the jailer who responds to the message of Paul and Silas (Acts 16:25-34).

Chapter III: The Servant-Ethic in the Johannine Writings

1   *Can Ethics Be Christian?* (Chicago: University of Chicago Press, 1975), 164–65.

2   The most thorough discussion of this question is found in C.H. Dodd, *Historical Tradition in the Fourth Gospel* (Cambridge: Cambridge University Press, 1965, especially 335–365). Dodd suspects that no direct literary dependence obtains between the Fourth and Synoptic gospels but discovers evidence for a core of tradition common to all. We do not seek evidence of literary dependence, but rather wish to demonstrate an intrinsic early Christian self-understanding by pointing to instances in which the gospel and epistles of John confirm the routine requirements of serving others that are scattered throughout theSynoptic tradition.

3   "Le Lavément," *RB* 71 (1964), 8.

4   B. Lindars, *The Gospel of John* (London: Oliphants, 1972), 448, emphasis his. Also see C. K. Barrett, *The Gospel According to John*, 2nd. ed. (Philadelphia: Westminster, 1978), 439. The historical-critical problem with v. 3, of course, is that this motive for Jesus' act is clearly from the hand of a redactor. In the verses which most scholars agree constitute the "kernel" of this episode (i.e., vv 4 and 5), no motive is mentioned.

5   Bernard, *The Gospel According to St. John* II (Edinburgh: T. and T. Clark, 1928), 464.
6   Ibid., 463–64. He also insists that the act reflects the dignity of service, an inference that is not necessarily justified.
7   Raymond E. Brown, *The Gospel According to John XIII–XXI* (New York: Doubleday, 1970), 562.
8   Ibid., 562. Brown sees the use of τίθημι in v.4 as indicating the laying down of life (cf. 10:11,15,17, 18). This understanding is confirmed by v.7b. Barrett agrees (*John*, 439). Herold Weiss is more interested in locating the significance of the footwashing within the Johannine community. He says that footwashing was practiced in the persecuted Johannine community and that it represented preparation for martyrdom ("Footwashing in the Johannine Community," *NovT* 21 [1979], 300). Weiss also says that John 13 and I Pet 2:22 are the only two passages in the New Testament which offer an "Example Christology." (323). Both communities apparently faced persecution and martyrdom and in both passages the example of Jesus is recalled as he faced his suffering and death. Brown, however, also points to Heb 13:12–13; II Cor 5:15; Phil 2:5–11; I Tim 6:12–13 as well as I John 3:16 as passages which encourage Christians to recall the example of Christ and to be prepared to imitate him (*The Epistles of John* [New York: Doubleday, 1982], 449).
9   *John XIII–XXI*, 561.
10   Bultmann, *The Gospel of John* (Philadelphia: Westminster, 1971), 478–79. See also, Marianne Meye Thompson, *The Humanity of Jesus in the Fourth Gospel* (Philadelphia: Fortress, 1988), 101.
11   In his article, "John 13:1–20, The Footwashing in the Johannine Tradition," F.F. Segovia makes the point that "the emphasis of this second explanation [i.e. vv12–17 as opposed to vv6–10], is on the ecclesiological implications of Jesus' act (*ZNW* 73 (1982), 46)." (In n.40, which accompanies this statement, Segovia suggests that "the failure to grasp the primary ecclesiological concerns of the washing in vv. 12–17 is, in my opinion, the fundamental weakness of those who interpret these verses primarily in terms of vv.6–10a.")
12   *John*, 459.
13   Ibid., 465.
14   (*John*, 440). He cites *Mekhilta Exod.* 21.2. B. Kötting in his article on footwashing claims that in the Jewish tradition a wife should wash her husband's feet not as a slave but out of love for him ("Füßwaschung" *RAC* VIII [Stuttgart: Hiersemann, 1950], 743–59). (Interestingly footwashing is omitted from the list of duties a wife should perform for her husband found in m.Ket. 5.5.) Arland Hultgren offers many examples of footwashing in antiquity including *Sifre Deut.* 355, in which a maid-servant washes her master's feet ("The Johannine Footwashing (13:1-11) as a Symbol of Eschatological Hospitality," [*NTS* 28 (1982), 545, nn13–16]).
15   Bultmann understands these details of vv 4–5 as a means to have the reader recognize the absurdity of the event (*John*, 466).
16   This is based in part perhaps upon typical evaluations of Johannine christology. The divine aspect of Jesus' nature reinforces the humiliation of the crucifixion (and the footwashing). The exaltation proceeds from the understanding that despite the self-sacrifice and self-abnegation of this person Jesus, his actions and sufferings reveal that the divine λόγος has penetrated the physical world. On Johannine christology and soteriology see S. Smalley, *John—Evangelist and Interpreter* (Greenwood, S.C.: Attic Press, 1983), 210–226. Smalley, in part, understands John to portray an

"exemplarist view of the cross," so that "Christ's passion and death are seen primarily as revealing the truth that self-sacrificial love lies at the heart of God's dealings with man, and also as an example which Christians are to follow in their own lives and relationships" (226). Following in this vein we may understand the footwashing as the initial phase of Jesus' passion which points forward to his death but also beyond to his resurrection and vindication. (This exemplary interpretation of the crucifixion calls to mind the words of Jesus to his disciples in Mark 10:42–45 par. as well as recalling John 15:12–14).

17   W. L. Knox says that John had an account of the Last Supper with a collection of sayings similar to that in Luke before him. The story of the footwashing is either a legend or a historical record unknown to Mark, according to Knox. The latter is less likely, Knox believes, because he feels that such a tradition would also have survived in the Synoptics ("John 13:1–30," [*HTR* 43 (1950)], 161–2). Brown notes that a lesson on humility and a reference to the disciples' future in the Father's kingdom or house are common to both John 13 and Luke 22 but notes that the wording is very different (*John XIII–XXI*, 557). We shall further consider the episode's relationship to the Synoptics below.

18   "John 13:1–30," 162, n.1. Barrett sees the passage as a Johannine construction "based on the Synoptic tradition that Jesus was in the midst of his disciples as ὁ διακόνων (Luke 22.27)" (*John*, 436).

19   *John XIII–XXI*, 562.

20   Ibid., 558. The papal practice on Holy Thursday is more in keeping with the Pope's role as Vicar of Christ than as a literal interpretation of vv 14–15. It hardly emulates Jesus' requirement of *mutual* foot-washing. See also I Tim 5:10, where again the practice seems anything but mutual.

21   See Bultmann, who says, "Jesus' action is an example binding on his disciples—whereby of course the footwashing is intended as a symbolic act, representative of loving service in general" (*John*, 475). Others, including Brown and Bernard, simply note that the church never took up the act as a sacrament (Brown, *John XIII–XXI*, 558; Bernard, *John*, 465–66). Boismard also notes the same ("Le Lavément," 19). Also see Morris' caustic note (*The Gospel According to John* [London: Marshall, Morgan and Scott, 1971], 612, n.3).

22   *Footwashing in John 13 and the Johannine Community* (Sheffield: Sheffield Academic Press, 1991), 109.

23   Ibid., 110.

24   For an exhaustive survey of "footwashing in the Jewish and Graeco-Roman environment," see Thomas, *Footwashing*, 26–60. He draws out the connotations of preparation, hospitality and cultic cleansing inherent in the practise.

25   *John*, 459.

26   ("Footwashing," 541). There is evidence that the Johannine community may have had geographical and chronological proximity to the church addressed in I Timothy (Ibid.," 542).

27   Reinhartz, "The Gospel of John" in *Searching the Scriptures*, II, ed. E. Schüssler Fiorenza (New York: Crossroad, 1994), 585. Other literature includes: Plato, *Symposium*, 175a, 213b. The appropriate passages Hultgren cites from *The Testament of Abraham* and *Joseph and Asenath* are more important, however. In the former, which according to Mathias Delcor (*Le Testament d'Abraham* [Leiden: Brill, 1973], 73–77) originated between 100 B.C.E. and 100 C.E., Abraham himself washes the feet

of his guest (the archangel Michael) although it is his son Isaac who is sent to fetch water (3:6–7). In the second text, which, according to Marc Philonenko (*Joseph et Asénath* [Leiden: Brill, 1968], 109), originated in Egypt at the beginning of the second century, there are three passages which describe foot-washing: 7:1; 13:12 and 20:3. In each passage the phrase νίπτειν τοὺς πόδας is used. In the first Pentephre, Asenath's father, washes Joseph's feet as a sign of hospitality. In 13:12 Asenath prays that she might become as a slave to Joseph and wash his feet all her life. In the final passage, Asenath refuses to allow a maid-servant to wash Joseph's feet, preferring to perform the act herself. The latter two of these references point beyond common courtesy and hospitality to an attitude of subservience and self-denial in 13:12 and to an expression of deep love in 20:3.

28   *Ethics*, 307–8.

29   *John*, 621.

30   See Thomas, *Footwashing*, 127–34 for a summary of the advocates of actual footwashing in the early Church (Tertullian, Athanasius of Alexandria, John Chrysostom, Ambrose, Augustine, John Cassian, Caesarius of Arles). Although all of these writers are late they demonstrate the pervasive appeal of the concrete act of washing one another's feet as indicative of the humble service of Christians.

31   *Die christliche Demut*, (Giezen: Alfred Topelman, 1906), 205.

32   The grammatical problems of the phrase εἰ ταῦτα οἴδατε, μακάριοί ἐστε ἐὰν ποιῆτε αὐτά (v.17) focus on doubts about the antecedent of ταῦτα. Commentators agree, however, that the meaning is clear: John 13:1–16, as Morris says, "sets out principles of conduct and Christ's followers are to act on them" (*John*, 622). Barrett points to a similar construction at Matt 7:21, 24–7 (*John*, 444). The call to perform footwashing reflects the attitude of I John 3:11–24 which speaks of the blessedness of responding to others' needs.

33   *John*, 479.

34   *Love Command*, 134–35.

35   Ibid., 136, emphases his.

36   See Schrage, *Ethics*, 307. Schnackenberg also notes the exemplar theme as it is picked up in I John 3:16 (*Moral Teaching*, 324).

37   See Bultmann's comments on I John 3:16 and 17 in *The Johannine Epistles* (Philadelphia: Fortress, 1973), 55–56. Also see F.F. Bruce, *The Epistles of John* (Grand Rapids: Eerdmans, 1970), 96.

38   *Ethics*, 100.

39   Ibid., 98.

40   See Wayne Meeks, *The Moral World of the First Christians*. (Philadelphia: Westminster, 1986), 99.

41   *Ethics*, 316–17.

42   Ibid., 317–18. See also Furnish, *Love Command*, 147. Even the Qumran community, like many of their Jewish contemporaries, saw no value in seeking retaliation (I QS 10:17–19). Vengeance was to be left to God.

43   Verhey claims that scholars such as Sanders are arguing from silence (*The Great Reversal*, 144), and Furnish agrees, saying that "the commandment to 'love one another' need not be regarded in itself as *excluding* love for 'neighbors' and 'enemies'" (*Love Command*, 148). Schnackenburg also rejects the "exclusive" interpretation of John (*Moral Teaching*, 328).

44   *Ethics*, 318.

45 Stricter limitations seem to be in place in the Johannine epistles. Here we find conditions placed upon hospitality to others. Only true Christians may be welcomed (II John 10), although they may be strangers (III John 5). It is well to note that those who are to be refused hospitality in II John 10 are "deceivers" rather than simply "non-Christians," i.e., they are not simply Pagans or Jews, or even as Brown says, "well-meaning Christians who are in error" (*Epistles of John*, 690).

46 See Brown *Epistles of John*, 690–691. Brown understands passages such as Matt 18:17; I Cor 5:4–5; Tit 3:10: II John 10–11 and Rev 2:2 as New Testament examples of early attempts to separate former Christians from the community.

47 *Jesus in History: An Approach to the Study of the Gospels* (New York: Harcourt Brace Jovanovich, 1977), 220.

48 *Love Relationships in the Johannine Tradition* (Chico: Scholars Press, 1982), 166.

49 *Ethics*, 309.

50 Schrage believes that it is indeed persecution that is the historical source for the restrictive nature of love in John (Ibid., 317).

51 Ibid., 316.

52 *The Great Reversal*, 144.

53 E.g. Outka, *Agape: An Ethical Analysis*, 37–40.

54 Ibid., 40.

55 "The Inadequacy of Selflessness," 213.

56 Ibid., 221.

57 "The Footwashing (John 13:1–20): An Experiment in Hermeneutics." *CBQ*, 43, 1 (1981), 84–85.

58 Ibid., 87.

59 Ibid., 91.

60 *Can Ethics Be Christian?*, 164–65.

61 *Love Command*, 202.

62 Barrett, *John*, 436. Brown disagrees with Barrett's suggestion that the footwashing episode was concocted by the writer of John to illustrate the saying in Luke 22:27. (*John XIII–XXI*, 568).

63 Brown, *John XIII–XXI*, 569. James Dunn also notes the thematic connection of the footwashing with Mark 10:42–45 ("The Washing of the Disciples' Feet in John 13:1–20" [*ZNW* 61 (1970)], 249).

Chapter IV: The Undisputed Pauline Epistles and the Servant-Ethic

1 Pheme Perkins, "Paul and Ethics" (*Int* 38 [1984]), 277.

2 Victor Paul Furnish, *Theology and Ethics in Paul* (Nashville: Abingdon, 1968), 204, emphases his. He also cites I Thess 3:12.

3 "Interchange in Christ and Ethics," (*From Adam to Christ: Essays on Paul*. Cambridge: Cambridge University Press, 1990), 56.

4 C. E. B. Cranfield's translation (*The Epistle to the Romans* II [Edinburgh: T and T Clark, 1979], 618).

5 The use of the verb δοκιμάζω points to the result of what is being tested—thus it can refer both to the process of testing and the outcome of the test. In this verse the renewing of one's mind that comes about when one is not conformed to this αἰών leads to the discernment of God's will and what is "good, acceptable and perfect."

6   Cranfield, *Romans* II, 618.

7   In the context of the structure of the passage I would opt for the former (contra RSV) because Paul alternates "formal" gifts (prophecy, teaching, exhortation) with the more unassuming ones of service, giving and mercifulness. Although this pattern is not an exact one of alternation it seems to fit with Paul's insistence that all members of the body are one in Christ. Alternatively, διακονία can be read in the sense of what later came to be an ecclesiastical office (deacon) in which case the "higher" gifts of prophecy, διακονία, teaching and exhortation are listed first followed by the more general ones of giving, aiding and showing mercy. In his short commentary on Romans 12–13, Cranfield is especially non-committal on the meaning of ὁ προϊστάμενος, offering several options including the ruler of the church, the administrator in charge of charitable work or the rich protector of the church who provided for the poor. Of these three options Cranfield seems to favor the second (*Romans* II, 625–627). Cranfield sees all seven gifts as being rather formal and referring to particular positions or offices in the church.

8   *Romans* II, 629.

9   The exact interpretation of τῇ τιμῇ ἀλλήλους προηγούμενοι in v.10 is disputed. The RSV translates it as "outdo one another in showing honour." Blass and Debrunner, however, prefer to interpret προηγέομαι in the sense of "to prefer" rather than "outdo" (BDF, 84). It can then be translated: "Concerning honour (or esteem) give preference to the other [rather than oneself]." BAGD suggests, "As far as honor is concerned, let each one esteem the other more highly (than himself)" (706), and see Cranfield, *Romans* II, 632–33.

10   *A Commentary on Romans* (London: SCM Press, 1980), 345.

11   *A Commentary on the Epistle to the Romans* (London: Adam and Charles Black, 1957), 242.

12   *Romans*, 348–49.

13   *Love Your Enemies*, 116.

14   Ibid., 117–118.

15   Ibid., 118–119.

16   *Love of Enemies*, 120–121.

17   Ibid., 121.

18   Cranfield, *Romans* II, 648–650.

19   Klassen, *Love of Enemies*, 120.

20   Ibid., 121.

21   "Hate, Nonretaliation and Love: Coals of Fire" *Meanings* (Philadelphia: Fortress, 1984), 146.

22   It is possible, however, that 14:21 speaks to the need for the believer to overcome the temptation to seek revenge, which is evil, with the call to love one's enemies, which is good, and was, of course, advocated by Jesus. For further comparisons of the command to love one's enemies in Paul and Jesus, see Piper and his discussion of the intention of the command (*Love Your Enemies*, especially 111).

23   See Klassen, 119–122.

24   Cranfield, *Romans* II, 650. V.18 perhaps expands this empathetic approach to the enemy in Paul's admonition to live peaceably with all. Christians must be careful not to incite their enemies to persecution or to evil acts through deliberate provocation. Christians are partly responsible for the actions and reactions of others.

25   B. Sabb 31a.

26 See S. Westerholm, "Letter and Spirit: The Foundation of Pauline *Ethics*" *NTS* 30 (1984), 243–44.

27 *Chapters in a Life of Paul* (New York: Abingdon, 1950), 139.

28 For an evaluation of "improper" and "proper" judgment in Paul's thought see J. Paul Sampley, *Walking Between the Times: Paul's Moral Reasoning* (Minneapolis: Fortress, 1991), 66–69.

29 *Slavery as Salvation*, 123.

30 See Barrett, *I Corinthians* (London: Adam and Charles Black, 1971), 139. As Davies (*Paul and Rabbinic Judaism* [London: SPCK, 1955], 138) and Longenecker (*Paul: Apostle of Liberty* [Grand Rapids: Baker Book House, 1976], 189–90) have pointed out there are several verses in Romans (12:14,17,21; 13:7,8–10; 14:10,13,14) where Paul seems dependent upon Jesus' words. According to Longenecker, however, Paul does not understand the "word of the Lord" to be "law" in the Jewish sense. The tradition of Jesus' teaching "partakes of the nature of a principle; a principle which points the way to the solution in the particular circumstances but which must be applied anew to differing situations" (*Paul*, 192). Piper also insists that I Cor 6:7 as well as Rom 12:19, 20 and I Pet 2:20 are examples of how the sayings found in Matt 5:39–42 and Luke 6:29–30 have been incorporated into the paranetic tradition, although indirectly: "His commands were so specific that they were apparently unsuitable for moral instruction . . . . Even so his commands control the development of the paraenesis" (*Love Your Enemies*, 59).

31 Barrett raises the possibility of irony here, citing I Cor 8:1, but also says that "Paul may have in mind the Jewish *hakam*, a scholar of lower grade than a rabbi, capable of acting as judge" (*I Corinthians*, 138). In response to his suggestion that I Cor 8:1 may be applicable here I would suggest I Cor 3:18–4:5 as more relevant, especially vv 3:18,19; 4:3 and 5. To my mind it is only by interpreting v.5 as ironical that vv7–8 make sense. On this view 6:1–6 as a unit is not a model for resolving disputes, at least at Corinth. That such intra–church procedures were undertaken to settle grievances, however, is confirmed by Matt 18:15–17.

32 *Ethics*, 193. Meeks also believes that the whole passage is harmonious: "The fact that the second half of the passage (vss. 6–11) chides them for having suits at all and urges an other-regarding ethic that would eliminate such competition does not cancel the practical directive [of vv 2–5]" (*The First Urban Christians*, 104).

33 Schrage, *Ethics*, 215–216.

34 See Bornkamm, *Paul* (New York: Harper and Row, 1971), 216.

35 The use of the verb ἀρέσκω here tempers the connotations of status Dale B. Martin awards it in Rom 15:1–2 (*Slavery as Salvation*, 123).

36 That Paul understands marital rights to be equal for both the husband and the wife in matters of sex is, as Barrett says, a "striking assertion" (*I Corinthians*, 156), and militates against the view expressed most vehemently perhaps by George Bernard Shaw that Paul has become "the eternal enemy of Woman" ("The Monstrous Imposition upon Jesus" in *The Writings of Saint Paul* [New York: W.W. Norton and Co., 1972], 299).

37 "Conscience in I Corinthians 8 and 10" *NTS* 33 (1987), 252. Verses 28–30 are difficult to interpret but seem to mean that one refuses to eat not because of one's own scruples but because of the other's. (See Barrett, *I Corinthians*, 243). Richardson, however, detects an inconsistency here and wishes to bracket vv 28–29a in order that v29b follows on from v27. He says that "It seems that weak Christians were using

their weakness aggressively, to keep others from doing things that offended them . .
. . This is illegitimate" (*Paul's Ethic of Freedom*, 129).

38   In Romans the issue appears to have more to do with the intrinsic cleanness of the food
rather than its possible history as a cultic sacrifice. This suggests that the "weak" are
of Jewish origin or have been influenced by Jewish Christians, while in I Corinthians
the pagan religious milieu sparks the debate. Barrett, however, notes "there is . . .
no definite indication in Rom.14;15 that either idolatry or Judaism is in mind" ("Things
Sacrificed to Idols," *Essays on Paul* [Philadelphia: Westminster, 1982], 42.) Also see
Cranfield and his commentary on Rom 14:14. He notes that the passage refers to
believers who have not yet come to a full understanding that Christ has rendered literal
obedience to the law redundant. They have not yet achieved full liberty in Christ.
Consequently, "the meats, which had been forbidden, though no longer ritually unclean
in themselves objectively, are still for them, subjectively, unclean" (*Romans* II, 690–98,
and 713–14). In both Romans and I Corinthians Paul recognizes all food as part of
God's creation and therefore good. The only thing which overrides this conviction is
the misgivings of a fellow Christian, or the critical judgment of a non-believer. In both
cases Paul urges his readers to take care not to cause damage to others' relationship
with God, whether real or potential. (It is interesting to note that in Romans 14 Paul
does not explicitly couch consideration of others' scruples in terms of service. In fact,
he deliberately avoids such language in v. 4 with the phrase σὺ τίς εἶ ὁ κρίνων
ἀλλότριον οἰκέτην and its implication that the strong Christian "is not the weak
Christian's slave, but another's, i.e., Christ's (or God's), and therefore not answerable
to the weak Christian" (Cranfield, *Romans* II, 703).

39   (Paul W. Gooch and Peter Richardson, "Accommodation Ethics," *TynBul* 29 (1978),
110, emphasis mine.) John Ziesler says, however: "Consideration for others, and their
existing or potential adherence to Christ is the guiding rule; in other words, love,"
(*Pauline Christianity* [Oxford: Oxford University Press, 1983], 118–9). V.4 simply
underlines that the Christian is first and foremost the servant of God, a fact which is
manifested in a desire to look to the interests of others.

40   "Consciousness and Freedom among the Corinthians: I Cor 8–10" *CBQ* 40 (1978),
587. Also see Wendell Willis, "An Apostolic Apologia? The Form and Function of
I Corinthians 9" *JSNT*, 24 (1985), 40.

41   "Pauline Inconsistency: I Corinthians 9:19–23 and Galatians 2:11–14" (*NTS* 26
[1980]), 356.

42   Ibid., 355.

43   Ibid., 356. See also Adele Reinhartz's comments on this verse (I Cor 11:1). She
suggests that part of Paul's motive for calling for imitation of himself is the defence of
his apostolic authority.("On the Meaning of the Pauline Exhortation: '*mimetai mou
ginesthe*—become imitators of me'" *SR* 16 [1987], 398). For Reinhartz, the
exhortations of Paul for believers to imitate him (I Cor 4:6, 11:1; Phil 3:17; I Thess
1:6) function as a defence of his right to admonish his readers by illustrating that he
himself, in his role as apostle, engenders the very qualities of humility and self-denial
that he seeks to promote in his churches.

44   Richardson suggests that if Galatians is earlier than I Corinthians, Paul may in fact have
learned his ethic of accommodation from Peter! ("Pauline Inconsistency," 361, n.43).

45   David Carson, "Pauline Inconsistency: Reflections on I Corinthians 9.19–23 and
Galatians 2.11–14" *Churchman* 100 [1986], 7–45.

46   Ibid., 15. Carson also notes that "the relation between model and imperative is

reminiscent of passages like Mark 10.43–45."

47   Ibid., 16, emphasis his. In relation to this question, Stendahl has pointed out how dangerous it would be were I Cor 9:19–22 to become itself the principle. Should this happen "it would be abhorrent and certainly lacking integrity" (*Paul Among Jews and Gentiles* [Philadelphia: Fortress, 1976], 62). Jacques Ellul also notes how such accommodation to the beliefs and principles of others of which Paul speaks in I Cor 9:19–23 can seem repellent. Like Stendahl he sees its justification in the primacy of the nature of Christian love (*The Ethics of Freedom* [Grand Rapids: Eerdmans, 1976], 202). Ellul understands the behaviour espoused by Paul in the Corinthian passage to be part of his own self-understanding as a Christian and not simply reserved for those who would call themselves apostles. Cultural and social distinctions become irrelevant in light of the gospel.

48   As Richardson suggests, this is perhaps the dilemma that Peter faced in Gal 2:11–14 ("Pauline Inconsistency," 360–362).

49   Ibid., 356. Troels Engberg-Pedersen argues, however, I Cor 11:16 illustrates Paul's practice of accommodation. He understands Paul to be saying in 11:6, "Christians are not contentious—so *I* will not be contentious; I will not *insist*" ("I Corinthians 11:16 and the Character of Pauline Exhortation" *JBL* 110 [1991], 686, emphasis his). Also see R. Alistair Cambell, "Does Paul Acquiesce in Divisions at the Lord's Supper?" *NovT* 33 (1991), 61–70, who argues that in I Cor 11:19 Paul is acceding to the Corinthians' habit of honoring an elite stratum within their membership.

50   Barrett, *The Second Epistle to the Corinthians* (London: Adam and Charles Black, 1973), 134.

51   See Eph 4:28; I Tim 5:3–8. See also the apparent contradiction between Gal 6:2 and 6:5 which Furnish resolves by saying that "Brotherly love requires mutual caring and serving, but the members of the body retain their individuality and stand always personally responsible under the sovereign law of Christ" (*The Love Command*, 100). On this assertion by Furnish, Gene Outka notes:

> Matters are not as simple and uncontroversial as this statement suggests, but it serves nicely, nevertheless, by ascribing importance to care of others *and* to an individuality and personal responsibility which are always retained and retained by all ("On Harming Others" (*Int* 34 [1980], 386).

52   Schrage, *Ethics*, 231–232.

53   Ibid., 231.

54   (New York: Abingdon, 1957), 243.

55   On Gal 5:13, see Franz Müssner, *Theologie der Freiheit nach Paulus* (Freiburg: Herder, 1976), 36.

56   See Enslin, *Ethics of Paul*, 242–3.

57   *CBQ* 49 [1987], 271.

58   Ibid., 286, emphasis his. Hays's article is also illuminating on the question of *imitatio Christi* as a motive for Paul's call to self-sacrifice and service to others.

59   F.F. Bruce, *The Epistle to the Galatians* (Grand Rapids: Eerdmans, 1982), 241.

60   *A Critical and Exegetical Commentary on the Epistle to the Galatians* (Edinburgh: T. and T. Clark, 1921), 293.

61   Rengstorf, "Δοῦλος," 274.

62   *Galatians* (Philadelphia: Fortress, 1979), 274.

63   The Greek here, as F.W. Beare points out, is vague (*A Commentary on the Epistle to the Philippians* [London: Adam and Charles Black, 1959], 73). The meaning,

however, is clear: the Philippians are not only to be concerned about their own interests (rights/affairs/things) but also the interests of others. Ralph Martin rejects the interpretation that Paul is encouraging his readers to remember their responsibility to seek the best interests of others in favor of one which understands the phrase to encourage the Philippians to regard each other's way of life as motivation in their own Christian walk (*Philippians* [London: Oliphants, 1976], 90).

64   Clearly, Paul's multiple use of cognates of the verb φρονέω in this passage (and Phil 1:7; 3:15,16,19; 4:2) reveals an interest in encouraging unity, especially since all of the uses of the verb push for unanimity (1:7 and 3:19 excepted). J. Paul Sampley sees in the use of this verb correspondence with the Roman idea of *societas* or partnership concerning a central purpose. "As long as all the partners are disposed in the same way, the contract continues. *Societas* terminates with the loss of unanimity, singlemindedness, among the partners" (*Pauline Partnership in Christ*, [Philadelphia: Fortress Press, 1980], 62).

65   *The Cost of Authority: Manipulation and Freedom in the New Testament* (Philadelphia: Fortress, 1982), 62–63.

66   *The Early Christians: Their World Mission and Self-Discovery* (Wilmington, Delaware: Michael Glazier, 1986), 184.

67   Ibid., 203.

68   Cranfield resists the interpretation of Rom 15:31 that sees evidence here of serious tension between Paul and the Jerusalem church. The anxiety Paul expresses about his service being acceptable, for Cranfield, is natural apprehension that anyone experiences whens embarking on a benevolent campaign. (*Romans* II, 778).

69   *Paul, Apostle of Liberty*, 229.

70   Schrage points out that in some cases the primary concern is to be for the other person and not necessarily for God. He says that "above all Paul sees conscience or its dictates as being limited by love." The question of eating meat offered to others "is decided ultimately by reference to others, not to God. Paul states explicitly that love can even lead one to forgo what one's conscience has determined to be necessary and proper (I Cor 8:2)" (*Ethics*, 196). Paul would not, however, have acknowledged such a dichotomy. He sees Christian service to others as service to God, as shown by his understanding of his own evangelistic activity.

71   Robert Banks, *Paul's Idea of Community* (Exeter: Paternoster Press, 1980), 58.

72   *Pauline Partnership*, 66.

73   Ibid., 67–68.

74   *Humility: Solidarity of the Humiliated* trans. John Bowden (Philadelphia: Fortress, 1988), 16–35.

75   *Theology and Ethics in Paul* (Nashville: Abingdon, 1968), 119

76   Ibid., 121, emphasis his.

77   *Paul, the Law and the Jewish People* (Philadelphia: Fortress, 1983), 156.

78   Ibid., 157, emphasis his.

79   On why some object to the notion that the New Testament speaks of the imitation of Christ, see John Webster, "Christology, Imitability and Ethics" *SJT* 39 (1986), 312–313.

80   See Schrage, *Ethics*, 207–208. He cites W.D. Davies, who maintains that Paul does not artificially separate the teaching of Jesus from the person of Jesus: "He [Paul] holds up certain qualities of the historic Jesus which were to be imitated" (*Paul and Rabbinic Judaism*, 147). Davies cites Rom 15:3; II Cor 10:1; Phil 2:5–6 and II Cor

8:9–10. Schrage, however, disagrees and says:

> What we have said about the life of Jesus [i.e. that it does not provide an ethical paradigm] does not apply in the same way to his message. The significance of Jesus' words is not subject to the same negative verdict as his significance as an earthly person or an ethical model, even though Paul is undeniably much more interested in Jesus' saving work than in his words (*Ethics*, 209).

81   Hays, "Christology and Ethics in Galatians," 294. Hays cites Furnish among others who oppose Davies and Dodd (See *Theology and Ethics in Paul*, 264–65.) The most important element of understanding the phrase "the law of Christ," however, is determining what Paul means by "law." As Stephen Westerholm says, "the phrase ["the law of Christ"] is used loosely, by analogy with the Mosaic code, for the way of life fitting for a Christian. No specific collection of commands is in view" (*Israel's Law and the Church's Faith: Paul and his Recent Interpreters* [Grand Rapids: Eerdmans, 1988], 214, n.38). Also see S. Lyonnet who says that "the law of the Spirit is by its very nature radically different from the old law: It is no longer a code . . . but . . . a principle of action, a new, interior dynamism" ("Christian Freedom and the Law of the Spirit According to St. Paul" in *The Christian Lives by the Spirit* [New York: Alba House, 1971], 158). Davies, however, sees Gal 6:2 as part of the evidence "that there was a collection of saying of the Lord to which Paul appealed" ("The Moral Teaching of the Early Church" in *Jewish and Pauline Studies*, [London: SPCK Press, 1984], 286).

82   *Ethics*, 208–209. "What is to be 'imitated' is concern for the good of others rather than self as exemplified by Christ, who humbled himself 'for us' (cf. [I Cor] 10:33)." Earlier Schrage says that, "The love manifested in Christ is also the criterion of Christian conduct. Paul can even find a substantial correspondence between the conduct of Christ and the conduct of those who belong to him" (173).

83   The most important verses for Hays are Gal 2:19b–20 which "give clear evidence that Paul understands his own life as a recapitulation of the life-pattern shown forth in Christ" ("Christology and Ethics," 280).

84   W.P. De Boer, *The Imitation of Paul: An Exegetical Study* (Kampen: J.H. Kok, 1962), 62. Also see De Boer, (75–80) for a discussion of how the readers of Ephesians are to imitate God (Eph 5:1) "by being kind to one another, tenderhearted, forgiving one another, as God in Christ forgave you" (4:32). They are also to "walk in love, as Christ loved us and gave himself up for us" (5:2).

85   Jo-Ann Martens understands the concept of "mimesis" in Paul as found in I Cor 4:16–17, 10:32–11:1; Phil 3:17; Eph 4:31–5:2; I Thess 1:5–6, 2:14 and II Thess 3:6–9, as a means to realize "the ethical principle that one should subordinate personal interests and privileges to the good of the community" ("Pauline Mimesis: The Realization of an Ethic" [M.A. thesis, McMaster University, 1986], 4). She says further:

> *Mimesis* is a process in which the imitator expresses the essence of an idea in concrete form. For Paul, this form is conduct. In all cases, the standard to which these communities' *mimesis* conforms is the ethic that one should subordinate his or her rights to the interests of others (Ibid., 21).

86   *Strenuous Commands*, 180.

87   "Interchange in Christ and Ethics," 64–65.

88   "Philippians 2:6–11" *From Adam to Christ: Essays on Paul* (Cambridge: Cambridge

University Press, 1990), 90–91.

89   Ibid., 91.

90   A. Dihle, *"Demut"* (*RAC* III [Stuttgart: Hiersemann, 1950]), 749. Hooker also acknowledges this aspect of the passage by pointing out that Paul does not introduce the hymn with the phrase ἐν Χριστῷ but rather with ἐν Χριστῷ Ιησοῦ. She sees particular significance in this: "The life which should be demonstrated in the lives of those who are ἐν Χριστῷ, which is possible only because of the salvation events, is precisely the kind of life seen in Jesus Christ" ("Philippians 2:6–11," 154). Also see Webster, "Christology, Imitability and Ethics," 320.

91   See, for example, Ralph P. Martin, *Carmen Christi: Philippians ii. 5-11 in Recent Interpretation and in the Setting of Early Christian Worship* (Cambridge: Cambridge University Press, 1967), 88.

92   *A Commentary on the Epistle to the Philippians* 2nd ed. (London: Adam and Charles Black, 1959), 73. Also see Bornkamm, "On Understanding the Christ-Hymn" in *Early Christian Experience* (New York: Harper and Row, 1969), 112.

93   *The Story of Christ in the Ethics of Paul* (Sheffield: Sheffield Academic Press, 1990), 92–95.

94   Ibid., 59. Bornkamm sees Christ's taking the form of a slave as directly related to his becoming incarnate and suffering human bondage to world powers ("On Understanding the Christ-Hymn,"115–116). C.A. Wanamaker also understands the enslavement to be directly related to becoming human—it is the consequent enslavement to sin and death ("Philippians 2:6–11: Son of God or Adamic Christology?" *NTS* 33 [1987], 189. L.W. Hurtado comes to similar conclusions to Fowl although he prefers to read δοῦλος as describing Christ's relationship to God: "While it is not expressly stated in 2:7 that Jesus was δοῦλος to God, neither is it expressly stated that Christ became *δοῦλος to evil powers* . . . and there are better reasons for taking the former meaning than the latter." He offers three justifications for his interpretation:

i)He notes that in the letters of Paul δοῦλος and its cognates are used most often to refer to Christian life and service "and is *never* used to mean human existence as such."

ii)In the immediate context, the contrast between the ἁρπαγμός which is put aside and the taking the form of a slave "suggests that what is meant is service toward God, or for his sake."

iii)Hurtado thinks that the most crucial reason for the correctness of his interpretation is "the striking διὸ of 2:9, and the fact that God is the actor in 2:9–11, show that the service of 2:7–8 must be seen as offered to God, and that 2:9–11 is the divine response." Paul therefore "makes God's act of exaltation a consequence of Christ's obedience" rather than simply contrasting the acts of God and Christ ("Jesus as Lordly Example in Philippians 2:5–11" in *From Jesus to Paul: Studies in Honour of Francis Wright Beare* [Waterloo, Canada: Wilfrid Laurier Press, 1984], 122–23). Hurtado also makes the point that theδοῦλος word-group often refers to general Christian life in Paul whereas διάκονος and cognates more often refers to church service (ibid., 122, n.36).

95   *Carmen Christi,* 88.

96   Dihle, also, is perhaps overly apprehensive in his concern that humility not be cultivated with a view to receiving some kind of divine blessing (*"Demut,"* 751).

97   Webster, *Christology,* 321.

98   "Philippians 2.6–11," 92. Harvey confirms this reading. He says that Philippians 2 "is

an 'example' only in the sense that divine action in Christ becoming man can inspire acts of human self-abandonment and generosity" (*Strenuous Commands*, 181). (His use of the adverb "only" is somewhat puzzling since the divine action is astonishing and its consequences, self-abandonment and generosity, profound.)

99   "Humility and Self-Denial in Jesus' Life and Message and in the Apostolic Existence of Paul" *Paul and Jesus* (Sheffield: JSOT, 1989), 155–56.

100   *The Great Reversal*, 107–8.

101   *Freedom and Obligation: A Study of the Epistle to the Galatians* (London: SPCK, 1985), 73.

102   Ibid, 67.

103   *The Ethics of Paul*, 243.

104   Humility as a mark of the elect underlies many of the texts we have considered. It is explicit in Gal 5:13; Eph 4:1–3; Col 1:25, 3:12, but all of the texts which promise a reward or exaltation for the humble may also be considered in this category.

Chapter V: The Servant-Ethic in Other New Testament Writings

1   Johnson, *Literary Function*, 216.

2   *Acts* (Philadelphia: Fortress, 1983), 66. A more graphic depiction of the failure to surrender is in Acts 5:1-11 which describes thefate of Annanias and Sapphira, who seek to withhold their wealth from the community, and then pay dearly for their deception.

3   *Literary Function*, 213.

4   *The Letter to the Colossians* (Minneapolis: Augsburg, 1982).

5   *The Epistles of Paul the Apostle to the Colossians and to Philemon.* (Cambridge: Cambridge University Press, 1968).

6   Fortunately we do not need to establish the authenticity of the epistle to see if the servant-ethic figures in its ethical content. For the sake of convenience, however, we shall refer to the author as Paul.

7   Schweizer finds in these verses evidence that Paul is not the author of Colossians since the passage "exceeds" what Paul says of himself in Rom 15:15–21 and I Cor 2:6–16 concerning his role as apostle (*The Letter to the Colossians*, 100).

8   F.F. Bruce and E.K. Simpson, *A Commentary on the Epistles to the Ephesians and the Colossians* (Grand Rapids: Eerdmans, 1957), 215–16.

9   Ibid., 216.

10   Ibid., 216–17. This idea is taken up by Moule, who understands such an interpretation to be the dominant one, although both this and the idea that Christ suffers in his members' suffering are pertinent (*Colossians and Philemon*, 76–78). Moule believes that "Paul and his contemporaries were familiar with this way of looking at things: a definite quantity, known to God, if hidden from men, of sins, sufferings and conversions must precede the End" (78). Schweizer, on the other hand, rejects this interpretation: "The idea of a precisely predetermined measure of such sufferings is scarcely present here" (*Colossians*, 105).

11   *Colossians*, 106–107.

12   Schweizer never explicitly says that Col 1:25 implies that Paul's "office" is to be a "minister" (διάκονος) but his commentary on v. 25 certainly implies such an understanding. See Moule, *Colossians and Philemon*, 80. Moule is very clear in

understanding Paul's office or task assigned by God to be that of "fully proclaiming God's message."

13   *The Writings of St. Paul* (New York: W.W. Norton and Co. 1972), 113.

14   See Thieme, *Die christliche Demut*, 19. Thieme claims Philippians was written after Colossians and Ephesians so that the word ταπεινοφροσύνη came to Paul through the heretics in Colossae (!)

15   In Francis and Meeks, *Conflict at Colossae* (Cambridge, Massachussetts: Scholars Press, 1975). See also, for example, Ralph P. Martin, *Colossians: The Church's Lord and the Christian's Liberty* (Exeter: Paternoster Press, 1972), 121.

16   "Humility and Angelic Worship," 167–171.

17   The correct translation of the last part of 2:23 is difficult to determine. The RSV offers two alternatives: "But they are of no value in checking the indulgence of the flesh" or "they are of no value, serving only to indulge the flesh."

18   For a full discussion of Ephesians' dependence upon Colossians, see C.L. Mitton, *The Epistle to the Ephesians* (London: Oliphants, 1962), 55–74.

19   *Humility*, 53.

20   The passage concerning marriage differentiates the Ephesian *Haustafel* most clearly from those found in Colossians and I Peter. Verhey notes that the point of the passage is not to assert the husband's authority but to put that authority "into the context of mutual subjection, reciprocal obligations, loyalty to Christ, and the fundamental obligation to love the neighbor, including and especially the neighbor who is one's wife" (*The Great Reversal*, 126). Fiorenza aptly notes, however, that "one could say that the exhortations to the husbands [in the Ephesian *Haustafel*] spell out what it means to live a marriage relationship as a Christian, while those to the wives insist on the proper social behavior of women" (*In Memory of Her*, 270).

21   Verhey is more blunt in his assessment: "The spirit of the ethic here is indisputably more pedestrian and prosaic . . . . The gospel gradually has become identified with 'sound doctrine'" (*The Great Reversal*, 126).

22   *The Love Command*, 127–128.

23   *The Pastoral Epistles* (Oxford: Clarendon, 1963), 26. Barrett continues: "It is God himself who commands the Good Life."

24   *Ethics*, 266–67.

25   There are difficulties with interpreting the meaning of the Greek in this verse. The verse can also be understood to read: "Enter honorable occupations so as to satisfy necessary needs"; i.e., "Get a good job so as to put food on the table." See Barrett, *Pastoral Epistles*, 148; A. I. Hanson, *Pastoral Epistles* (Grand Rapids: Eerdmans, 1982), 196–97; and J. N. D. Kelly, *A Commentary on the Pastoral Epistles* (London: Adam and Charles Black, 1963), 258.

26   *Theology of the New Testament* II (Grand Rapids: Eerdmans, 1982), 257.

27   Harold W. Attridge, *The Epistle to the Hebrews* (Philadelphia: Fortress, 1989), 22–23.

28   *Ethics*, 110.

29   *Ethics*, 29. For the shift in eschatological focus from the imminent and universal to the eventual and personal, see Goppelt *Theology* II, 265 and Attridge *Hebrews*, 27–28.

30   *Ethics*, 106.

31   *Ethics*, 109.

32   The question of chapter 13's place in the epistle has been debated although it is now generally considered to be original despite its tenuous link with the first 12 chapters.

See Attridge *Hebrews*, 384–5. Also see J. Héring, who suggests that chapter 13 is a letter to a specific congregation attached to a general homily (*The Epistle to the Hebrews* [London: Epworth, 1970], 119). H.W. Montefiore rejects the suggestion that chapter 13 is Pauline and, like Hering, says the style and content "are sufficiently explained by the author's adaptation of his original homily to the needs of an epistle" (*A Commentary on the Epistle to the Hebrews* [London: Adam and Charles Black, 1964], 238).

33 (*Ethics*, 323). In 12:3 Jesus is referred to as an example of one "who endured from sinners such hostility against himself." While the accent here is not upon serving others but upon resisting sin, the characteristic of Jesus that is chosen is his endurance of hostility.

34 See Attridge, *Hebrews*, 357–8, who notes the parallels between Jesus and Moses at this point and the paradigmatic role of the former here.

35 See 6:12, in which the addressees are called to imitate those who through faith and patience inherit the promises. This verse points ahead perhaps to chapter 11 and the examples therein.

36 See Montefiore, *Hebrews*, 223; and B. Lindars, *The Theology of the Letter to the Hebrews* (Cambridge: Cambridge University Press, 1991), 114.

37 For a thorough discussion see Martin Dibelius, *James* trans. Michael A. Williams (Philadelphia: Fortress, 1976), 51–57.

38 *Paul and His Letters* (Philadelphia: Fortress, 1979), 91.

39 See Dibelius, *James*, 21–2.

40 Ibid., 3–5.

41 *Divine Impartiality* (Chico: Scholars Press, 1982), 180.

42 *The Epistle of James* (Grand Rapids: Eerdmans, 1982), 112.

43 See Adamson, *James: The Man and his Message* (Grand Rapids: Eerdmans, 1989), 254.

44 *James*, 125.

45 See Schrage, *Ethics*, 285.

46 As Victor Furnish has pointed out, in James divine Wisdom is "the essence of God's gift, to be sought and received by faith and then exhibited in an upright life" (*The Love Command*, 181).

47 *The Epistle of James* (London: Marshall, Morgan and Scott, 1966), 137.

48 *James*, 140.

49 See, for example, Elsa Tamez, *The Scandalous Message of James* (New York: Crossroad, 1990). Although questions of authorship are not our focus it is notable that in Eusebius' account of Hegesippus' report of the martyrdom of James the Just (bishop of Jerusalem), the scribes and Pharisees seek to coax the people away from Christianity with James's testimony. In that passage these officials describe James as "just and no respecter of persons" (Eusebius, *Ecclesiastical History*, xxiii).

50 R. Schnackenburg, *The Moral Teaching of the New Testament*, 365–66.

51 Ibid., 366.

52 See I Peter 1:15. E. G. Selwyn traces this back to Matt 5:16 (*The First Epistle of St. Peter* [London: Macmillan, 1964], 170, 373).

53 "The Literary and Theological Structure of I Peter 1:3–12," in *Perspectives on First Peter* (Macon, Georgia: Mercer University Press, 1986), 112.

54 See also Beare who notes that "the regenerate life is lived in the community of God's people and finds its necessary expression in the 'love of the brethren' (1:2) and in

mutual service (4:8–10)" (*The First Epistle of Peter* [Oxford: Basil Blackwell, 1961], 39).

55   *Ethics*, 274.

56   Ibid., 275.

57   Furnish, *Love Command*, 164. The double commandment is not so limited in the Synoptic literature. (Beare insists that v.16 is "not to be taken as subordinated to the imperatives in the following verse" [*I Peter*, 117].)

58   Peter H. Davids points to Jas 3:10–12 and m.Aboth 4:1 as expressions of the same point (*The First Epistle of Peter* (Grand Rapids: Eerdmans, 1990), 103.

59   *The Great Reversal*, 138.

60   *Moral Teaching*, 370.

61   For a brief discussion of ethical motivation in I Peter see Schrage, *Ethics*, 269: "The real and ultimate basis for ethical exhortation [in I Peter] is christological and soteriological." He admits that sometimes this motivation is "sounded somewhat formulaicly" as in 3:16 and 2:13, but also points to other passages in which the motivation is more completely described and readers are reminded of the suffering Christ endured to complete his salvific work (3:17–18; 2:21–25).

62   L. Goppelt, *Theology of the New Testament* II, 167.

63   The Christian wives who seek to win their husbands "without a word" exemplify the missionary strategy of I Peter (Schrage, *Ethics*, 274).

64   See, for example, Fiorenza, *In Memory of Her*, 251–270, and Jack T. Sanders, *Ethics*, 75, 85.

65   John H. Elliott, "I Peter: Its Situation and Strategy," in *Perspectives on First Peter* [Macon, Georgia: 1986], 71, emphasis his. For a full discussion of Christian attitudes to slavery see John M.G. Barclay, "Paul, Philemon and the Dilemma of Christian Slave-Ownership" (*NTS* 37 [1991], 161–186). Barclay points out that while slaves were assured "freedom in Christ," this did not translate into a movement towards abolition of the social institution of slavery.

66   *Ethics*, 85, emphasis his.

67   See David Balch, *Let Wives be Submissive* [Altanta: Scholars Press, 1981], 121.

68   *The Politics of Jesus* (Grand Rapids: Eerdmans, 1972), 192.

69   Beare, *I Peter*, 41.

70   Ibid., 40–41.

71   *Ethics*, 275.

72   *The Great Reversal*, 139.

Chapter VI: Conclusions and Implications

1   Stanley Hauerwas, *The Peaceable Kingdom* (Notre Dame, Indiana: Notre Dame University Press, 1983), 44.

2   *Jesus and the Ethics of the Kingdom*, 3.

3   *The Politics of Jesus*, 190–191.

4   *Theological Ethics of the New Testament* (Minneapolis: Fortress, 1991), 220.

5   See E. C. Gardner, *Biblical Faith and Social Ethics* (New York: Harper and Row, 1960), 257–259.

6   *Method in Theology*, (New York: Seabury Press, 1972), 54.

7   Ibid., 55.

8   *Justice* (New York: Pantheon Books, 1955), 96–97.

9   Ibid., 107.

10   Schweizer, *Lordship and Discipleship*, 53.

11   *The Common Life in the Body of Christ* (London: Dacre Press, 1963), 27.

12   Modern scholarship in the social sciences has sought to discover whether true altruism is ever displayed in human behaviour. According to many experiments, one would be correct in assuming that no human action is motivated by pure disinterestedness or altruistic concern for the other. Acts which appear to be motivated out of concern for another's suffering are in reality a means to increase one's stature in the eyes of onlookers or to alleviate feelings of guilt, etc. Nevertheless exceptions to this principle seem to have been discovered, which for some scholars offer possibilities by which disciplines such as social psychology can inform and illuminate theology (See Paul Rigby and Paul O'Grady, "Agape and Altruism: Debates in Theology and Social Psychology" *JAAR* 57 [1989], 719–37).

13   Lonergan, *Method in Theology*, 53.

14   *Situation Ethics: The New Morality* (Philadelphia: Westminster 1966).

15   Ibid., 57–86.

16   *Gospel and Law*, 44–45.

17   "The Ethics of the Pauline Epistles," 297. Nevertheless, Dodd believes that a catechism of ethical instruction developed very early in Christian history and traces of (or even excerpts from) it are detectable in the New Testament. This catechism was a "scheme of practical precepts for everyday living" (*Gospel and Law*, 25).

18   See W.D. Davies, "Conscience and Its Use in the New Testament" in *Jewish and Pauline Studies* (Philadelphia: Fortress Press, 1984), 254–56 . Davies notes that in the non-Pauline epistles conscience and faith are tied together despite the claims that the Pastorals (especially) promote a "bourgeois morality."

19   *TDNT* II, 499.

20   "The Freedom of a Christian," 344.

21   *Method in Theology*, 253.

22   *Ethics and Infinity* (Pittsburgh: Duquesne University Press, 1985), 98.

23   *Totality and Infinity* (Pittsburgh: Duquesne University Press, 1969), 75.

24   *Hospitality to the Stranger* (Philadelphia: Fortress, 1985), 56.

25   The neighbour as representative of God or Christ is thematic in the New Testament, especially the Synoptic gospels (Mark 9:37, par; Matt 25:31–46). Ernst Kasemann applies this within the context of the Church. He notes that humility (ταπεινοφροσύνη) must be practised in the presence of Christ "even when—indeed precisely when—I encounter this presence embodied in the person of my brother who has also his charisma" ("Ministry and Community in the New Testament," in *Essays on New Testament Themes* [London: SCM Press, 1964], 80).

26   Eduard Lohse, *Theological Ethics*, 165

27   *Hospitality to the Stranger*, 39.

BIBLIOGRAPHY

Adamson, James B. *James: the Man and his Message*. Grand Rapids: Eerdmans., 1989.

Albright, W. F., and C. S. Mann. *Matthew*. Anchor Bible Commentary, vol 26. New York: Doubleday, 1971.

Allen, Joseph L. *Love and Conflict: A Covenantal Mode of Christian Ethics*. Nashville: Abingdon, 1984.

Andolsen, Barbara Hilkert. "*Agape* in Feminist Ethics" in *Journal of Religious Ethics* (Spring 1981), 62-83.

Aristotle. *Nichomachean Ethics*. Translated by H. Rackham. LCL, 1962.

Attridge, Harold W. *The Epistle to the Hebrews*. Philadelphia: Fortress, 1989.

Balch, David. *Let Wives be Submissive: The Domestic Code in 1 Peter*. Atlanta: Scholars Press, 1981.

Banks, Robert. *Paul's Idea of Community*. Exeter: The Paternoster Press, 1980.

Barclay, John M. G. "Paul, Philemon and the Dilemma of Christian Slave-Ownership." in *NTS* 37 (1991) 161–186.

Barrett, C.K. *A Commentary on the Epistle to the Romans*. London: Adam and Charles Black, 1957.

_____ .*The First Epistle to the Corinthians* 2nd ed. London: Adam and Charles Black, 1971.

_____ . *Freedom and Obligation: A Study of the Epistle to the Galatians*. London: SPCK, 1985.

_____ . *The Gospel According to John*, 2nd ed. Philadelphia: Westminster, 1978.

_____ . *The Pastoral Epistles*. Oxford: Clarendon, 1963.

_____ . *The Second Epistle to the Corinthians*. London: Adam and Charles Black, 1973.

_____ . "Things Sacrificed to Idols" in *Essays on Paul*, 40–59. Philadelphia: Westminster, 1982.

Bartchy, S. Scott. *First Century Slavery and I Corinthians 7:21*. Atlanta: Scholars Press, 1971.

Barth, Karl. *Church Dogmatics* III/4. Edited by T. F. Torrance. Translated by G. W. Bromily. Edinburgh: T. & T. Clark, 1961.

Bassler, Jouette M. *Divine Impartiality*. Chico: Scholars Press, 1982.

Beare, F.W. *A Commentary on the Epistle to the Philippians*. New York: Harper and Brothers, 1959.

_____ . *A Commentary on the Epistle to the Philippians*. 2nd ed. London: Adam andCharles Black, 1959.

_____ . *The First Epistle of Peter*. Oxford: Basil Blackwell, 1961.

_____ . *The Gospel According to Matthew*. Oxford: Basil Blackwell, 1981.

Bernard, J.H. *The Gospel According to St. John* Vol II. Edinburgh: T. & T. Clark, 1928.

Best, Ernest. *Following Jesus: Discipleship in the Gospel of Mark*. Sheffield: Sheffield Academic Press, 1981.

Betz, Hans Dieter, "Cosmogony and Ethics in the Sermon on the Mount" in *Essays on the Sermon on the Mount* 89–123, Translated by L.L. Welborn. Philadelphia: Fortress, 1985.

_____ . *Galatians*. Philadelphia: Fortress, 1979.

Beyer, H.W. "Διακονέω, διακονία, διάκονος," TDNT II 81–93.

Boismard, M.-E. "Le Lavement de Pieds," *RB* 71 (1964): 5–24.

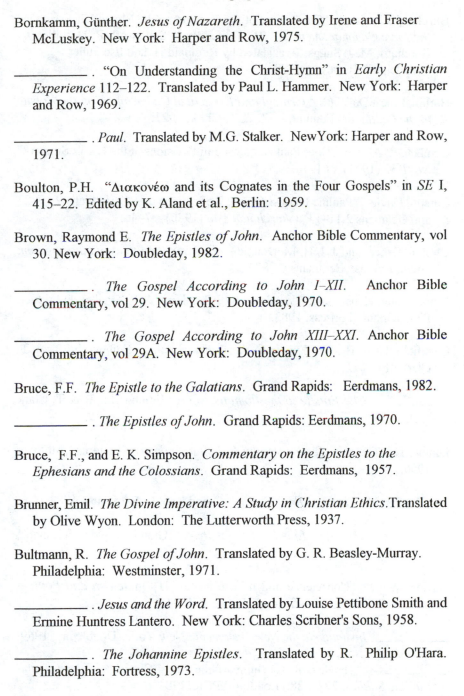

Bornkamm, Günther. *Jesus of Nazareth*. Translated by Irene and Fraser McLuskey. New York: Harper and Row, 1975.

_____ . "On Understanding the Christ-Hymn" in *Early Christian Experience* 112–122. Translated by Paul L. Hammer. New York: Harper and Row, 1969.

_____ . *Paul*. Translated by M.G. Stalker. NewYork: Harper and Row, 1971.

Boulton, P.H. "Διακονέω and its Cognates in the Four Gospels" in *SE* I, 415–22. Edited by K. Aland et al., Berlin: 1959.

Brown, Raymond E. *The Epistles of John*. Anchor Bible Commentary, vol 30. New York: Doubleday, 1982.

_____ . *The Gospel According to John I–XII*. Anchor Bible Commentary, vol 29. New York: Doubleday, 1970.

_____ . *The Gospel According to John XIII–XXI*. Anchor Bible Commentary, vol 29A. New York: Doubleday, 1970.

Bruce, F.F. *The Epistle to the Galatians*. Grand Rapids: Eerdmans, 1982.

_____ . *The Epistles of John*. Grand Rapids: Eerdmans, 1970.

Bruce, F.F., and E. K. Simpson. *Commentary on the Epistles to the Ephesians and the Colossians*. Grand Rapids: Eerdmans, 1957.

Brunner, Emil. *The Divine Imperative: A Study in Christian Ethics*.Translated by Olive Wyon. London: The Lutterworth Press, 1937.

Bultmann, R. *The Gospel of John*. Translated by G. R. Beasley-Murray. Philadelphia: Westminster, 1971.

_____ . *Jesus and the Word*. Translated by Louise Pettibone Smith and Ermine Huntress Lantero. New York: Charles Scribner's Sons, 1958.

_____ . *The Johannine Epistles*. Translated by R. Philip O'Hara. Philadelphia: Fortress, 1973.

Burchard, Christoph. "The Theme of the Sermon on the Mount" in *Essays on the Love Commandment*, 57–91. Edited by L. Schottroff, R. H. Fuller, C. Burchard, M. J. Suggs. Translated by Reginald H. and Ilse Fuller. Philadelphia: Fortress, 1978.

Burton, Ernest De Witt. *A Critical and Exegetical Commentary on the Epistle to the Galatians*. Edinburgh: T. & T. Clark, 1921.

Cambell, R. Alistair. "Does Paul Acquiesce in Divisions at the Lord's Supper?" *NovT* 33 (1991): 61–70.

Carson, David. "Pauline Inconsistency: Reflections on I Corinthians 9.19–23 and Galatians 2.11–14" *Churchman* 100 (1986): 7–45.

Chilton, Bruce, and J. I. H. McDonald. *Jesus and the Ethics of the Kingdom*. Grand Rapids: Eerdmans, 1987.

Conzelmann, Hans. *Acts*. Translated by J. Limburg, A.T. Kraabel, D.H. Juel. Philadelphia: Fortress, 1983.

Cranfield, C. E. B. *The Epistle to the Romans*, vol. I. Edinburgh: T. & T. Clark Ltd., 1975.

_____ . *The Epistle to the Romans*, vol. II. Edinburgh: T. & T. Clark Ltd., 1979.

Daube, D. *The New Testament and Rabbinic Judaism*. London: Athlone, 1956.

Davids, Peter H. *The Epistle of James*. Grand Rapids: Eerdmans, 1982.

_____ . *The First Epistle of Saint Peter*. Grand Rapids: Eerdmans, 1990.

Davies, W. D. "Conscience and its use in the NT" in *Jewish and Pauline Studies*, 243–256. Philadelphia: Fortress, 1984.

_____ . *Invitation to the New Testament*. New York: Doubleday, 1969.

_____ . "The Moral Teaching of the Early Church" in *Jewish and Pauline Studies*, 278–288. London: SPCK, 1984.

_____ . *Paul and Rabbinic Judaism*. London: SPCK, 1955.

_____ . *The Setting of the Sermon on the Mount*. Atlanta: Scholars Press, 1989.

Davies, W. D., and Dale C. Allison. *The Gospel according to Saint Matthew*, vol I. Edinburgh: T. & T. Clark, 1988.

_____ . *The Gospel according to Saint Matthew*, vol II. Edinburgh: T and T Clark, 1991.

De Boer, W.P. *The Imitation of Paul: An Exegetical Study*. Kampen: J.H. Kok, 1962.

Delcor, Mathias. *Le Testament d'Abraham*. Leiden: E.J. Brill, 1973.

Dibelius, Martin. James. Translated by Michael A. Williams. Philadelphia: Fortress, 1976.

Dibelius, Martin, and Hans Conzelmann. *The Pastoral Epistles*. Translated by Philip Buttolph and Adela Yarbro. Philadelphia: Fortress, 1972.

Dihle, A. "Demut" *RAC* III, 735–78.

Dodd, C.H. "The Ethics of the Pauline Epistles" in *The Evolution of Ethics*. Edited by E. Hershey Sneath. New Haven: Yale University Press, 1957.

_____ . *Gospel and Law*. New York: Columbia University Press, 1951.

_____ . *Historical Tradition in the Fourth Gospel*. Cambridge: Cambridge University Press, 1965.

Dunn, James D. G. *Unity and Diversity in the New Testament*, 2nd ed. Philadelphia: Trinity Press International, 1990.

_____ . "The Washing of the Disciples' Feet in John 13:1–20" *ZNW* 61 (1970): 247–52.

Elliott, John H. "I Peter, its Situation and Strategy" in *Perspectives on First Peter*, 61–78. Edited by Charles H.Talbert. Macon, Georgia: Mercer University Press, 1986.

Ellul, Jacques. *The Ethics of Freedom*. Translated by Geoffrey W. Bromiley. Grand Rapids: Eerdmans, 1976.

Engberg-Pedersen, Troels. "I Corinthians 11:16 and the Character of Pauline Exhortation" *JBL* 110 (1991): 679–689.

Enslin, Morton Scott. *The Ethics of Paul*. New York: Abingdon, 1957.

Epictetus. *The Discourses*, vols. I and II. Translated by W. A. Oldfather. LCL, 1966, 1967.

Epstein, I., ed. *The Babylonian Talmud*. London: Soncino Press, 1938.

Fiorenza, Elisabeth Schüssler. *In Memory of Her: A Feminist Theological Reconstruction of Christian Origins*. New York: Crossroad, 1984.

_____ . *But She Said*. Boston: Beacon, 1992.

Fitzmyer, Joseph A. *The Gospel according to Luke I–IX*. Anchor Bible Commentary, vol 28. New York: Doubleday, 1981.

_____ . *The Gospel according to Luke X–XXIV*. Anchor Bible Commentary, vol 28A. New York: Doubleday, 1981.

Flescher, Paul V. *Oxen, Women, or Citizens? Slaves in the System of the Mishnah*. Atlanta: Scholars Press, 1988.

Fletcher, Joseph. *Situation Ethics: The New Morality*. Philadelphia: Westminster, 1966.

Fowl, Stephen E. *The Story of Christ in the Ethics of Paul*. Sheffield: Sheffield Academic Press, 1990.

Fox-Genovese, Elizabeth, and Eugene D. Genovese. "The Divine Sanction of Social Order: Religious Foundations of the Southern Slaveholders' World View" *JAAR* 55 (1987): 211–33.

Francis, Fred O. "Humility and Angelic Worship in Col 2:18" in *Conflict at Colossae*. Edited by Fred O. Francis and Wayne A. Meeks. Cambridge, Massachusetts: Scholars Press, 1975.

Friedlander, G. *Jewish Sources of the Sermon on the Mount*. New York: Ktav Publishing House, 1969.

Funk, Robert W. *Parables and Presence*. Philadelphia: Fortress, 1982.

Furnish, Victor Paul. *The Love Command in the New Testament*. New York: Abingdon, 1972.

——————— . *Theology and Ethics in Paul*. Nashville: Abingdon, 1968.

Gardner, E.C. *Biblical Faith and Social Ethics*. New York: Harper and Row, 1960.

Gerhardsson, Birger. *The Ethos of the Bible*. Translated by S. Westerholm. Philadelphia: Fortress, 1981.

——————— . "Sacrificial Service and Atonement in the Gospel of Matthew" in *Reconciliation and Hope*, 25–35. Edited by Robert Banks. Grand Rapids: Eerdmans., 1974.

Gnilka, Joachim. *Das Evangelium nach Markus*, vol II. Köln: Benziger Verlag, 1979.

Gooch, Paul W. "Conscience in I Corinthians 8 and 10," *NTS* 33 (1987): 224–254.

Gooch, Paul W., and Peter Richardson. "Accomodation Ethics" *TynBul* 29 (1978): 89–142.

Goppelt, L. *Theology of the New Testament*, vols I and II. Translated by John E. Alsup. Grand Rapids: Eerdmans, 1982.

Graham, Susan Lochrie. "Silent Voices: Women in the Gospel of Mark." *Semeia*, 54 (1991): 145-158.

Grundmann, W. "ταπεινός" *TDNT* VIII, 1–26.

Gustafson, James. *Can Ethics Be Christian?* Chicago: University of Chicago, 1975.

_____ . "Moral Discernment in the Christian Life" in *Norm and Context in Christian Ethics*, 17–36. Edited by Gene H. Outka and Paul Ramsey. New York: Charles Scribner's Sons, 1968.

Gutierrez, Gustavo, *A Theology of Liberation*, Translated by Sister Caridad Inda and John Eagleson. Maryknoll, New York: Orbis Books, 1988.

Hallett, Garth. *Christian Neighbor-Love*. Washington D.C.: Georgetown University Press, 1989.

Hanson, A.T. *The Pastoral Epistles*. Grand Rapids: Eerdmans, 1982.

Harvey, A.E. *Strenuous Commands: The Ethic of Jesus*. London: SCM Press, 1990.

Hauerwas, Stanley. *The Peaceable Kingdom*. Notre Dame: University of Notre Dame Press, 1983.

Hays, Richard B. "Christology and Ethics in Galatians: The Law of Christ," *CBQ* 49 (1987): 268–290.

Hengel, Martin. *The Charismatic Leader and his Followers*. Translated by James C.G. Greig. Edinburgh: T. & T. Clark, 1981.

Héring, Jean. *The Epistle to the Hebrews*. Translated by A.W. Heathcote and P.J. Allcock. London: Epworth Press, 1970.

Hooker, Morna D. "Interchange in Christ and Ethics" *From Adam to Christ: Essays on Paul*, 56–69. Translated by Barnabas Lindars and Stephen S. Smalley. Cambridge: Cambridge University Press, 1990.

_____ . "Philippians 2:6–11" in *From Adam to Christ: Essays on Paul*, 88–100. Cambridge: Cambridge University Press, 1990.

Horsley, Richard A. "Consciousness and Freedom among the Corinthians: I Cor 8–10," *CBQ* 40 (1978): 574–589.

Hultgren, Arland J. "The Johannine Footwashing (13. 1–11): as a Symbol of Eschatological Hospitality" *NTS* 28 (1982): 539–546.

Hurtado, L. W. "Jesus as Lordly Example in Philippians 2:5–11" in *From Jesus to Paul: Studies in Honour of Francis Wright Beare*, 113–26. Edited by Peter Richardson and John C. Hurd. Waterloo: Wilfrid Laurier University Press, 1984.

_____ . *Mark*. San Francisco: Harper and Row, 1983.

Jeremias, Joachim. *New Testament Theology*. Translated by John Bowden. London: SCM Press, 1971.

_____ . "Die Salbungsgeschichte Mk 14:3–9" in *Abba*, 107–120. Göttingen: Vandenhoeck and Ruprecht, 1966.

Johnson, Luke T. *The Literary Function of Possessions in Luke-Acts*. Chico: Scholars Press, 1977.

Käsemann, Ernst. *A Commentary on Romans*. London: SCM Press, 1980.

_____ . "Ministry and Community in the New Testament" in *Essays on New Testament Themes*, 63–94. Translated by W.J. Montague. London: SCM Press, 1964.

Keck, Leander E. *Paul and His Letters*. Philadelphia: Fortress, 1979.

Kee, Howard Clark. *Jesus in History: An Approach to the Study of the Gospels*, 2nd. ed. New York: Harcourt Brace Jovanovich, 1977.

Kelly, J. N. D. *A Commentary on the Pastoral Epistles*. London: Adam and Charles Black, 1963.

Kendall, David W. "The Literary and Theological Function of I Peter 1:3–12" in *Perspectives on First Peter*, 103–120. Edited by Charles H. Talbert. Macon, Georgia: Mercer University Press, 1986.

Kierkegaard, S. *Works of Love*. Translated by Howard and Edna Hong. New York: Harper Torchbooks, 1962.

Klassen, William. *Love of Enemies: The Way to Peace*. Philadelphia: Fortress, 1984.

Klausner, Joseph. *Jesus of Nazareth*. Translated by Herbert Danby. New York: Menorah Publishing Co., 1925.

Knox, John. *Chapters in a Life of Paul*. New York: Abingdon, 1950.

_____ . *The Ethics of Jesus in the Teaching of the Church*. New York: Abingdon, 1961.

Knox, W. L. "John 13:1–30," *HTR* 43 (1950):   161–63.

Kötting, B. "Füßwaschung" in *RAC* VIII, 743–59.

Lagrange, M.-J. *L'Évangile selon Saint Mark*. Paris: Libraire Lecoffre, 1966.

Lane, William L. *The Gospel According to Mark*. Grand Rapids: Eerdmans, 1974.

Lemcio, Eugene E. "The Unifying Kerygma of the New Testament," *JSNT* 33 (1988):   3–17.

Levinas, Emmanuel. *Ethics and Infinity*. Translated by Richard A. Cohen. Pittsburgh: Duquesne University Press, 1985.

_____ . *Totality and Infinity*. Translated by A. Lingis. Pittsburgh: Duquesne University Press, 1969.

Lillie, William, "The Christian Conception of Self-Denial" in *Studies in New Testament Ethics*, 151–162. Edinburgh and London: Oliver and Boyd, 1961.

Lindars, Barnabas. *The Gospel of John*. London: Oliphants, 1972.

_____ *The Theology of the Letter to the Hebrews*. Cambridge: Cambridge University Press, 1991.

Lohfink, Gerard. *Jesus and Community*. Translated by John P. Galvin. Philadelphia: Fortress, 1984.

Lohse, Eduard. *Theological Ethics of the New Testament*. Minneapolis: Fortress, 1991.

Lonergan, Bernard. *Method in Theology*. New York: The Seabury Press, 1972.

Longenecker, Richard N. *Paul: Apostle of Liberty*. Grand Rapids: Baker Book House, 1976.

Lull, David, J. "The Servant-Benefactor as a Model of Greatness (Luke 22:24–30)," *NovT* 28 (1986): 289–305.

Luther, Martin. "A Treatise on Christian Liberty" in *Luther's Works*, 31, 327–77. Translated by W.A. Lambert. Philadelphia: Muhlenberg Press, 1957.

Luz, Ulrich. *Matthew 1–7*. Minneapolis: Augsburg Fortress, 1989.

Lyonnet, S. "Christian Freedom and the Law of the Spirit According to Saint Paul" in *The Christian Lives by the Spirit*, 145–74. New York: Alba House, 1971.

Malherbe, Abraham J. *Social Aspects of Early Christianity*, 2nd ed. Philadelphia: Fortress, 1983.

Mann, C.S. *Mark*. Anchor Bible Commentary, vol. 27. New York: Doubleday, 1986.

Manson, T.W. *The Sayings of Jesus*. London: SCM Press, 1949.

Marcus Aurelius Antonius. *Speeches and Sayings*. Translated by C.R. Haines. LCL, 1961.

Marshall, L.H. *The Challenge of New Testament Ethics*. London: Macmillan, 1946.

Martens, Jo-Ann. "Pauline Mimesis: The Realization of an Ethic." M.A. thesis, McMaster University, 1986.

Martin, Clarice J. "Womanist Interpretations of the New Testament: The Quest for Holistic and Inclusive Translation and Interpretation" *JFSR* 6 (1990): 41–61.

Martin, Dale B. *Slavery as Salvation*. New Haven: Yale University Press, 1990.

Martin, R. P. *Carmen Christi: Philippians ii.5–11 in Recent Interpretation and in the Setting of Early Christian Worship*. Cambridge: Cambridge University Press, 1967.

_____ . *Colossians: The Church's Lord and the Christian's Liberty*. Exeter: Paternoster Press, 1972.

_____ . *Philippians*. London: Oliphants, 1976.

Mathews, Shailer. *Jesus on Social Institutions*. Edited by Kenneth Cauthen. Philadelphia: Fortress, 1971.

Meeks, Wayne A. *The First Urban Christians*. New Haven: Yale University Press, 1983.

_____ . *The Moral World of the First Christians*. Philadelphia: Westminster, 1986.

_____ . *The Origins of Christian Morality*. New Haven: Yale University Press, 1993.

_____ . *The Writings of St. Paul*. New York: W.W. Norton and Co. 1972.

Meyer, Ben F. *The Aims of Jesus*. London: SCM Press, 1979.

_____ . *The Early Christians: Their World Mission and Self-Discovery*. Wilmington, Delaware: Michael Glazier Inc., 1986.

Mitton, C.L. *The Epistle to the Ephesians*. London: Oliphants, 1962.

_____ . *The Epistle of James*. London: Marshall, Morgan and Scott, 1966.

Montefiore, C.G. *The Synoptic Gospels* I and II. London: Macmillan and Co., 1927.

Montefiore, H.W. *A Commentary on the Epistle to the Hebrews*. London: Adam and Charles Black, 1964.

Morris, Leon. *The Gospel According to John*. London: Marshall, Morgan and Scott, 1971.

Mott, Stephen, *Biblical Ethics and Social Change*. New York: Oxford University Press, 1982.

Moule, C.F.D. *The Epistles of Paul the Apostle to the Colossians and to Philemon*. Cambridge: Cambridge University Press, 1968.

Müssner, Franz. *Theologie der Freiheit nach Paulus*. Freiburg: Herder, 1976.

Niebuhr, Reinhold. *An Interpretation of Christian Ethics*. New York: Meridian Books, 1956.

_____ . *Love and Justice*. Philadelphia: Wesminster, 1957.

Nygren, Anders. *Agape and Eros*. Translated by Philip S. Watson. Chicago: University of Chicago Press, 1953.

Ogletree, Thomas W. *Hospitality to the Stranger*. Philadelphia: Fortress, 1985.

_____ . *The Use of the Bible in Christian Ethics*. Oxford: Basil Blackwell, 1983.

Osborn, Eric F. *Ethical Patterns in Early Christian Thought*. Cambridge: Cambridge University Press, 1976.

Outka, Gene. *Agape: An Ethical Analysis*. New Haven: Yale University Press, 1972.

_____ . "Character, Conduct, and the Love Commandment" in *Norm and Context in Christian Ethics*, 37–65. Edited by Gene H. Outka and Paul Ramsey. New York: Charles Scribner's Sons, 1968.

_____ . "On Harming Others" *Int* 34 (1980): 381–93.

Perkins, Pheme. "Paul and Ethics" *Int* 38 (1984): 268–280.

Philo, "The Contemplative Life" IX. Translated by F.H. Colson. LCL, 1967.

_____ . "Every Good Man is Free" IX. Translated by F.H. Colson. LCL, 1967.

Philonenko, Marc. *Joseph et Asénath*. Leiden: E.J. Brill, 1968.

Pieper, Josef. *Justice*. Translated by Lawrence Lynch. New York: Pantheon Books, 1955.

_____ . *Prudence*. Translated by Lawrence Lynch. New York: Pantheon Books, 1959.

Piper, John. *Love Your Enemies: Jesus' Love Command in the Synoptic Gospels and in the Early Christian Paranesis*. Cambridge: Cambridge University Press, 1979.

Post, Stephen G. "The Inadequacy of Selflessness: God's Suffering and the Theory of Love," *JAAR* 56 (1988): 213–228.

_____ . *A Theory of Agape*. Lewisburg: Bucknell University Press, 1990.

Reinhartz, A. "John." in *Searching the Scriptures*, vol II. Edited by E. Schüssler Fiorenza. New York: Crossroad, 1994.

_____ . "On the Meaning of the Pauline Exhortation: '*mimētai mou ginesthe*—become imitators of me.'" SR 16 (1987): 393–403.

Rengstorf, K.H. "Δοῦλος" *TDNT* II, 261–280.

Reumann, John. *Variety and Unity in New Testament Thought*. Oxford: Oxford University Press, 1991.

Richardson, Peter. "Pauline Inconsistency: I Corinthians 9:19–23 and Galatians 2:11–14" *NTS* 26 347–362.

_____ . *Paul's Ethic of Freedom*. Philadelphia: Westminster, 1979.

Rigby, Paul, and Paul O'Grady. "Agape and Altruism: Debates in Theology and Social Psychology" *JAAR* 57 (1989): 719–737.

Robertson, Archibald, and Alfred Plummer. *A Critical and Exegetical Commentary on the First Epistle of St. Paul to the Corinthians*. Edinburgh: T. & T. Clark, 1914.

Sampley, J. Paul. *Pauline Partnership in Christ*. Philadelphia: Fortress, 1980.

_____ . *Paul's Moral Reasoning: Walking Between the Times*. Minneapolis: Fortress, 1991.

Sanders, E.P. *Paul, the Law, and the Jewish People*. Philadelphia: Fortress, 1983.

Sanders, Jack T. *Ethics in the New Testament*. Philadelphia: Fortress, 1975.

Schlier, Heinrich. "Ἐλεύθερος" *TDNT* II, 487–502.

Schnackenburg, Rudolf. *The Moral Teaching of the New Testament*. Translated by J. Holland-Smith and W.J. O'Hara. London: Burns and Oates, 1975.

Schneiders, Sandra. "The Footwashing (John 13:1–20): An Experiment in Hermeneutics," *CBQ* 43 (1981): 76–92.

Schottroff, Luise. *Lydia's Impatient Sisters*. Translated by Barbara and Martin Rumscheidt. Louisville: Westminster John Knox, 1995.

_____ . "Non-violence and the Love of One's Enemies" in *Essays on the Love Commandment*, 9–39. Edited by L. Schottroff, R. H. Fuller, C. Burchard, M. J. Suggs. Translated by Reginald H. and Ilse Fuller. Philadelphia: Fortress, 1978.

Schrage, Wolfgang, *The Ethics of the New Testament*. Translated by David E. Green. Philadelphia: Fortress, 1988.

Schweizer, Eduard. *The Letter to the Colossians*. Minneapolis: Augsburg Publishing House, 1982.

_____ . *Lordship and Discipleship*. London: SCM Press, 1960.

Segovia, Fernando, F. "John 13:1–20, The Footwashing in the Johannine Tradition," *ZNW* 73 (1982): 31–51.

_____ . *Love Relationships in the Johannine Tradition*. Chico: Scholars Press, 1982.

Seim, Turid Karlsen. *The Double Message*. Translated by Brian McNeil. Nashville: Abingdon, 1994.

Selwyn, E.G. *The First Epistle of Saint Peter*. London: Macmillan and Co., 1964.

Shaw, George Bernard. "The Monstrous Imposition upon Jesus" in *The Writings of Saint Paul*, 296–302. Edited by Wayne A. Meeks. New York: W.W. Norton and Co., 1972.

Shaw, Graham. *The Cost of Authority: Manipulation and Freedom in the New Testament*. Philadelphia: Fortress, 1982.

Smalley, Stephen. *John—Evangelist and Interpreter*. Greenwood, S.C.: Attic Press, 1983.

Spicq, C. *Agape in the New Testament* I. Translated by Sister Marie Aquinas McNamara and Sister Mary Honoria Richter. St Louis: B. Herder Book Co., 1963.

Stauffer, E. "Αγαπάω" *TDNT* I, 21–55.

Stendahl, K. "Hate, Nonretaliation and Love: Coals of Fire" in *Meanings*, 137–149. Philadelphia: Fortress, 1984.

_____ . *Paul Among Jews and Gentiles*. Philadelphia: Fortress, 1976.

Stuhlmacher, P. *Reconciliation, Law, and Righteousness*. Translated by E.R. Kalin. Philadelphia: Fortress, 1986.

Swartley, Willard M. *Slavery, Sabbath, War, and Women*. Kitchener, Ontario: Herald Press, 1983.

Tamez, Elsa. *The Scandalous Message of James*. New York: Crossroad, 1990.

Taylor, Vincent. *The Gospel according to Mark*. London: Macmillan, 1953.

Thieme, K. *Die christliche Demut*. Giezen: Alfred Topelmann, 1906.

Thomas, John Christopher. *Footwashing in John 13 and the Johannine Community*. Sheffield: Sheffield Academic Press, 1991.

Thomas, George F. *Christian Ethics and Moral Philosophy*. New York: Charles Scribner's Sons, 1955.

Thompson, Marianne Meye. *The Humanity of Jesus in the Fourth Gospel*. Philadelphia: Fortress, 1988.

Thornton, L . S. *The Common Life in the Body of Christ*, 4th ed. London: Dacre Press, 1963.

Tillich, Paul. *Morality and Beyond*. New York: Harper and Row, 1963.

Urbach, E.E. "The Laws Regarding Slavery as a Source for Social History of the Period of the Second Temple, the Mishnah and Talmud" in *Papers of the Institute of Jewish Studies, London*, vol I. Edited by J.G. Weiss. Jerusalem: Magnes Press, 1964.

Verhey, Allen. *The Great Reversal*. Grand Rapids: Eerdmans, 1984.

Via, Dan O. Jr. *The Ethics of Mark's Gospel: In the Middle of Time*. Philadelphia: Fortress, 1985.

Wanamaker, C. A. "Philippians 2:6–11: Son of God or Adamic Christology?," *NTS* 33 (1987): 179–193.

Webster, John. "Christology, Imitability and Ethics" *SJT* 39 (1986): 309–326.

Weiss, Herold. "Foot Washing in the Johannine Community," *NovT* 21 (1979): 298–325.

Wengst, Klaus. *Humility: Solidarity of the Oppressed*. Translated by John Bowden. Philadelphia: Fortress, 1988.

Westerholm, Stephen. *Israel's Law and the Church's Faith: Paul and his Recent Interpreters*. Grand Rapids: Eerdmans., 1988.

_____ . "On Fulfilling the Whole Law," *SEÅ* 51–52 (1986–87): 229–237.

_____ . "Letter and Spirit: The Foundation of Pauline Ethics," *NTS* 30 (1984): 229–248.

Willis, Wendell. "An Apostolic Apologia? The Form and Function of I Cor 9" *JSNT* 24 (1985): 33–48.

Windisch, Hans. *The Meaning of the Sermon on the Mount.* Translated by S. Maclean Gilmour. Philadelphia: Westminster, 1951.

Wire, Antoinette Clark. "Gender Roles in a Scribal Community" in *Social History of the Matthean Community.* Edited by David Balch. Minneapolis: Fortress, 1991.

Wolff, Christian. "Humility and Self–Denial in Jesus' Life and Message and in the Apostolic Existence of Paul" *Paul and Jesus* 145–160. Edited by A.J.M. Wedderburn. Sheffield: JSOT, 1989.

Yoder, J. H.. *The Politics of Jesus.* Grand Rapids: Eerdmans, 1972.

Ziesler, John. *Pauline Christianity.* Oxford: Oxford University Press, 1983.

Zimmerli, W. "Παῖς Θεοῦ" *TDNT* V, 654–717.

Index to Biblical Passages